RAISING SUSAN

RAISING SUSAN

A MAN, A WOMAN, AND A GOLDEN EAGLE

BILL BURNS

Published in 1999 by Stoddart Publishing Co. Limited
34 Lesmill Road, Toronto, Canada M3B 2T6
180 Varick Street, 9th Floor, New York, New York 10014

Distributed in Canada by:
General Distribution Services Ltd.
325 Humber College Blvd., Toronto, Ontario M9W 7C3
Tel. (416) 213-1919   Fax (416) 213-1917
Email customer.service@ccmailgw.genpub.com

Distributed in the United States by:
General Distribution Services Inc.
85 River Rock Drive, Suite 202, Buffalo, New York 14207
Toll-free Tel. 1-800-805-1083   Toll-free Fax 1-800-481-6207
Email gdsinc@genpub.com

03 02 01 00 99   1 2 3 4 5

Canadian Cataloguing in Publication Data

Burns, Bill, 1944–
Raising Susan: a man, a woman, and a golden eagle

ISBN 0-7737-3161-X

1. Susan (Eagle). 2. Hyndman, Cecil. 3. Hyndman, Adele.
4. Featherland (B.C.). 5. Bird Refuges — British Columbia.
6. Human-animal relationships — British Columbia.
I. Title.

SF473.E2B87 1999   598.9'423'092271128   C98-932658-6

Jacket Design: Bill Douglas @ The Bang
Text Design: Tannice Goddard

Photographs appearing on the jacket and in the photo
inserts reprinted with permission of the author.

Printed and bound in Canada

*Stoddart Publishing gratefully acknowledges the Canada Council for the Arts and
the Ontario Arts Council for their support of its publishing program.*

For my two daughters:
Danielle, who was with me
the first time I visited Cecil,
and Cehra, who was with me
the last time;
and for Debbie and
Bryan McGill, who
made this book possible

Love is a powerful attraction, whether it involves a human or bird. Being the unpredictable will-o'-the-wisp that it is, love answers to no master. To ignore that truth is to court failure in relations with a bird. In humanity it is often disaster. Our affair with the golden eagle Susan demonstrates that sometimes reciprocal love chooses not to materialize. But when it does, there is no limit in how far one can go — or where it can lead.

— CECIL HYNDMAN

CONTENTS

Prologue *xi*

one Susan 1

two Featherland 11

three The Arrival 22

four Susan's First Year at Featherland 34

five An Uphill Battle 50

six A Brush with Death 64

seven A Love Affair 76

eight The Rift 97

nine A Busy Time 107

ten Progress 123

eleven Ups and Downs 136

twelve Eagle Song 161

thirteen The Miracle 171

fourteen An Eventful Winter 180

fifteen Tough Going 189

sixteen A New Era 208

seventeen The Grasp 227

eighteen Twilight Years 246

nineteen Farewell 266

Epilogue 275

Acknowledgments 283

PROLOGUE

Saturday, April 30, 1994, was an unusually hot spring day, so hot that I rolled down the window of my car as we exited the busy highway onto rural Burnside Road, which winds through the gently rolling countryside outside Victoria on Vancouver Island. The recent rains had softened the landscape, turning it into a lush green. My daughter Danielle said, "Look, Dad, the trees have beards," pointing to the long strands of lichen hanging from the gnarled limbs of the oak trees.

Ahead drove Debbie McGill, who was guiding us to Cecil Hyndman's cottage. Debbie, an interior design consultant who had befriended Cecil, had told her husband, Bryan, the editor of *Beautiful B.C.* magazine, about the colorful "eagle man." Bryan, in turn, had told me about him. I planned to write a magazine article about Cecil's life with Susan, his golden eagle. After I had gained his trust, perhaps he would even allow me to write a book about his and his wife's unique relationship with the magnificent bird.

Years earlier I had found a copy of Cecil's self-published book about Susan, *The Grasp*, in a used book shop. From reading the book, I knew that he must have been well into his eighties by now.

I didn't know what to expect from Cecil because I had heard contradictory opinions about him. "Hyndman? He's a crank, don't take him seriously," dismissed one source. Another person claimed Cecil was badly misunderstood, "like all true prophets."

Cecil had turned his back on a successful film production career when he married Adele Gordon, and they agreed to devote their lives to birds. From what I had heard, he had worn many hats: showman, promoter, writer, photographer, painter, inventor, vet, poet, and producer. How could one man be all these things?

As we rounded a bend in the road, Danielle spotted a weathered sign that read "Featherland," barely visible in the trees. We followed Debbie up a gravel driveway. The outline of a small cottage flickered through the thick foliage. We made our way up the overgrown pathway toward the cottage on foot.

The back door creaked open and Cecil stepped outside. He resembled a highly intelligent bird, his alert stare intensifying his hawk-like profile. He was extremely lean, even bony, weighing less than 100 pounds.

We followed him into the cottage. A faint but sickly smell of heating oil hung in the overheated room. Cecil introduced us to Quite So, his African gray parrot, explaining that the bird needed the heat. Then he said, "Without any fat reserves, I always feel cold."

Cecil's vivid watercolors and small engravings brightened the wooden walls. Tree stumps on rollers acted as tables and rush mats were strewn across the wooden floor. A thin layer of dust covered everything, cobwebs laced the corners of the room, and ivy crept down the walls, sneaking in from outside. I thought about how nature was slowly reclaiming the inside of the cottage. And age and

natural decay were reclaiming Cecil. He looked alert, but I thought
that surely a man his age must tire easily.

I needn't have worried. On my next visit, with tape recorder running, Cecil spoke for six hours. I staggered out of his cabin afterwards,
exhausted. Despite his eighty-three years, Cecil never tired, never
repeated himself, and only once asked me, "Now, where was I?"

Back at my motel after that visit, I felt so drained that I had to lie
down for a while before supper. I tried to sleep, but as I lay on the
bed I thought about something Cecil had said. Cecil had explained
that when he stared at the ceiling from his cot, people he knew from
his childhood would appear in front of him as clearly as if they were
standing in his cottage, as if the movie of his life was being replayed
for him. Maybe his visions accounted for his passion. Had he been
reliving his life during our long interview? Of course he had. But I
sensed that something else, something deeper, drove him.

Over the next few months I returned to Cecil's cottage a number
of times. We settled into a comfortable routine. Cecil would take the
dust covers off his tape recorders and plug my recorder's leads into
the overhead microphone system he used to record his birds. His
expertise with sound recording impressed me. (We had a number of
things in common, including sound editing jobs with the CBC.)
During these sessions, Cecil animated his "performances" with
vocalized sound effects. His beautifully modulated voice complemented his narrative skills.

Our relationship deepened into something curious and surprisingly complex. The closer we became, the more I realized the
distance that separated us.

Cecil had tried to tell his story of raising Susan for years. He had
turned down offers from publishers, offers that had too many
strings attached. Cecil was stubborn, determined to tell his own
story his way. Now, his advancing years made that task impossible.
Perhaps I represented his last chance, but first I had to earn his trust.

What was not expressed between us was probably more

important than what was. In my conversations with Cecil, I saw a man attempting to validate his unique life. He was in essence a man forgotten, his life's work scorned. But what he wanted most was to be heard. I sensed that Cecil looked at me and wondered, "Anyone can sit and listen, but can you deliver?"

At that moment, our roles reversed. Up to that point, Cecil had been the father figure, passing along his life's story to a man thirty years his junior. Now he looked particularly vulnerable.

"I promise I'll get Susan's story out in a book," I told him, and admitted that I wasn't sure how, or when.

Cecil became uncharacteristically silent, then smiled. "You better get going on it, I'm not getting any younger." He made no demands, nor did he ask for any conditions. Instead, we shook hands, striking a deal based on the firmest of bonds — *a man is his word*. Finally, I had won his trust.

Cecil committed himself fully to the project after my bold promise. A night owl all his life, he'd call me late at night. Or he would write, enclosing clippings, his artwork, poems, or lengthy "reminiscences." The flood of material threatened to overwhelm me, but I managed to send out some proposals.

Cecil was in the hospital when I found a publisher. The news seemed to improve his condition. The terrible wheeze and sputter that had accompanied his every breath faded. Still, his weight was a major concern. I helped to feed him, joking that he had to put on weight for the interviews after the book came out.

Cecil died on April 17, 1997, the same date his wife, Adele, had passed away seven years earlier.

A week after my daughter Cehra and I attended Cecil's simple burial, I returned to Victoria. With the permission of Cecil's executor and with Marie Thomas's help, I planned to retrieve Cecil's written records. Most of the older material, as well as numerous cans of sound tapes, were stored in Talon Hall. Part of the roof had collapsed, and Marie warned me that the fifty-year-old floor had rotted.

I laid planks over the decaying wood so that I could walk across and reach the rows of boxes. The first few I opened contained only wet pulp. His old "paper tapes" were a stinking and soggy mass in their metal cans.

Without warning, a rotted beam gave way beneath me while I was looking through Cecil's things, and I crashed through the floor, injuring my ribs. Was this a sign of things to come?

After returning home to Vancouver, I had to separate each damp page of Cecil's notes, then dry the mold-encrusted paper. All of the material I salvaged was damp, moldy, or covered with bird and animal droppings. My ribs were sore from my fall, so my father helped me pin the paper to the wooden siding of my house. What the neighbors thought of a house plastered with paper, I can only guess.

The next step was to transcribe 300 hours of taped interviews, which ran to almost 300,000 words. Cathy Gibson, a fellow writer, handled a good deal of these transcriptions. After that, I had to go through 10,000 photographs.

The preliminary sorting of Cecil's written material took months. I hired my daughters to help me. Whether from the fungus on the paper or from the bird and mouse droppings, my two daughters and I developed respiratory difficulties during this period. Eventually, I came down with pneumonia.

When I had recovered, I sealed every single sheet of paper in plastic before handling them again. I deciphered Cecil's scratchy handwriting and retyped the contents to disk. Slowly (there was no other way), I read every scrap of Cecil's notes and letters in chronological order, beginning with some of his love letters to Adele from the 1940s. The experience was emotionally draining, but at the same time I felt energized. Cecil had become my daily companion. I acquired a great understanding of the man as I read his notes, seeing his life through his eyes.

I began to realize how Cecil's life was affecting mine while trekking through Burns Bog (no relation) after my first book, *Discover Burns Bog*, came out. A newspaper reporter, Dawn Hanna, photographer Don DeMille, and I stumbled across a distressed bald eagle. When I approached the bird, it flapped its wings, raised its hackle feathers, and, I swear, spat at me.

Dawn knew that I was writing a book on the "eagle man," and assumed I knew everything about eagles, including how to capture one. The eagle was displaying such aggression that I was ready to give up and admit I'd never captured an eagle before. Then I swear I heard Cecil's voice saying, "Get a coat over its body and grab the talons at the same time."

With the late eagle expert whispering instructions to me, I outlined his "swoop and grab" technique to my companions. I undertook the frontal approach, and Don came up behind the bird. As he threw his coat over the eagle, I grabbed its talons. The next step was "hooding" it, as falconers do, with Dawn's coat. We took the eagle to the nearby OWL (Ophaned Wildlife Rehabilitation Society) bird sanctuary, where it was diagnosed as having pesticide poisoning. Within fifteen minutes, the eagle was operated on, and months later it was safely released back into the wild.

I like to think that Cecil was proud of me that day. And I hope this book does justice to his, Adele's, and Susan's unique story.

one

In March of 1955, a large wooden box arrived at Featherland, the avian sanctuary operated by Cecil and Adele Hyndman outside Victoria, B.C. Inside shrieked an enraged young female golden eagle. When Cecil peeked into the box, four inches of talon shot through the air hole.

This violent introduction began a long and stormy relationship involving a man, a woman, and a golden eagle. Their strange love story would continue for almost a quarter of a century. The golden eagle's "acts of love" not only astounded the scientific community but resulted in hundreds of articles in newspapers and magazines, as well as radio and TV shows, a book, and a short film. No one else has lived in such intimate contact with such a large bird of prey for such long time.

The story of this unique love triangle had its beginning some

1,000 miles from the Hyndmans' Victoria sanctuary, on a mountain ledge near Whitehorse, in the Yukon Territory. Two golden eagles rose on invisible air currents, soaring higher and higher. The larger one, a female, maintained position behind the smaller male as they gained altitude over the forested slopes and plateaus of the Yukon far below. It was a warm spring day in 1954. The deep blue of the sky contrasted with the white snow-capped mountains.

The eagles rode the uplifting thermals of warm air until they became two specks against the clear Yukon sky. With superb control, they adjusted their wingtips to keep rock-steady as they glided over their vast territory.

Suddenly the male rolled and tucked his wings close to his body for a steep dive. He picked up speed as he plummeted, reaching a velocity of 150 miles per hour. After falling like a rock for hundreds of meters, he swooped back up like the arm of a pendulum, then surprised the female with an aerial somersault at the top of this arc.

She flipped over, displaying her talons, as he flashed past. Calling loudly, she closed her wings and plunged after him. Both gained speed as they hurtled downward like bullets. The air rushing past their furled wings caused a loud ripping noise, like a cloth being torn. They pulled out of their dive and swiftly rose with powerful wingbeats.

High in the Yukon sky, their courtship progressed. The male displayed more than the female. Again and again he stooped at her as if attacking. Each time, she countered with a lightning-quick roll. At times their upstretched talons almost touched. Their vocalizing became louder with excitement as they looped and rolled, sometimes almost stalling in mid-air.

For hours they continued their aerial ballet. Then the female executed a slow roll to the right and glided toward a cliff face far below. The male followed, his wingtip almost touching hers.

Following this prenuptial display, the female gracefully landed on a rocky ledge near their nest. Excitedly the male mounted her.

Weeks later the female laid two eggs on their nest. For the next month and a half, both eagles shared incubation duties. In the summer of 1954, two golden eagle chicks were born. One grew up in the wild; the other had a unique future ahead of her — she was to become one of the most famous birds in history.

A few weeks later, a brawny young Whitehorse forestry firefighter, Danny Nowlan, climbed toward a golden eagle's nest. The huge size of these aeries, almost three feet deep and up to six feet across, made them easy to spot on cliff ledges. Danny had found this nest earlier in the spring, when it was still empty. But a pair of golden eagles soaring above it had convinced him the nest was in use, and he hoped to find an eagle egg, or even a chick, today.

An experienced falconer, Danny knew North America's highest density of breeding golden eagles is found in the southern Yukon, where the alpine-like terrain suits the birds perfectly.

Danny, originally from northern Saskatchewan, had since childhood shown a keen interest in wildlife, keeping hawks, owls, and a wide variety of animals, including minks. Years later he became the first person to successfully breed Dall sheep in captivity.

Although he had trapped many birds of prey, this was Danny's first attempt at capturing a golden eagle. He was in luck; eggs had not only been laid, but had hatched. Adult golden eagles are large birds — females weigh up to fifteen pounds, and the populations of the far North are the largest in North America. But the chicks begin as three-ounce balls of whitish fluff.

Danny started scaling the cliff toward the golden eagle's nest. He felt no fear, climbing almost casually, despite the fact the golden eagle is perhaps the only bird of prey capable of severely injuring, if not killing, a man. He knew these fierce predators would defend their territory from other birds of prey; often remains of goshawks, gyrfalcons, and ravens are found in eagle nests. Yet, while other, smaller birds of prey will attack any human intruding on their nest, golden eagles always retreat if a human approaches, leaving their nest undefended. And the nearsighted young presented no danger. Unlike many other young birds, such as baby gulls, which are extremely active from birth, young eagles spend most of their early life passively awaiting the food they need to bulk up.

So Danny was certain that he faced no threat as he climbed the last few feet and snatched a downy eaglet from the nest.

Danny attempted to raise the eagle, which he named Susan, in the busy forestry firehall where he worked outside Whitehorse. Perhaps it was the noisy background, but as the eagle grew, putting on muscle and acquiring strength, her temper worsened. Within six months, she became so rough that Danny had no alternative but to find Susan a new home. He contacted another falconry enthusiast, Wilf Blezard.

Wilf worked at the weather forecast office at Watson Lake in the southern Yukon. Born in the Yukon, son of a wildlife ranger, Wilf had a reputation as an expert trapper of birds of prey. Older and more experienced than Danny, he was confident he could control Susan. He planned to train her as the ultimate hunting bird — the dream of every falconer.

Wilf consulted falconry experts, who confirmed what Danny had learned through first-hand experience — that golden eagles were dangerous. Deliberate attacks on trainers, Wilf learned, were common among golden eagles, especially those trained to hunt.

The acknowledged eagle expert in the province in the 1950s was Frank Beebe, of the Royal Museum of British Columbia, author of *Hawks, Falcons, and Falconry*. Beebe candidly warned:

Susan

Golden eagles are in a class by themselves. Of all the birds used for hunting, they are perhaps the least predictable. It is this characteristic, combined with their great size and strength, which makes them so hazardous. Golden eagles are difficult to make secure, heavy to carry, hard to hood, and dangerous to their trainer and to any other humans in the area.

Wilf accepted the challenge. The first step was to fit Susan with jesses, the leather leg ties used in the sport of falconry. Attached to these jesses was a length of rope, which Wilf tethered to a stand outside his house.

Susan's training progressed extremely slowly — so slowly that Wilf wondered if Susan was simply too vicious to be trained at all. One day a dog spotted her tied up outside and attacked — a fatal mistake. Susan killed the dog with her talons. This "blooding" of Susan — her first kill — worried Wilf, who had young children.

Ultimately, Wilf's neighbors complained to the local mayor, who declared the bird "a danger to the community" and demanded that Wilf get rid of her immediately.

When he too reluctantly realized he could not keep the eagle, Wilf thought of Cecil Hyndman. Cecil ran an avian sanctuary near Victoria, British Columbia, with his wife, Adele. The two were considered somewhat eccentric, keeping dozens of birds in their home as well as in enclosures and outbuildings on the property they called Featherland. Featherland was a combination of zoo, scientific research colony, bird hospital, and extended collection of pets. But Wilf knew Cecil's passion for birds was serious, however unusual his lifestyle. Over the years, Wilf had sent Cecil various birds, including a baby owl, a raven, and hawks. Wilf recalled that Cecil had expressed an interest in golden eagles, especially young ones. Susan's fierceness made her a special case and Wilf wondered if Cecil could control her.

On a chilly February morning a letter arrived at Featherland bearing a postmark from Watson Lake, Yukon Territory. Adele Hyndman's eyes lit up as she read Wilf's letter: *Did the Hyndmans want a golden eagle?*

As Cecil came in the back door of the cottage for a cup of coffee, she excitedly waved the letter at him. "Cecil, send a reply this minute. We must have Susan," she said.

"Whoa. Susan? Who is Susan?" Cecil poured his coffee, warming his cold hands on the mug. "What's this all about?"

Adele was so animated that she thrust the letter at Cecil, then handed her husband pen and paper. "Wilf is offering us a young female golden eagle."

Although they already had a number of birds of prey, including both great horned owls and snowy owls, the offer of a golden eagle, the most impressive bird of prey of the Northern Hemisphere, caught Cecil by surprise. His first reaction was disbelief.

When they had first opened Featherland, Cecil had made inquiries about golden eagles, but local bird experts had explained that they did not nest on Vancouver Island. Even seeing one was a rare event, and provincial regulations made it almost impossible to capture or own one within B.C. Discouraged by his initial inquiries, Cecil had stopped asking.

Now, as Cecil read the words "young female golden eagle," he became so excited he had to sit down. Could his dream of acquiring the fiercest of all the birds of prey be really coming true? But his sense of elation abated as he read the last part of the letter. Wilf explained that he had attempted to train Susan for falconry, but Susan had never advanced to being "flown." Wilf cautioned Cecil about Susan's violent behavior and suggested Cecil contact a zoo as a backup, since she would likely grow even more ferocious in time. Wilf stated that the Bronx Zoo in New York had already expressed interest in acquiring Susan.

Susan

Doubts began to surface in Cecil's mind. Wilf was a serious falconer, and much younger and athletic than he was himself. Cecil also knew Danny Nowlan, who had sent him a snowy owl and a hawk owl. Would he be able to succeed where these two falconers, both experienced in raising birds of prey, had given up?

At the same time, he knew this chance to add a truly rare bird to Featherland's collection might never come again.

"Cec, you must reply." Adele hovered over him. "We simply must have Susan."

Adele's face glowed with animation. Cecil, however, wanted time to consider the decision. But time was one thing they didn't have; Wilf's letter stressed he needed an immediate reply.

"This opportunity might never happen again," Adele said.

Her nature had an impulsive side. She was quick to make a decision and rarely wavered once she had decided on a course of action. While her approach was direct and emotional, she was never fickle. Adele always backed up her decisions with a quiet determination.

While Adele tended to be spontaneous, Cecil was more deliberate. Where she looked at the whole picture and made an instantaneous decision, he tried to weigh all the details, mentally plotting out the ramifications of any decision. His approach tended toward the philosophical, a fact that sometimes led to friction with Adele.

But together they were an extraordinary pair — Adele the heart and Cecil the brains, their mutual passion for birds bonding them together. Friends used to remark that the chances of two people who shared such an intense fixation for birds meeting and marrying was one in a million.

With Adele fighting back her impatience, the pair discussed the pros and cons of taking on Susan — the most important decision they would ever make at Featherland.

Cecil's first concern was the most obvious: money. Featherland had ongoing financial problems. It seemed irresponsible to go even further in debt by purchasing Susan when they were already so short of money. Even the cost of crating and transporting an eagle from the Yukon was beyond their means.

"We've always managed somehow in the past," Adele reminded him.

Then there was the possibility that Susan's violent tendencies might be impossible to overcome. Cecil suspected that the eagle's already fierce temperament had been encouraged by the attempts to train her for falconry. Was Susan too old to be deconditioned from her falconry training? With its rigid human master and bird servant relationship, falconry differed radically from the Hyndmans' approach to birds at Featherland.

"The moldability of the young was vitally important to us at Featherland," Cecil wrote in his journal. Except for injured birds, they always tried to raise their birds from eggs or acquire very young birds.

Adele pointed out that Susan's violent outbursts might in fact indicate that she had not fully responded to her falconry training. Susan was about six months old, but still young enough, Adele argued, that there was "some hope of remolding her life."

In truth, the very characteristics that troubled Cecil — Susan's strength and power — at the same time attracted him. When he was a young boy ill at home in Edmonton, he had passed the time in his father's library. His reading had included a great deal about golden eagles, which had a long tradition as a symbol of imperial power. Belshazzar of Babylon first used the eagle emblem in the sixth century B.C. Later the Egyptians and Persians featured the eagle on their battle standards.

In the first century B.C., Caius Marius, Julius Caesar's uncle, introduced the golden eagle standard to the Roman legions as a symbol of strength. Each legion carried an eagle emblem on a pole into battle, and after a victory, sacrifices were offered to the eagle idol. A legion that lost its eagle battle standard in defeat faced disbandment.

The eagle continued as the symbol of power during the Christian era. Charlemagne began with the Frankish eagle as his badge. He adopted the two-headed eagle when he became the Holy Roman emperor in 800. Succeeding Holy Roman emperors and the eastern Roman Empire also used the eagle to represent their power. Later the Russian czars and late Austrian emperors used eagles in their heraldry.

In medieval Europe, with falconry at its peak (before the introduction of guns and clearing of the great forests), birds "had become symbols of freedom," wrote Sir Kenneth Clark. "Under feudalism, men and animals were tied to the land. Few could move about."

The United States adopted the bald eagle as its national emblem. Many disagreed, including Ben Franklin, who cited the bald eagle's "bad moral character," by which he meant that it fed off carrion. But the bald eagle won out as the new republic's emblem of freedom. It was chosen instead of the more powerful golden eagle for the simple reason that the less fierce bald was the only species of eagle native to North America. Later, Mexico adopted the golden eagle as its national emblem.

Cecil knew that the golden eagle's reputation for fierceness and aggression was no myth. In the wild, golden eagles are capable of attacking and killing formidable prey, including foxes and coyotes. Cecil had read an eyewitness report of two eagles cooperating in attacking deer. During winter, golden eagles in Canada have also been known to attack other animals much larger than themselves, including reindeer, antelope, and mountain goats.

Golden eagles trained for falconry in Asia regularly attacked and killed wolves. The practice dated back to China in the time of Genghis Khan and lingered in central Europe up to the start of World War II. Two eagles once took thirty-two foxes and eighteen wolves in one season. One extraordinary female is reputed to have killed thirty-six wolves before losing a foot attacking the thirty-seventh. Small wonder the golden eagle had long been used as the symbol of war.

As the discussion by the kitchenette dragged on, Adele began to grow frustrated. "I simply don't see why you're so hesitant," she said. Cecil did not reveal his main concern: if he took a chance and accepted this ferocious bird, would he be endangering Adele?

"We have to decide today," Adele said. Wilf was under intense pressure from the Watson Lake authorities to move Susan.

"Our dream could turn into a living nightmare," Cecil told Adele.

"With us," Adele countered, "Susan can be world famous. I have a premonition about it."

In the end, Adele's emotion won out against Cecil's reason. The Hyndmans agreed to take Susan in at Featherland.

two

FEATHERLAND

Featherland was a labor of love for Cecil and Adele Hyndman. They were very much in love with one another, but also shared a passion for birds so deep they wanted nothing more than to devote their lives to them.

Although considered odd — if not downright eccentric — in their choice of lifestyle, both Cecil and Adele came from fairly distinguished backgrounds. The path that led these two people together, and then to their unique paradise on the slopes above Victoria, was unusual.

Cecil Hyndman was born in Edmonton in 1911. He came from a long line of judges and politicians. His father was a Supreme Court justice and his grandfather was Sir Louis Davies, Chief Justice of Canada. But from an early age, Cecil's interests lay outdoors. As a small boy, Cecil and his parents were visiting Sir Louis when a

messenger arrived with a set of documents for Sir Louis to sign —
Canada's declaration of war. Solemnly, Sir Louis gathered together
the family to witness the historic event. But he grew impatient
when he counted heads and found Cecil missing; he had headed
outdoors. Sir Louis bellowed, "go get that drat of a boy playing in
the garden. This is an historic occasion!"

At an early age Cecil became fascinated with birds. When five
years old, he earned twenty cents helping to dig the garden. When
his mother asked him what he wanted to buy, the blond, curly-
haired Cecil firmly replied, "a bird." His mother hitched the buggy
and drove to the farmers' market, where Cecil bought his first bird,
a hen.

Soon he acquired mallard ducks, who laid eggs deep in the straw
in the barn all winter. The venture prospered; Cecil sold the eggs
from his thirty ducks to his Uncle Harry, a lawyer in partnership
with future prime minister R. B. Bennett.

Cecil suffered from ill health through most of his formative years.
At age thirteen he suffered from a bout of scarlet fever. At first
the doctors thought the illness had affected his eyes, and for over
a month, Cecil was quarantined in a section of his parents' house
in Edmonton. A private nurse attended to him while he remained in
semi-darkness. When he recovered, the family doctor recommended
Cecil take a year off school to recuperate outdoors in the fresh air.
No one knew at that time that the illness had damaged the lining
and valves of his heart.

His family sent him to a farm to improve his health. But instead
of letting him rest, the sheepherders took advantage of Cecil —
working the thirteen-year-old from before dawn until after dusk.
His weakened heart "blew up to three times its normal size, doing
125 to 130 beats a minute even lying down," Cecil recalled. Finally
his parents came to take him away.

A heart specialist confirmed he had an enlarged heart and prescribed complete rest for almost a year. Cecil's continuing heart and

health problems prevented him from attending high school, although he took correspondence courses during his lengthy convalescence. His scarred heart kept him out of the war.

He was never a hardy boy, but he always had an affinity for birds. During the winter of 1929, he worked on a poultry farm at Qualicum under very primitive conditions — no running water, no electricity, and very cold at night. During the spring, the man who ran the poultry farm rushed off to Vancouver, leaving teenaged Cecil alone with 2,000 eggs in a huge incubator. The oil lamps and heaters had to be manually operated and checked, twenty-four hours a day. When the owner came back ten days later, the chicks were hatching and the owner praised Cecil for a near perfect incubation.

Cecil also became an expert horseman, working on ranches in Alberta, and later spent some time in agricultural college. After his family moved to Ottawa, Cecil briefly studied pre-medicine at Queen's University.

In 1932 he quit to become the CBC's first sound effects specialist, working on live radio dramas for five years. Medically unfit for service in World War II, Cecil spent the war years with the newly established National Film Board (NFB). He shepherded film crews from Fox Movietone News and the March of Time across the country, traveling over 200,000 miles. He submerged in submarines and flew high over convoys at sea. He survived car accidents, an aircraft crash landing, and narrowly escaped death in a horrific train wreck in the Rocky Mountains.

Toward the end of the war, Hyndman met Adele Gordon. Adele had been a debutante; her father was the Deputy Minister of National Defence. He was immediately smitten by this beautiful woman, whose lithe frame and high cheekbones gave her the appearance of a fashion model. Adele found Cecil equally attractive, with his blue eyes, handsome features, and muscular frame — he had taken up working out under the guidance of some wrestlers, and his sinewy arms were as taut as steel cable and his waist was almost as small as Adele's. They made a striking pair while courting in Ottawa.

They carried on a long-distance courtship while Cecil was still busy traveling across the country for the NFB. Finally they married late in the war. On an impulse, Cecil bought a baby budgie for his bride. Adele, who had never "seen a feather outside a hat shop" up until then, became fascinated with the bird, which she named Macdougal. While Cecil was away on film trips, she concentrated her energy on teaching the bird to talk.

Adele displayed an instinctive understanding of birds, a rare gift few people possess. When she focused all her attention on the tiny bird, "something indefinable about her voice, manner and touch brought a remarkably similar response in Macdougal. Adele believed in flesh to flesh contact, rubbing faces with Macdougal and physically handling him. Not only was Adele fixated with Macdougal, he in turn focused all his attention on her," Cecil wrote.

Adele quickly made a breakthrough in teaching Macdougal to speak, recognizing the budgie repeated phrases faster than they were spoken. If the reproduction was too fast, then the words jammed together and became indecipherable. Up to this point, few speech trainers had done the obvious.

"If you taught a budgie 'Merry Christmas,'" Cecil explained, "it would come back spoken so quickly that the phrase was almost incomprehensible. So you had to speak very slowly, stretching out the words 'M..e..r..r..y C..h..r..i..s..t..m..a..s.' If the teaching is done at half speed, when the budgie doubles this speed, then the reproduction sounds normal to a human."

Adele accidentally discovered another technique that stimulated speech. At the time, they were living in a little room and when a streetcar rumbled past, the noise would stimulate Macdougal's speech. Adele experimented and found other ways to induce the budgie to talk if he was reluctant. She made a crinkling sound with paper or ran a tap. Within a few short months, Adele "made of her pupil a phenomenon of human-toned, crystal clear talking ability. His speech was more colourful and spirited than most human voices."

"A singular rapport built up between this minute bird and ourselves," Cecil said about the deep bond that was to shape the rest of their lives. As they discussed the bird's ability to mimic speech, they wondered what mental abilities lay in recesses of the bird's mind. Macdougal's apparent ability to understand raised the question of whether birds had higher mental faculties.

Up until then, birds had been a hobby or side interest for Cecil. During his teenage illnesses, he had become familiar with Charles Darwin from reading books in his father's large library. Of this tiny budgie's effect on him, Cecil later wrote:

I glimpsed at last that added dimension that I had groped for since childhood. Now with a vision of what might be found in the grey cells of some [birds], I had broken through a confining wall. Beyond it I might uncover truths to which humanity had been blind.

Tiny Macdougal's arrival that cold winter of 1945 reignited Cecil's passion for birds, as well as awakening in Adele an equally consuming passion. This doubled the attachment between Cecil and Adele. Not only did they love each other, they shared a love of birds. Once they discovered this mutual dream, they talked about building a pastoral retreat and devoting their lives to rearing birds in a human environment. But where?

During the severe Ottawa winter they nearly froze in their flat while blizzards raged across the Parliament Buildings in the nation's capital. "My hatred of cold made me think of Victoria, where the temperature seemed almost tropical in comparison," wrote Cecil. In February of 1946 Cecil resigned from the NFB, feeling burned out, no longer capable of keeping up the frantic pace he had followed for years. (The final impetus behind his decision to quit was the subject of his next production assignment at the film board: a documentary on an insane asylum!)

The newly married couple escaped Ottawa's freezing temperature and headed west. Cecil was familiar with the Pacific coast as his family had often vacationed on Vancouver Island and he had fond memories of warm summers spent by the sea. The character of Victoria in the late 1940s could best be described as "tweedy Old English." This quiet city of 50,000 dressed its traffic police in English "bobby" uniforms. The pace of life matched the slow growth of ivy spreading across Victoria's brick buildings.

After establishing a base at a small motel on the outskirts of Victoria, the newlyweds rented a car to search for their dream property. Although Adele was eager to embrace this new life on the West Coast, she had never lived away from the city, with its paved roads and stores. Her life as a deputy minister's daughter had been a social whirl, with teas, parties, and balls. Now she was living in an old motel, bouncing over narrow rural trails. After weeks of futile searching, her spirits sagged. Finding their Eden was proving elusive — especially as their meager finances limited what they could afford.

In early April, driving along a narrow road that twisted west of Victoria, they passed a highland area. Adele suggested they stop and take a closer look. The site looked promising; the lower stretch, fairly level and bare, would be perfect for the cottage they planned on building.

Excited by the natural beauty of the landscape, they pressed upward toward the cloud-enshrouded peak, climbing the tiers of domed rocks that resembled a massive stone staircase. The earth-filled depressions between the "stairs" bloomed with wildflowers. Huge oaks slumbered like bearded giants with lacy Spanish moss falling from their twisted limbs, giving the highlands a dreamy, almost surreal appearance. Cecil speculated that some of the giant oaks towering above were so old they "had known rain and sun before the start of recorded Canadian history." The Hyndmans wondered if they were the first humans to intrude on this primeval terrain.

They reached the highest point of land just as banks of cloud lifted, revealing the snowy peaks of the Olympic Mountains across the Strait of Juan de Fuca. Seven miles south was the famous Empress Hotel. As the two sat in silence enjoying the vista, they could hear deer browsing. The magic moment lengthened as twilight came. From the top the lights of Victoria twinkled invitingly, appearing much closer than in reality.

"Cec, I feel at home here." Finally Adele spoke.

Nothing more was said. Nothing more needed to be said. Looking down at distant Victoria, they decided this was to be their home — their Eden.

After the purchase of their dream property, an almost overwhelming series of obstacles stood between the Hyndmans and the idyllic life they planned. The unserviced site had no power, water, or telephone. (In fact, it took until the early 1950s before they were hooked up to telephone service.) Although the war had ended, Canada in 1946 had still not made the transition to a peacetime economy. Basic building supplies, like nails and lumber, were difficult to obtain. Consumer items were even harder to come by, and household appliances like toasters were unobtainable.

The first problem facing them was the water supply. The nearest municipal water line ended about half a mile away. To purchase enough pipe they had to travel up and down the island, visiting every hardware store. Digging a trench and laying the pipe was exhausting work, especially for Cecil. Only a few years earlier he had nearly broken his back in a train crash in the Rockies and it still bothered him years later. The last stretch of the water line had to cross a paved road. They couldn't afford mechanical equipment so Cecil used a pickaxe to tear through the asphalt. Although he had little experience in construction, and none in plumbing, fifty years later the pipe Cecil laid still supplied water to his cottage.

Once the water line was in place, they began building a tiny cottage. To save money the Hyndmans put up the siding themselves. They also erected another building, which they called Talon Hall — a two-story wooden structure with white clapboard, on a grassy field set back 100 yards from the road.

Cecil put his experience in the saddle to good use. He acquired a semi-wild draft horse from the Prairies, named Queen, and harnessed her to a homemade stoneboat — a flatbottomed wooden sled. She turned out to be more temperamental than regal. She "could buck like the part bronco she was," and more than once she bolted, overturning the stoneboat, or ran away while hauling rock from the hills to make a driveway.

Yet slowly and steadily the Hyndmans' rustic Eden began to take shape. "Featherland. That will be the name of this little world of ours," Adele announced one evening in 1946.

Like two nesting birds, Cecil and Adele wanted to create the perfect environment. They decided against planting flower beds, instead enjoying the wildflowers that bloomed in colorful carpets of white, red, blue, and purple. Each season brought a new flowering, beginning as early as January when clusters of tiny white flowers would appear on Indian plum shrubs to herald the approaching spring.

The Hyndmans used native plants, digging up sword ferns and replanting them close to the creek and wooden bridges. When they decided that the stump-littered lowland needed a ground covering, ivy filled the bill, while being easy on their pocketbook. A tiny pot, planted fifteen yards from the front porch of the cottage, spread until the cottage was surrounded "by a sea of ivy."

Even before they started constructing their cottage, the Hyndmans had planted their first tree, a birch, which soon towered over the front door. Other trees followed in the late 1940s, some starting from tiny seedlings only inches high. Eventually the Hyndmans planted over 400 trees of various species, including weeping willow, cypress, maple, fir, cascara, and cherry and other fruit trees. They never transplanted the Garry oak seedlings that sprouted from acorns, but protected them from numerous deer and rabbits.

When they had a little money, Cecil splurged on buying concrete to build a series of interconnected ponds. They also constructed rustic bridges to cross a stream they named Burble Creek, after the burbling sound it made. The stream only flowed in winter, when rainwater collected in basins high up in the hills. The stream cascaded down the rocky slope over a series of beautiful waterfalls Cecil described as "mini Niagaras."

In their quest to achieve natural landscaping, the Hyndmans were years ahead of their time. Their use of native plants and trees created an attractive backdrop for Featherland that followed the rolling contours of the land. Clumps of ferns and native flowers complemented the ponds of Burble Creek. The Lombardy poplars, planted as seedlings, grew over the years into a stand that shot skyward over thirty yards and was visible from miles away. The huge, gnarled limbs and massive crowns of the native oaks swathed in Spanish moss gave Featherland an informal, pastoral beauty. Commentators would later write about Featherland's "extravagant feeling, ivy and ferns adding to the graceful setting. The lofty hedge of Lombardy poplars looming like the towers of some medieval castle."

Purchasing their dream site and erecting buildings left them "poor as church mice." While their financial situation was bleak, they owned the land and had a roof over their heads. To finance their Eden, they attempted a number of commercial ventures. First they raised poultry, using clapboard-sided Talon Hall to house 3,500 birds. In only their second year of poultry farming, they broke the Canadian flock egg-laying record. But when a highly contagious disease began devastating nearby farms, they decided the poultry business was too risky. They closed their operation in 1951 and never again had another chicken on their property.

The next bird-related venture they tried was the pedigree breeding of budgerigars. These Australian parakeets, known as budgies, had first appeared on the scene in Canada around the start of the 1940s. The tiny birds could be trained to talk and became very popular. The Hyndmans' own Macdougal, who had a 300-word vocabulary, became something of a sensation. Unfortunately, Macdougal died shortly after Featherland opened, after being exposed to gas in a hotel.

The Hyndmans soon had 300 budgies housed in an outbuilding on their rolling property. They shipped birds all over Canada. But raising budgerigars turned out to be both difficult and time-consuming, and their market share fell as the number of breeders increased.

Next they acquired a number of tropical birds from a failed pet dealer in Vancouver. They taught many of the birds to speak and opened Featherland to paying visitors. It quickly acquired the name "Land of Talking Birds." They planned to use the revenue from exhibiting birds to fund research into both the psychological and physical makeup of birds. Adele and Cecil led personal tours, charging adults fifty-five cents and children thirty cents. They opened the doors to Featherland every day, except Mondays, at two in the afternoon for years afterward.

In another attempt to combine his passion for birds with profit, Cecil produced the first of many commercial sound recordings, *Quiz Kids of Featherland*, featuring talking myna birds. Cecil had bought a used tape recorder from a radio station. The finished production played on local radio and on the CBC and helped promote Featherland.

The mid-1950s were difficult times for the Hyndmans. They had started a family — a winged one. "We knew we would never be able to devote time to children. It had to be one or the other. We chose birds," Cecil explained. As more and more birds arrived at their avian sanctuary, often dozens of feathered companions shared their small cottage, some even occupying their bed at night. As they stumbled from one financial crisis to the next, sometimes the birds ate and they didn't. Often they resorted to collecting bottles to return for money. But there was no turning back. They had put down roots and begun their bird family. And with the arrival of Susan the golden eagle in 1955, this already unusual family was about to acquire a new member with a unique personality — one who would change the lives of those who became close to her forever.

three

THE ARRIVAL

After the Hyndmans had accepted the challenge of raising Susan, the next few days passed in a frenzy of activity. Adele became so excited, Cecil wrote in his journal, "she seemed to float over the ground. I told her that she need not bother to use the door — in her state she could easily fly out the window." His own initial excitement slowly deflated as one practical difficulty after another presented itself.

Somehow he had to raise the necessary money, help make complicated travel arrangements to transport Susan, and build an enclosure — all within a few days.

When they contacted Wilf to accept his offer, an even more immediate snag developed. Wilf pointed out that Danny Nowlan also had to approve the transfer, as they were co-owners of Susan. Wilf also reminded Cecil that some well-financed American zoos had expressed interest in obtaining Susan. Suddenly there was no guarantee they would even get Susan, now that they had their hearts set on it.

"The wait is agonizing," Cecil wrote. "Even Dell is becoming somewhat discouraged. The money issue remains unresolved — not only the purchase of Susan but the future of Featherland itself."

Featherland at that stage was undergoing a transformation. From a zoo-menagerie, or performing bird-animal sanctuary — "Land of Talking Birds" — the Hyndmans were in the progress of shifting the focus to large birds of prey. The addition of Susan — if they could obtain her — would be a big step in the new direction.

Cecil also took inventory and updated the ads for Featherland in newspapers, as well as the pamphlet they distributed through tour companies and the chamber of commerce. His inventory of their menagerie for 1955 included:

one talking Malayan myna, one talking budgie, one talking and performing blue fronted Amazon parrot, one performing cockatiel, one performing budgie, one performing mountain crow, one Assam Indian myna being trained to talk, one baby Yukon magpie being trained to talk, one northern raven trained to talk and perform in combination with wild donkey, one Mexican raven, three hand-raised uniquely tamed screech owls, one great horned owl, one baby Canada jay, one Stellar's jay, three black-capped chickadees, two hand-raised northwestern crows, one extremely rare Indian blossom head parrot, one hand-raised sparrow hawk, one pair of mated bare-eyed cockatoos (from New Zealand), one performing baby spider monkey (trained to wear clothes), one adult ringtailed monkey from Brazil, one young black-faced white ringtail (from Colombia), one young male golden spider monkey, one male Mexican donkey (burro), two eastern flying squirrels, one horse, and one dog (spaniel).

He further listed over a dozen waterfowl and game birds, includ-ing "two Indian ducks (unique on Vancouver Island), one male

California quail, two white Chinese ganders, two Toulouse geese, and Muscovy ducklings." The new count came to forty-seven species and varieties of birds and animals.

Cecil debated adding Susan's name to the promotional literature, as well as raising the admission price.

Finally they heard from Wilf Blezard. He still had not completely resolved the legal issues surrounding Susan's future, but he felt confident enough to begin making travel arrangements. Thrilled, the Hyndmans got to work, helping Wilf arrange the shortest flight south they could find. They feared Susan might injure herself if she was confined too long. Equally important were handling arrangements. If her box was mishandled or dropped, Susan could panic and try to take off. The airlines co-operated to work out the shortest connecting flights between Watson Lake and Victoria.

While Wilf built a large wooden box with padding for Susan's long journey, the Hyndmans scrambled to construct a special enclosure at Featherland. They ordered lumber from a local yard, then carried the load up the slope they called Huff and Puff Hill to Talon Hall.

Given Susan's violent tendencies, Cecil decided the female golden eagle needed a quiet enclosure. He suspected her temperamental outbursts might have been triggered by all the noise and activity in the firehall where Danny Nowlan had raised her. They began framing a flight enclosure twenty-five feet long by fifteen feet wide.

"Susan's been tethered outside in Watson Lake. How is she going to react to being confined?" Adele asked as they worked on the first wall of the enclosure.

"We'll keep a dim light on at night," Cecil replied.

He reasoned that if Susan suddenly became alarmed, her first instinct would be to take to flight. In taking off, she could accidentally crash into a wall in the dark. Where this might not be a problem with a smaller and lighter bird, given Susan's weight, she could badly injure herself.

The Arrival

As the day of Susan's arrival neared, the preparations reached a fever pitch. Adele's eyes shone with excitement as they pulled wire across the front of Susan's future pen, completing the construction. When they returned to Ookpik Cottage, a letter from Wilf awaited them. Cecil grabbed two cups of coffee as Adele opened the letter.

The news from Watson Lake was mixed. The good news was that Danny Nowlan had approved the transfer of Susan to Featherland and Wilf Blezard confirmed that the flight plans had been finalized. The bad news came in the form of even more serious warnings from the co-owners about Susan's behavior.

Both falconers warned Adele and Cecil that Susan's temperament was unlike any other bird of prey they had ever encountered. Where golden eagles normally do not attack humans unless confronted or cornered, Susan had no fear of humans as she had been raised in the firehall.

Wilf, a rugged outdoorsman, admitted Susan had scared him a number of times. "She's become disturbingly violent and threatens to become even more so," he cautioned Cecil. He stressed that the "fantastic power" of Susan's taloned feet, coupled with her ability to strike faster than the human eye could follow, gave her the capability to attack and badly injure or even kill a man. His advice: "Don't ever, ever, let your guard down with her."

Wilf went on to list a number of trigger points that might provoke an attack. Susan reacted to anyone wearing a furred glove or clothing. She was especially dangerous when eating. People staring at her often provoked a violent response. So unpredictable were her attacks that Wilf threatened not to ship Susan unless Cecil outfitted himself with both body armor and a face guard.

The letter concluded by asking the Hyndmans to reconsider if they wanted Susan, mentioning that the Bronx Zoo was still interested in acquiring her. Wilf asked them to write back and confirm.

"What do you make of this, Cec? Sounds like they're getting cold feet," Adele told Cecil.

The chilling warnings had failed to cool the excitement rising in Adele. She had made her decision, and was not about to waver. She noticed that Cecil had grown silent. "You haven't changed your mind?"

For a moment Cecil did not reply. The whole focus of Featherland was not to simply display birds, but rather to interact with them. But how could they achieve this intimacy with Susan given her violent temperament?

"Cec, what is it?" Adele said. "Second thoughts?"

"No, I'm just trying to figure out how I can get all this protective gear made up in time."

But the truth was, as much as he admired Adele's positive approach, Cecil knew they were taking a chance. Not only was acquiring Susan a financial risk, but if what Wilf said was true, they were also risking injury — perhaps even death.

The next morning, Cecil looked up fencing schools in the Yellow Pages of Victoria's phone book in search of a fencing mask.

Adele's bubbly enthusiasm about Susan's arrival could not be contained. She joked that his beaked nose required a special mask. Cecil played along, conceding that a fencing mask would make him look even sillier. He did not have the heart to destroy her elation by confiding his deep fear. He knew not only from books but from his sheep-herding days how a golden eagle kills its prey: It folds its wings close to its body and dives from the sky, talons clenched. After stunning its prey with a lightning strike from above, it drives its long and curved talons through the prey's eye sockets and into the brain.

The next step in the preparations took Cecil to town. Wilf had recommended thick leather gloves — standard gear in falconry — as well as heavy leather body protection. Cecil soon discovered he could not afford the expense of handmade leather gloves and arm guards. So he settled for a much cheaper but poorly fitting alternative: double-thickness welder's gloves. Much later he would regret this decision when the loose fingers of the bulky welder's gloves made him lose his grip on Susan's jesses.

Luckily he already had a pair of heavy leather chaps, saved from his ranch days in Alberta. But he had to order a pair of lace-up cowhide arm guards for his upper arms. The shop owner stared at him strangely when he placed his order, but took measurements and agreed to have them ready later that afternoon.

While he was in Victoria, Cecil took the opportunity to spread the word about Susan's imminent arrival. The newspapers seemed interested, but when, at the various shops he visited, he mentioned that a golden eagle was arriving in Victoria, he quickly discovered few others shared his enthusiasm.

In the 1950s many people regarded the golden eagle as a savage killer with a well-deserved bounty on its head. During this era, Canadian fisheries patrol boats used 50-caliber machine guns mounted on their bows to destroy killer whales because they were thought to decimate valuable salmon stocks off the West Coast. Wildlife officials offered bounties on cougars and wolves. Coyotes were exterminated by the thousands using carcasses laced with poison.

From personal experience Cecil knew the terrible reputation eagles had among sheepherders in North America. When he was thirteen, for six months he had risen each morning at 4:00 a.m. to herd a flock of 400 sheep. He knew that herders regarded golden eagles as predators who killed lambs. Each spring thousands of eagles migrating to Mexico were shot, poisoned, or trapped. In the U.S. Southwest, the eagle spring kill was an annual event for nearly a century, approved by the Department of Agriculture, which supplemented the kills by a poisoning campaign, using hares laced with strychnine.

The slaughter intensified with the formation of "plane clubs." Members of these organized eagle-hunting clubs maneuvered alongside eagles in aircraft and blasted them out of the air with shotguns. The aerial killing was chillingly effective. In one Texas district, sixty eagles died from poisoning during a single spring and fall, while a single aircraft accounted for twenty-three eagles in six hours. One pilot from west Texas claimed to have killed 8,000 eagles between 1945 and 1952. The United States' Congress did not end this practise until 1962.

By mid-afternoon, Cecil had only one piece of protective equipment left on his list: a mask to protect his face. He visited a fencing school and talked to the Master of the Swords, a small, hawklike man who stiffened when Cecil explained his plight. The master seemed offended, especially as Cecil added he had no money to buy a fencing mask.

"He spoke in a succession of vocal jabs with edges on them in keeping with those things in scabbards hanging on the dingy studio walls," Cecil recalled.

But eventually the instructor relented, lending Cecil an old and battered fencing mask. The metal grille and thick padding provided good protection but made the mask very heavy; Cecil felt like it was made from solid lead.

Finally, it was the last night before Susan's arrival. After some gentle prodding, Cecil tried on the mask and leather body armor — clumsy cowhide arm pieces, heavy chaps, and gauntlet gloves. Adele started to laugh, and soon triggered a fit of laughter from Cecil, providing a few moments of relief from anxiety.

"Ready or not, Susan arrives tomorrow," Adele said between fits of laughter.

On March 14, 1955, Adele and Cecil paced anxiously, waiting for news of Susan's flight. In late afternoon the phone rang, announcing Susan's arrival at Vancouver. The first leg of her flight from the Yukon was complete. The airline official informed Cecil that the eagle seemed relatively calm, although she occasionally flapped her wings. Cecil could only hope the thick padding inside the custom-made box prevented Susan from injuring herself. Another flight would take her across the Georgia Strait to Victoria. From the airport, the box would be driven by bus to the express terminal.

Later that evening, Cecil drove Adele in the Hyndmans' old '33 Dodge six miles to the bus station. The day had been a long and anxious one, and it was almost midnight when they arrived. They were surprised to find a scrum of reporters and photographers surrounding the plywood box containing Susan. The photographers demanded Cecil pry open the box so they could snap a photo of the first golden eagle to be imported to Victoria.

Cecil refused this dangerous request. The press insisted. Not wanting a confrontation, Cecil patiently explained what would happen if he released Susan at the terminal. The three press photographers protested vigorously that the airlines had promised them a photograph. Why else would they show up and waste an evening? For a few anxious minutes, the press refused to leave. But eventually the photographers stormed out indignantly. This would not be the last time Cecil had a run-in with the media.

After the unpleasant exchange with the press, a more concrete problem faced Cecil and Adele. Could the two of them move the large crate? As they struggled with the heavy and bulky box, Cecil mentally calculated the dimensions and concluded the box would not fit inside their old car.

"I don't think we can get this in at any angle," he told Adele as they rested the box beside the car door.

"Don't be silly, Cecil. We have to," Adele replied. "That's all there is to it."

They managed to fit the oversized box into the car, shattering a car window in the process and scraping their hands. Cecil wondered on the drive back to Featherland if this was a bad omen. Sounds of movement inside the box reassured them Susan was alright.

Arriving back at Featherland, they had more difficulty squeezing the box through the narrow opening of Susan's enclosure in Talon Hall. Cecil's greatest worry was that Susan, after being confined so long, might react to the jerky handling by flinging herself against the sides of the box.

"One final attempt," Cecil told Adele as he remeasured the opening, "then we'll have no choice but to widen it."

By tilting the plywood box sideways, they managed to squeeze the crate into Susan's new quarters. Adele hugged her husband.

Exhausted but elated that they'd succeeded, Cecil knelt to assure Susan they would soon have her out. He tried to sound comforting as he spoke, squinting through one of a series of tiny air holes to check on the eagle's condition.

Bang! Four inches of talon shot through the hole, making a sound like a pistol going off. Instinctively Cecil bolted backward, landing on his rear.

For a moment Cecil sat dazed on the wooden floor as the sturdy plywood box rocked from inside, then finally settled. He realized he had come close to of losing his eye. Wilf had warned the Hyndmans that Susan could move so fast the human eye could not follow.

"What did you do?" Adele asked Cecil. "You've upset Susan."

᾿ *"What did I do?"* Cecil sputtered.

"Susan wants out," Adele calmly informed her husband.

"She's made that very obvious," Cecil said.

One more hurdle faced them. They had to dismantle the box to release Susan and somehow get out of her pen safely. Cecil's recent first-hand experience with Susan's rage made him consider their approach very carefully.

They worked on opposite sides of the box, from the bottom up. They first pulled the nails out as slowly as possible. Susan began to move around, forcing them to pause until she quieted down. The next step involved loosening the screws holding the sides together. The plan was to keep the top on until the last moment, then bolt for the door.

Susan's agitation grew as they loosened the four sides until only the top held the plywood box together. Cecil waved at Adele to leave the enclosure but she refused, pointing out it would be much easier for them to take the top off together.

On the count of three, they both pried, and with a deafening wooden squeak, the top came off in one motion. Adele and Cecil sprinted toward the door, almost stumbling over one another.

A gold-black form exploded out of the box as its sides collapsed. Although the Hyndmans had raised large hawks and owls, the size of the golden eagle surprised them. When, after thrashing about for a few moments, Susan stretched her wings, they spread so wide they seemed to touch either side of the enclosure. She stood a good two feet tall. Her wide set legs bulged with muscle, her thighs three inches in diameter. Feathers covered her legs down to her thick yellow feet. Her chest bulged with pectoral muscles strong enough to power her wings — already seven and a half feet wide. The noise she made by riffling her huge wings filled the room.

For a few moments Susan wobbled unsteadily as she adjusted to her new freedom. Then suddenly she adopted a threatening stance, appearing even larger and more intimidating than before. Susan's stride became a swagger as she moved in her pen.

It was the talons, scraping on the wooden floor, that impressed Cecil most of all. There were four on each foot, up to four inches long and designed to kill. The curved talons reminded Cecil of black sabres. "They radiated the impression of spring steel. They forced the word grasp to one's mind if not to the lips," he later wrote of how they had struck him that day.

While the Hyndmans stared awestruck at Susan, the golden eagle turned to face them. For the first time, Cecil and Adele encountered the piercing stare of a golden eagle. Her large yellow-brown eyes, set at a forward slant under cliff-like brows, fixed on Cecil. The feathered bony protrusion above each eye, which acts like a shield to protect the eye below, extenuated the forward thrust of her face. Her massive hooked beak was highlighted by the bright yellow corners of her mouth. The beak was tipped in black and obviously designed to tear flesh.

Of that first moment of contact, Cecil later wrote:

something strange but big happened deep inside both Adele and myself — a magnetic Goddess capturing us to the core on sight and for life, come what may. She "owned" us then and has never relaxed that magic grip.

Cecil slowly stepped closer to the pen, speaking quietly to Susan, trying to reassure her. But instead of calming down, Susan glared in agitation.

"Her hackle feathers, each one tipped with gold, slowly rose and remained on end in hostile stiffness while I stood there voicing greetings," Cecil recalled. She riffled her raised hackle feathers while compressing her other feathers. Cecil knew what that reaction meant. It was a sign of hostility. And since Susan had been raised with humans, he knew the hostility was not general, but personal. The raised hackle feathers signaled a rejection of Cecil.

As Cecil stepped back, deeply disappointed, Adele approached the edge of the pen and greeted Susan in her soft, lilting voice. The eagle responded with a twittering noise from deep in her throat. At the same time her collar hackles relaxed and her expression softened.

Susan's thin and shrill voice — "tweeters of pleasure" — surprised Cecil. The sound reminded him of a canary — hardly what you would expect from such a fierce and magnificent bird. He realized what her vocalizations meant. "This was meaningful in an almost ominous sense," he wrote. "Susan had made a clear choice between us. It was Adele and she only. She melted for Adele. She bristled toward me."

four

Susan's First Year at Featherland

Ordinarily Cecil enjoyed the night chorus at Featherland, with the hooting of the many owls providing a soft backdrop to the higher-pitched chirping of other birds. But as the Hyndmans made their way back to their cottage, the night seemed strangely silent. Sleep did not come easily to Cecil the night of Susan's arrival. While Adele dozed off, he lay awake, concerned over the long-term implications of his initial encounter with the eagle. He knew from his years of handling other birds of prey that first impressions tended to be long lasting.

If Featherland had been just a zoo, Susan's rejection would not have presented a problem. In many zoos, large birds of prey are fed through slots in the bars of their cages. Hoses shoved through the bars clean their pens. Zoo-kept eagles rarely come into human contact and, if they need to be handled, the keepers can wear protective gear.

But Cecil did not want merely to display Susan for revenue as a "rarely seen captive raptor." He wanted to personally handle her in close contact; to truly cultivate her in order to probe her intelligence.

Cecil also worried about the possibility of danger to Adele. Both Adele and Cecil had been bitten by various other birds. But no bird they had handled possessed four-inch talons.

As Cecil faded off that night, he remembered his one previous encounter with a golden eagle. While researching film locations in the foothills of southern Alberta during the war, Cecil had stopped the pickup truck to admire two golden eagles soaring overhead. Without warning, the pair had folded their wings and swooped out of the sky. He watched in awe, not overly concerned since he had never heard of a wild eagle attacking a man. But the driver became rattled and pulled Cecil back into the car. And to Cecil's amazement, instead of pulling out of their dive-bombing attack, the wild pair of eagles smacked the roof of the pickup with their feet.

Susan's first few days at Featherland passed quickly. The very sight of the latest addition to their feathered family never failed to thrill Adele. Cecil was equally impressed, although he had less time to stand and admire Susan in all her majestic glory. He was busy formulating a plan to reduce Susan's hostility toward him.

Cecil hoped her behavior might mellow once she adjusted to her new surroundings. But every time he approached her that first week, his greetings brought a hostile response from Susan. Her defiant posture reaffirmed to Cecil that she had made her choice that first evening and did not intend to waver from it.

Each time Adele approached the pen, Susan would twitter and sway back and forth. Her physical mannerisms and excited vocalizations made it obvious whom she preferred. By the end of the week, despite Cecil's determined efforts, Susan had not swayed from her decision.

Cecil and Adele discussed their next move. They agreed that they could not put off the inevitable direct contact any longer. But while Adele argued that she should be the one to go in as she was sure Susan would not attack her Cecil maintained that he could not allow his wife into such a dangerous situation.

Their debate raged on and off late into the night, continuing in bed. Adele insisted she should establish contact. When she refused to concede, Cecil offered her a test.

"If you can lift and keep those ten-pound weights of mine on your outstretched arm for ten minutes, then you can enter Susan's pen," he said.

"We'll see," Adele said, hopping out of bed to accept the challenge.

She knew why Cecil insisted on this weight-lifting trial. Wilf had warned them about Susan's habit of flying up to the arm of anyone within reach. Susan's in-flight momentum, coupled with her weight of nearly seventeen pounds, could easily knock over a person.

Adele found the ten-pound weight Cecil used to exercise and locked her elbow to hold it steady in her hand. Within minutes her arm began to throb. She tried to ignore the pain, but her knees gave out and she crumpled to the bare wooden floor.

"If you fell holding Susan, she might instinctively strike," Cecil said. "She's already been blooded by her kill of that dog at Watson Lake."

Adele stopped pestering Cecil. But she sensed something was holding him back from entering Susan's enclosure. Each morning over the next three days, when she brought up the subject, Cecil delayed — telling Adele the postponement gave Susan time to adjust to her new indoor quarters. Furthermore, they had scheduled a handyman to frame a new outbuilding. But on the tenth day after Susan's arrival, Adele gentled chided Cecil.

"You're not afraid, are you?" she asked.

She had intuitively put her finger on the one major barrier that remained — a psychological one. Although Cecil would never admit it to Adele, he was afraid.

He tried to make a joke of it. "Perhaps I better go in today — before I lose my nerve."

Cecil felt like an ancient gladiator preparing to enter the arena. With Adele's help, he donned his protective gear: leather riding chaps, a thickly padded coat, leather arm coverings, the double-thickness welder's gloves, and finally, the borrowed fencing mask. He was barely able to stagger under the unwieldy weight. Adele broke out in hysterical laughter at what she described as "this Man from Mars apparition."

Once inside Talon Hall, Cecil hesitated.

"Now what's the matter?" Adele asked, excited but exasperated.

"I feel almost naked," Cecil confessed.

Despite his cumbersome assortment of protection, one vital article of clothing was missing. Adele rushed to find his well-worn felt hat.

Squashing his felt hat over the fencing mask, Cecil eased open the door to Susan's pen. Adele passed him the lure — thin slices of juicy red meat. Susan immediately stiffened inside her pen, the talons on her powerful feet flexing. As if to get a better position to attack, she hopped up on the box stand.

Summoning up his courage, Cecil entered the room, slowly extending the red meat he carried in his hand, never taking his eyes off Susan. He was not sure what to expect.

Susan lowered her head menacingly while raising her hackle feathers. Not a good sign. Their eyes locked and Cecil felt transfixed by her stare. He could feel sweat stain his clothes. Slowed he plodded forward, almost waddling from the bulky clothing and loose chaps.

Susan instantly uncoiled, like a feathered spring, using her huge wings to launch herself into the air. With only a few powerful flaps, she flew to Cecil's padded left arm — just as Wilf had predicted she would. The weight of the bird and the grip of her talons nearly toppled Cecil, who only weighed 135 pounds himself. As Cecil reached out to grab the jesses attached to Susan's feet, the eagle struck, gouging the padding on his shoulder.

Clumsily Cecil tried again to grab both straps, cursing the loose welder's gloves. They were as much use in gripping an object as boxing gloves. Finally he managed to grab one of the leather thongs, then the other. Susan did not seem to object; her huge eyes remained fixed on the meat Cecil held.

Slowly Susan's talons tightened on Cecil's arm. At first he could not believe the strength of her grasp. As the relentless force increased, Cecil became frightened. Wilf had warned him that the power of her grip exceeded her physical proportions.

Through the caged mask, straining under the weight and feeling his arm getting numb, Cecil watched Susan's rapier beak rip apart the chunk of red meat and swallow it quickly.

Then he swung her off his arm in the direction of her box stand. Immediately she shot back to his arm and began to scream excitedly in a small voice. His arm sagged under Susan's weight and the extra weight of his protective gear. Cecil swung Susan off again. Once again she instantly rebounded, "like a great, live boomerang."

Cecil inwardly cursed falconry, with its fixation on food rewards. Traditionally, falconers operated on the simple principle of birds of prey associating their owners with food. The falconer began by teasing hungry birds with bits of food. Often the captured hawk refused it. This contest of willpower left the owner with little choice; he could release the bird as untrainable or starve it until it accepted food from him or died.

Cecil desperately tried to hold his arm steady. His blood circulation was being cut off by Susan's four-inch talons squeezing like curved vices on his arm. His muscles ached from extending his arm level with an extra seventeen pounds on the end.

As he feared, as his arm dropped slightly, Susan instinctively eyed the highest point: Cecil's thinly padded shoulder. Cecil in turned eyed the door behind him. With his arm almost completely numb, he had to find a way out without exposing his unprotected neck and back to Susan. She could easily plunge her talons into his spinal column. Wilf had also warned Cecil that Susan used her wings like blunt knives. A double-winged swipe was powerful enough to knock a man down.

"Get the door ready," Cecil told Adele as he edged backward toward the door.

He let his arm drop suddenly, which caused Susan to loosen her grip. She flapped wildly, but before she could land on his shoulder, Adele opened the door and Cecil managed to escape.

Cecil's arm was so numb it took five minutes of deep massage from Adele before the blood began to circulate again. Somehow Susan's conditioned response of flying to an outstretched arm to feed had to be reversed.

"Remolding Susan's bad habit is going to be even more difficult than forming it in the first place," Cecil said.

"Promise me that you'll try," Adele replied, "I still want to go in with Susan."

Over the next few weeks, Cecil accustomed Susan to being fed regularly, like the rest of birds at Featherland. Since she was still in her growing stage, she was fed twice every twenty-four hours. The Hyndmans cut up pieces of meat, put them in a dish, and slipped the small bowl through the bars on the floor. Gradually Susan learned to accept food while standing on the floor.

Cecil and Adele differed from most bird handlers in their approach to feeding birds of prey. They believed food must not be a reward for any action or performance. Years ago Cecil had realized that the practice of reward feeding ultimately became self-defeating: If it becomes the standard motivator, an animal will refuse to learn unless fed.

Cecil worked on deconditioning Susan from her expectation of receiving food from his gloved hand. The first few times he approached her empty-handed, she grabbed at his hand, bloodying it on more than one occasion with her sharp bill. Adele remained supportive, encouraging Cecil when he complained of taking "two steps back for every single step forward."

Gradually, Susan's impulsive grabbing waned. While the activity never completely disappeared, it encouraged Cecil to see that Susan's behavior could be modified. Adele pointed out a number of small signs that Susan was becoming more tolerant. She only occasionally raised her hackle feathers, and she rarely flew in a rage inside her enclosure.

"Cec, do you realize it's been over a month since Susan arrived," she told Cecil in bed late one night. "I think it's time you start shedding some of your Man from Mars armor."

Cecil wasn't so sure. "It's only been a week since Sue last cut me."

He showed Adele the bandage to remind her of the incident. She dismissed the small cut as "an accidental scratch."

Cecil lay back in bed, knowing full well where the conversation was leading. Frankly, he was surprised Adele had not confronted him earlier. The protective gear had been intended as a temporary precaution. Continuing to wear it meant he could not achieve the closeness he wanted with Susan. And by prolonging wearing the layers of protection, he was taking the risk of conditioning her to only accepting him fully armored.

"Alright, tomorrow I'll start," he conceded.

This "disarmament phase," as Adele described it, initially went well. Cecil began by dropping some of the padding under the leather, which lightened the weight of the gear he wore and made physical movement easier. Although Susan studied him curiously, noting the changes, her actions showed no disapproval.

He then discarded the cowboy chaps. The loose rawhide, which he wore over work pants, had protected his lower half from hips to toes. Susan's reaction told Cecil that she had noticed his new slimness.

On his next visit, Cecil left off the handmade leather arm protectors. This time Susan glared, as if perplexed, at where the missing gear should be. Cecil stared back just as intently, checking for signs of hostility. But Susan made no attempt to attack.

Later, Cecil entered her room without the padded coat. Once again she slowly looked him over but showed no signs of violent behavior. If anything, her responses grew more friendly.

Finally, Cecil retained only his thick welding gloves and fencing mask. (And, of course, his fedora.) Adele continued to be bemused by the heavy mask with its iron grille. She told Cecil he reminded her of a living surrealist painting, dubbing him "the man in the iron mask with fedora." More seriously, she complained the mask prevented Cecil "from making direct contact with Susan."

"The heavy mask . . . was probably more a menace to safety than a protection," Cecil admitted later in his journal. "Its grille interfered with my vision and Susan showed signs of wanting to grab at it if she found an opportunity. Still, few people are completely logical and I could not bring myself to discard it."

But when the European fencing master called to demand the return of the mask, Cecil had no choice. The prohibitive cost of purchasing a new fencing mask meant he would have to do without.

The following day Cecil stepped inside Susan's pen for the first time with his face unprotected. Despite her dismissal of the mask's usefulness, he noticed how nervous Adele appeared as she waited by the door.

Cecil halted in mid-step as he spotted something unusual in Susan's stance and stare. Her body language did not express fear or anger, but a nervous tension that could go either way. For a moment Cecil and Susan eyed each other apprehensively. Neither budged. The scene reminded Cecil of a "Western movie where two gunfighters wait for the other's first move."

Finally Susan cocked her head anxiously and fixed her huge eyes on the puzzling maskless intruder in her enclosure. The intensity of her piercing stare froze Cecil to the spot. The impasse continued for what seemed like an eternity. Unsure of Susan's reaction and not knowing what she might do, he did not dare move. Without the mask he was virtually defenceless should Susan attack.

"Speak to her," Adele whispered from the door. "She's confused — reassure her it's really you."

Cecil spoke quietly to Susan, hoping for the right tone, although his throat felt dry and his voice sounded strained. To his surprise, Susan immediately softened her stance. Behind him, he could hear Adele exhale.

Cecil felt like doing the same. By gradually reducing his protective gear, piece by piece, he had discarded more than just items of thick clothing. He had also reduced the barriers between him and Susan. Only by rendering himself vulnerable could he make progress in their relationship.

The day Cecil faced Susan without his mask marked a turning point in their relationship. While he was still some way from being fully accepted, for the first time since Susan arrived, he sensed a bond developing between them.

"I should be jealous — I think she's beginning to like you," Adele said when Cecil left Susan's pen.

"Don't be, I have enough love for both of the women in my life."

The end of Susan's first spring at Featherland saw more than just the colorful carpeting of the rocky slopes with spring flowers. Late spring began the busiest part of the year at the sanctuary. Each year at this time, Cecil and Adele opened the gates to what seemed a never-ending stream of visitors, most arriving by carload, with the occasional bus group. Abandoned and injured birds also began arriving as word of their avian sanctuary spread. They prided themselves on never turning away an ill or injured bird.

On a sunny May morning, the Hyndmans sat to enjoy their first coffees of the day. Adele shifted uncomfortably when she saw the thickness of the note pad with the ominous words "chore list" scrawled across the cover in Cecil's handwriting. The list had grown considerably after they had deliberately delayed much of their annual maintenance work on Featherland's grounds and buildings to concentrate on Susan.

The phone rang and Adele quickly answered it.

"Cec, it's that press photographer after a photo of Susan," Adele called out, putting her hand over the mouthpiece. "Should I put him off again?"

"No, tell him to come along this afternoon — but he'll have to agree to follow my directions."

Cecil felt that, as Susan seemed somewhat calmer now, they could use the publicity to promote Susan as the latest addition to Featherland. He suggested they change the brochures to include her.

"What do you think of this caption, provided we get a usable photo?" he asked, and read aloud from a handwritten sheet: "Meet Susan, our majestic hand-reared golden eagle — a dramatic bird of incredible power who can be as gentle as a lamb or as dangerous as a tiger."

"Maybe we should see how the session goes today." Adele for once suggested a cautious approach.

The initial photographic session went well and the Hyndmans contacted the other newspapers that had expressed interest in Susan's arrival in Victoria.

Over the next few days, separate teams of reporters and photographers arrived. Cecil, who had a genuine rapport with people, could be a masterful showman when he wanted. His work for the CBC and then the NFB had given him first-hand experience of the tremendous publicity the media could generate.

He took each press team on a tour of Featherland, proudly showing off the natural gardens and wildlife. Before taking journalists inside to view Susan, he warned them that they must follow certain rules.

Only one photographer was foolhardy enough to laugh at Cecil's precautions. The photographer prided himself on his toughness and dismissed Susan as "nothin' but an oversized turkey. I expected something a little more fierce."

Although he had shed all his other protective gear, Cecil still wore the heavy and clumsy gloves whenever he entered Susan's enclosure. These were a necessity not just for protection, but also as a means of transporting Susan. Large birds of prey cannot be carried like cats or led on leashes like dogs. And to attempt to lift or confine a golden eagle in one's arms almost always results in an attack unless the bird is wounded or injured. The gloves also helped Susan maintain her balance; her talons could slip on loose flesh.

So instead of debating with the man, Cecil took off the gloves he wore and offered them to the photographer. Then Cecil dared him to put his hand into Susan's enclosure. The burly man laughed and began to put on the gloves — until he saw the length of the curved talons on Susan's feet. Cecil took back the gloves and went inside the enclosure while the pressman silently shot stills from outside.

The resulting publicity from the photographic sessions created tremendous excitement — not only in Victoria but across Canada.

Susan quickly became the star attraction of Featherland. How could she fail to impress visitors with her fierce gaze and large, powerful body? What initially impressed people was Susan's extraordinary size. Many experts who studied golden eagles remarked that she was the largest example of the species they had ever seen. Her wingspan now reached nearly eight feet. Cecil speculated the rich-beef diet supplied to the eaglet by Danny Nowlan at the Whitehorse forestry firehall accounted for her large size.

By late fall of 1955, the news of Susan's arrival had spread east. A Montreal newspaper article mentioning the golden eagle being exhibited in Victoria caught the attention of the NFB. Shortly after the article appeared, the film board contacted the Hyndmans, requesting permission to film a documentary on Featherland with the focus on Susan.

While Cecil found the offer flattering, he was hesitant. He confided his worries to his journal: "The questions raised by the NFB show their ignorance of Featherland and the difficulties involved in filming. They obviously regard Featherland as some private roadside zoo, with outdoor cages. They also think Susan can perform aerial acrobatics like some trained falcon."

Adele, however, could barely contain her excitement when she heard about the offer. "Think of it — our Susan on movie screens across Canada."

"We'll have to set conditions," Cecil said.

He knew only too well what was involved in a film shoot. He explained to Adele how the thick cables, camera, and microphones might cause the birds to panic and injure themselves.

Cecil went on to describe how filming inside required floodlights and reflector boards that could easily startle the birds when they were turned on. Such trauma might set back the speech training of a number of their birds. And how would Susan react?

He mentioned the embarrassing example of Captain C. W. R. Knight, a falconer who had climaxed his lecture at a National

Geographic Society gathering by releasing his trained golden eagle. A flashbulb blinded the eagle, who, instead of returning to the falconer's hand, landed on a lady's hat.

Adele refused to be swayed. As quickly as Cecil raised an objection, she dismissed it. This clash of temperaments played out often at Featherland — Cecil's rational practicality conflicting with Adele's romantic idealism. With Adele, it was all or nothing. Words like "compromise" or "practicality" did not exist in her vocabulary.

While Cecil wanted to wait and find out more about the offer, Adele wasted no time in deciding. She repeated to Cecil what she had said months ago: "With us, Susan can become world famous."

The debate continued over the next two days, flaring up whenever they came in contact with each other. Neither one gave, and an uneasy truce thickened the silence between them.

Three nights later in bed, Cecil, who suffered from insomnia all his life, had just drifted off to sleep when something jabbed him. He woke, thinking one of the birds that shared their bedroom had bitten him. Perhaps one of the gulls, as they were forever flapping into bed and using their sharp beaks to gain more space. But it was Adele who had nudged him.

"I just realized — there's something else, isn't there, the real reason why you can't decide about the NFB," Adele said.

"Yes, there is," Cecil admitted. "We'd better talk."

Once again Adele had intuitively grasped that something was troubling Cecil. He got out of bed and Adele made a pot of coffee. They sat and talked, Cecil telling Adele he had been charting Susan's adjustment over her first six months at Featherland. Recently her progress had not only stalled, but she had begun to display an aggression that worried Cecil.

Adele dismissed these as "just Sue's mood swings."

Cecil pointed out that Adele did not notice Susan's violent tendencies for the simple reason Susan behaved when Adele was present. In an attempt to encourage Susan to bond to him,

Cecil had recently tried to discourage Adele from attending their sessions.

"I worry we're pushing Susan too fast — maybe even too far," Cecil confessed, "exhibiting her might be overstressing her."

"So this debate's really over profit versus Susan's progress," Adele astutely summarized the dilemma. Even with the upturn in the numbers of visitors since Susan's arrival, financially Featherland was barely keeping afloat.

On the other hand, time was ticking away; Susan was going through her critical formative years. Like human children, young birds of prey have a narrow window in which their personalities can be molded. Unfortunately, no one had ever attempted to make such direct and intimate contact with a golden eagle before, so there were no guidelines as to when this window closed.

"It might already be too late — which limits us to keeping her behind bars with no contact or shipping her to a zoo," Cecil said.

As they talked out the problem, they agreed the first concern was Susan's well-being. Adele suggested she try bonding with Susan. Cecil still insisted the risk of personal injury was too great. It was almost dawn when they decided the only solution was to carry on in hopes that Susan was just going through a phase.

The other alternative was too drastic to contemplate. If they failed with Susan and shipped her off to a zoo, they faced the very real possibility of losing Featherland. Even with the extra revenue generated by this rare and majestic bird of prey, their money problems continued.

Cecil's father, Judge Hyndman, was providing the couple with financial support. But Cecil wondered if he would be willing to continue it if they failed at rearing their star attraction. Both Cecil's and Adele's families had serious doubts about their eccentric lifestyle. Without Judge Hyndman's support, they would have to give up their Eden.

Eventually Cecil agreed to the NFB's proposal to film a documentary at Featherland, finalizing arrangements with the NFB over the winter months. The small NFB crew arrived early in the spring of 1956. Cecil had asked that dummy equipment and lights be set up well before shooting began, so the Hyndmans could gradually condition the birds to their presence. "Our request was brushed aside as unnecessary and impractical," Cecil wrote in his journal. His worst fears were justified.

The team was led by a "red-headed cameraman-director full of youthful ego and with about as much finesse as a bull in a china shop." Filming took place over a period of ten days. During the initial phase, the crew busied themselves laying electric cables to supply the lights and setting up overhead microphones to record the speech of the birds. At first all the film equipment merely made the birds anxious.

The outdoor sequences were completed, showing the grounds of Featherland. Finally filming began indoors. Adele and Cecil waited tensely as the floodlights were switched on for the first time. The blinding light unnerved the birds inside Ookpik Cottage. Some froze in panic, others startled and took off but luckily none injured themselves.

Inside Talon Hall, the filming progressed slowly. Most of the birds were uncooperative. Not surprisingly, Susan proved the most difficult of all. When the bright lights pointed at her enclosure first came on, she signaled her displeasure with such force that the director ran for cover. Cecil was forced to step in and halt the filming before Susan became completely enraged. Adele's gentle voice seemed to calm Susan, but the director wisely postponed the sequence that featured the eagle.

"He's afraid of Susan," Adele informed Cecil, unable to suppress a smile.

"Maybe we should have some fun with him," Cecil suggested.

Now behind schedule, the director tried to speed up the pace as he filmed the sequences involving the other birds. By the end of the first week of filming, Adele and Cecil were as fed up as their feathered family.

The dramatic finale was the last to be shot. The script called for Susan to fly to Cecil's arms. The director demanded that the Hyndmans make Susan cooperate, putting the blame for the film's lateness on Susan. Cecil decided to extract a measure of satisfaction.

"I think you should place the camera inside Susan's pen," he deadpanned. "Otherwise, the shot will be ruined by filming through the cage wire."

For once the cocky director lost his composure, flatly refusing to entertain the idea. In the end, Susan was filmed from behind the safety of the wire mesh.

The completed black-and-white film played as a theatrical short at movie theaters across Canada. After it ran at the local Odeon in Victoria, Cecil and Adele were recognized in shops all over town. But they never went to see the documentary. Their ten minutes of fame did not offset their frustration at the way the film crew had upset their family.

Judge Hyndman, on the other hand, reacted with pride when he heard of the filming. With some bemusement, Cecil noted how that NFB film seemed to legitimize their work with birds in his father's eyes.

Many times over the next few months and years, as Susan's fame spread, other film and television companies contacted the Hyndmans. Each time they politely refused permission to film inside their buildings. When pressed, Cecil gave a standard answer: "We have no objection to interior filming, but the final decision's up to Susan. All the director has to do is to go into her enclosure and ask her personally for permission." No one ever took him up on this suggestion.

five

An Uphill Battle

"*You know what day it is?*" Adele asked Cecil one warm spring day in 1956. "The tenth anniversary of our arrival here on the West Coast."

"And it'll soon be Susan's first anniversary here," Cecil added.

The Hyndmans quietly celebrated Susan's first year with them. Instead of a cake, Susan was given extra strips of lean beef. She enjoyed the treats and put on her own high-spirited celebration, "churning up the air with her wings in storms of zesty vigor," in Cecil's words. Adele clapped her approval at Susan's exuberance.

Cecil marked Susan's anniversary by measuring her wingspan, which turned out to be slightly less than when she arrived. Cecil was not surprised. He knew that the first-year feathers of golden eagles are longer than those from subsequent molts, often by an inch. A golden eagle takes three to five years to reach maturity; Cecil wanted to record the changes in each of Susan's molts.

Susan had lost most of her sharply bicolored first-year plumage. These feathers were white at the base, with dark tops. When she was sitting, the overlapping feathers covered most of the lighter color, except at the base of her tail feathers. In full flight, with both wings outstretched and the band of white on each wing and her white-ringed tail, the immature golden eagle looked striking.

Susan's weight had increased slightly as she put on muscle. Cecil knew that the coming year or two of Susan's life would determine her fate at Featherland. As she approached the peak of her physical power, her "terrible teen" years, Cecil was determined to break through to her. He had to — or else admit defeat and ship Susan to a zoo.

News of another golden eagle in captivity offered little encouragement. Through Wilf Blezard and Danny Nowlan, Cecil learned that a falconer in Victoria had also acquired a female golden eagle. Young David Hancock visited Cecil with falconry expert and author Frank Beebe. Later David would go on to establish a career photographing wildlife, writing books, and producing documentary films — as well as setting up a publishing house devoted to wildlife.

David told Cecil how he had started by training a number of smaller hawks. His golden eagle was the falconer's ultimate dream. He had acquired her out of the nest, but soon found "her heavy weight was unmanageable, her temperament just a little too unpredictable, and the paralyzing strength of her talons just too much." David's experience with this spirited bird reinforced Cecil's fears that Susan would become even more aggressive as she approached maturity. Now when she flew to his arm, Cecil could feel the difference in her strength.

Early in his relationship with Susan, only weeks after her arrival, Cecil had experienced the unbelievable crushing effect of her feet on his arm. He had extended his gloved hand into Susan's pen to feed her. She landed on his outstretched arm, shifted her feet, and slowly exerted the full power of her talons. The four-inch talons acted like a tourniquet, restricting the blood flow.

Numbness quickly followed, eventually leaving rings of purple welts on Cecil's hand. It was a sensation he never forgot. "Tighter and tighter the pressure became until my very bones seemed to crack. It was a panicky feeling, yet there was no way of getting out of it, no way of withdrawing. It was all I could do to keep from crying out and fainting through fifteen long minutes of torture."

That had been when Susan was still a juvenile. Now when she turned on her full strength, the pain was simply overwhelming. Worse yet, Susan seemed to delight in exerting full force. Once during a tour, she squeezed Cecil's hand for only a few minutes, but it seemed like hours to him. Adele massaged the arm and restored the circulation, but it took some days before Cecil really recovered. He wrote:

I was positive I would never have the use of any part of my arm and hand again. For several days afterward until my hand and fingers returned to normal, I tried in vain to pick things up or use a pen or pencil. My wrist for a while was colorfully "tattooed."

An American falconer, Kent Durden, who had raised a golden eagle named Lady with his father, described a similar experience: "With slow, relentless force her talons tightened on my arm. I was frightened at her strength. . . . The circulation on my arm was cut off, my muscles ached. My arm now felt as if it belonged to someone else and I was just a horrified onlooker."

During that spring, Susan began to molt. Cecil began to collect Susan's feathers, hanging the prized twenty-four-inch-long flight feathers in the living room.

Cecil noted that the process of molting seemed to exhaust Susan. Like human youngsters going through a growth spurt, Susan had bursts of fantastic appetite. A golden eagle ordinarily consumes about six percent of its body weight in food each day. Given Susan's weight of seventeen pounds, she would have needed to eat one pound of food a day. But during this molt, she often ate two to three pounds of raw beef in two meals.

Soon the peak of the summer tourist season arrived. While the visitors brought in much-needed revenue, leading the tours exhausted the Hyndmans.

On a July evening at the end of two very busy weeks, Cecil hobbled into the cottage after the last tour of the long day. His boot was bloodied.

"Whose tattoo is that?" Adele chided Cecil as she helped him take off the boot. Adele rarely offered — or expected — much sympathy.

"Our darling Sue," Cecil admitted.

He explained that he had been so tired he dropped the broom while sweeping out Susan's stall between tours. As he picked it up, he turned to see her flick out one foot.

"The move was so fast it was a blur. I simply had no time to react."

Susan's middle talon punctured his thick shoe, piercing his foot to the bone. She withdrew it in a flicking motion too fast for the human eye to follow.

Cecil saw no malice behind the action. In fact, he realized he had been lucky. He had startled Susan and she had reacted impulsively. But she had not carried through with an attack.

As news of Susan spread, the number of visitors began to increase.

While Featherland boasted a number of exotic and rare birds and animals, including four monkeys, three screech owls, a great horned owl, and a sparrow hawk, the highlight of the tour was the rare golden eagle.

By now Cecil had progressed beyond merely showing Susan to staging a performance with her at the conclusion of the tour. But this grand finale for visitors to Featherland was nerve wracking. Cecil never knew from day to day whether she would cooperate and fly to his arm or launch a flying assault before he reached her pen, which delighted the visitors, but not Cecil.

On good days, he donned his minimal protective gear, a leather jacket, entered the pen, and called to Susan. She would excitedly flap her huge wings, launch herself, and fly to Cecil's outstretched hand. This short flight, coupled with Susan's huge wingspan and fierce expression, always brought a chorus of "ahhhs" from the visitors. But Cecil was never certain when she would act out her hostility by squeezing his arm until the blood stopped flowing.

He decided to practice his demonstration with Susan alone. Perhaps if he worked with her one-on-one, away from the distraction of the crowds, he could accustom her to fly to him "more calmly and on command."

At first the training sessions went extremely well. Pleased with the progress, he began practicing with Susan every day at noon in Talon Hall. Then one dull gray September day, Cecil entered her enclosure and called to Susan. Three times in succession she flew to his outstretched arm. Then Cecil made a costly mistake — one that would almost prove fatal.

When he tried to grasp her leg straps on her fourth flight to his outstretched arm, he fumbled and missed completely.

"From a blow out of nowhere, I found myself bowled flat to the floor. However Susan did it, no sledgehammer could have been more swiftly effective," he later wrote about the start of the attack.

As he struggled to his feet, he looked up in time to recognize that Susan was about to launch an airborne assault. She hovered, whipping the air with her huge wings, then pounced, her talons piercing Cecil's leg.

"Her great steely tongs pierced and locked into my left thigh. I jerked convulsively. Another talon fastened into my right hip. Those hooks of hers seared like fire into and out of my flesh." The intense pain of talons in his left thigh and right hip made him scream. Cecil thrashed desperately, which only seemed to excite, then enrage Susan.

His outburst brought a wing slap across his nose. Luckily it was only a light blow; a blow from Susan's wing edges delivered at full force had the power to sever like a scythe.

Down and injured, Cecil tried not to panic, knowing he was in serious trouble. He instinctively shouted for Adele, then realized she could not possibly hear him from the cottage. He recalled Wilf's warning of how Susan had attacked the dog. With her talons still stuck into his legs, Cecil attempted to inch backward, protecting his chest and abdomen with his hands.

Immediately Susan loosened one foot and struck again. He later recalled watching with a detached fascination as her talon shot straight at his unprotected eyes. He compared the eerie sensation to watching a bullet spinning toward his head in slow motion, knowing there was no way of moving fast enough to avoid being hit. Although his head instinctively snapped back, his movement was a split second too late.

The lightning-quick thrust knocked him backward. He felt "a hot sting, then wet red murk poured over and into my right eye. I could make out very little with the left one in the cloud of dust raised by all our thrashing and rolling on the floor."

Realizing he was in mortal danger, Cecil again shouted for Adele. Exhausted, he made desperate efforts to crawl toward the door. Susan continued to attack with both her wings and talons. Each time he lurched backward, Susan struck. Although she spread her wings and lowered her beak, her pale, thin tongue darting in and out, she never used her sharp bill. Golden eagles normally crush their prey with their talons — only afterward does the bill tear the flesh into manageable chunks. That knowledge gave Cecil little comfort as he rolled to force Susan to extract her talons, the pain searing and darkness threatening to engulf him.

Shock set in after a few minutes from his loss of blood and exhaustion. In his dazed condition, he almost welcomed the warm blackness as he passed out.

Later he woke to find himself outside the door to Susan's pen. He had no recollection of how he had escaped from Susan's talons. Or how he had somehow managed to shut the door behind him. Nor did he know if he had been unconscious for moments or minutes. He almost passed out again as he found he could not see out of his right eye.

Trembling with pain, he wiped his bloodied face, discovering that Susan's blow had split his brow but missed his right eye. As his vision returned, Cecil took stock, surprised at being able to stand. He stumbled off toward the cottage.

"What on earth have you been up to, you fool?" Adele greeted Cecil when he staggered through the door of their cottage. Her sharp tone changed when she saw the blood pouring from the cut above his eye. Then she noticed the red blotches on his legs. He could barely stand, but when he tried to sit, his body shook so badly he almost fell out of the chair.

Within minutes, Adele had catalogued the punctures, cuts, and slices, as well as itemizing the welts and bruises. None were serious, although some of the punctures were deep. Cecil did not feel her not-so-gentle prodding as she checked his wounds and rinsed the blood off. He sat in what he later described as "a semi-daze, delighted to be alive. Never had a drink of whisky ever tasted so good."

For the next few weeks, Adele took over feeding Susan to allow Cecil's wounds time to heal. She kept an eye out for any further signs of aggression in Susan. She also observed Cecil closely, to make sure he was not losing his nerve. Although he was keen to resume the performance he put on for visitors touring Featherland, for now this was impossible, as his injured legs caused him to limp and his bruised hand had swollen. The Hyndmans cancelled the grand finale of the tour for a few weeks.

Adele began to feed Susan between the bars, wearing heavy gloves as a necessary precaution. When she was overly excited, Susan sometimes used her feet to strike the meat as if it were prey. Even the thick gloves offered little protection from Susan's talons, as Adele found out the painful way.

One evening Cecil limped into the cottage to find Adele bathing a small wound on her hand. She tried to hide the injury from Cecil, but he recognized Susan's "tattoo mark" by the shape of puncture. While it was not deep, it was blunt.

"I see Sue's been a naughty girl," Cecil said to Adele.

"She apologized," Adele said. "Not in words, but I could read it in her body language."

As he had feared, Susan had punctured Adele's hand while striking for the meat. Adele gladly accepted these minor cuts as the price of getting close to Susan. After this incident, Susan's table manners slowly improved, as if she were making amends for injuring Adele.

As Adele spent more and more time with Susan, the eagle began to respond with gentle twittering to Adele's advances. Susan's behavior improved so much, in fact, that Adele secretly began to feed her out of her bare hands. Only after she had accomplished this feat a number of times did she casually announce her success to Cecil.

Ten days later, Cecil prepared to again enter Susan's pen. He confessed to Adele that the anticipation of returning to Susan's pen was unnerving; as a youngster in Alberta, he had always been taught to get back up if a horse threw him. But every time he passed Susan's enclosure, "her eyes burned with infuriation."

And yet, Cecil wrote, while his fear of Susan mounted "higher and higher, no corresponding hate for her grew in me. In fact, I would have killed anyone intending to harm her. From the first moment I laid eyes on Susan, hate for her was impossible."

One of the basic principles of bird handling at Featherland was that any bird had the right to injure humans, but they could not retaliate. "They're given that privilege, but we do not have the same return privilege. If we used force or violence to train a bird, we'd break their spirit. We want them to develop fully to enable them to exhibit their full faculties."

Cecil's temporary limp from Susan's attack meant he could not show visitors around the grounds of Featherland. Adele took over these duties, giving Cecil time to tend to a number of newly arrived birds at Featherland, including another golden eagle shipped from the Yukon. The male eagle, named Kluane, was much smaller than Susan and had a badly damaged wing. The Hyndmans also acquired a female bald eagle in 1956 called Lightning and a tiny male sparrow hawk called Rufus, who lived the next fourteen years in their living room, much of that time perched on Adele's shoulder or head.

The change in the routine also gave Cecil time to take detailed notes about Susan's behavior. Even the mundane task of cleaning her pen provided fascinating insights.

The enclosure featured a door at each end, and the pen itself was divided into two sections by a wire mesh partition. A door in the middle of the mesh was ordinarily kept open.

On the floor of the pen lay a mattress of straw, which served as litter. Every few days Cecil would sweep up the absorbent material and add new straw. He would enter and close the partition door, leaving Susan on one side while he cleaned the other side. Or Adele would sometimes enter the unoccupied side to clean.

The pen also featured a large pan filled with water, about four inches deep. This pan served almost exclusively as Susan's bathtub, not a source of drinking water. Golden eagles obtain all the moisture they need from their food. Rarely did Susan ever drink water "beyond a token sip of a drop or two in the hottest weather of one or two summers," Cecil recalled.

Susan delighted in her elaborate daily bath — as did Cecil, who spent time observing her and recording her routine. First came the wash, followed by a period of careful preening. "After lengthy primping and grooming she found it enjoyable to study her shadowy reflections in the water, turning her face this way and that as she peered," Cecil observed.

Adele and Cecil noticed that Susan's sharp eyes followed their every move when it came cleaning time — especially their movements from one side of the pen to the other. Before long Susan began to show a special interest in the door itself. She tried to duplicate the Hyndmans' moves and figure out how the door worked, using her talons for force, her beak for finesse.

As Susan came close to figuring out how to open the door, the Hyndmans talked about whether they should encourage or discourage this activity. On one hand, it would be relatively easy to reinforce the door to make it eagle-proof. On the other hand, if Susan could learn to open the door, this achievement would offer proof that eagles could solve problems. While this action might not qualify as a measurable test of intelligence, it would counteract the prevailing notion of the time that eagles were only capable of instinctive, unreasoning action.

Even Dr. Konrad Lorenz, famous for his insights into animal and bird life, thought little of eagles' intelligence. He wrote in his book *King Solomon's Ring* that all birds of prey were "extremely stupid creatures. This applies particularly to the golden eagle, 'the eagle' of our mountains and our poets, which is one of the most stupid among them, much more so indeed than any barnyard fowl."

The Hyndmans decided to leave the door as it was, and soon Susan figured out how to open and close the door dividing her pen. Watching her swagger proudly back and forth between the two sections of her pen for the first time, Cecil felt a surge of pride. The sensation was as strong as that of any father watching a daughter's first steps, or performing at a dance recital. Susan seemed to bask in the admiration, twisting her head to glare proudly at him with her big brown eyes under her thrusting brows.

By late 1956, Susan had firmly established herself as the star attraction of Featherland. Cecil wrote, "Our murderous yet beloved Susan was the keystone, supported by other trained eagles, both golden and bald, who came to us shortly after Susan arrived. These and other birds of prey as well as a host of whimsical, cultivated bird personalities and a scattering of mammals made up the cast."

Cecil and Adele tried to tailor the show as far as possible to suit the varying groups that arrived at Featherland's gate. Some visitors were so impressed with the natural landscaping they took them on short hikes along the creek to a series of pools where ducks and geese swam. By now the Lombardy poplars they had planted a decade ago shot skyward to a height of eighty-two feet. Even the artificial portions of the grounds, the twisting paths and concrete ponds, blended into the lacy fern backdrop.

Each informal tour was personally led by either Cecil or Adele. While they strove to be informative, the tours "steered away from the dryly pedantic." The Hyndmans wanted the Featherland experience "to embrace something of the artistic and most of all, the dramatic — combined sometimes with a few grains of relaxing humor and nonsense."

Cecil kept up a running commentary on the birds, enlivening the tours by pointing out the idiosyncrasies of each one. For example, while showing visitors through the cottage, where many birds resided, Cecil would introduce Goliath, the Arctic raven. The sight of this massive bird taking a bath with its feet in the air always amused the visitors. A hand-reared gull named Winkin would come when called and step up to Cecil's hand on command. The talented gull could also turn the pages in a book when asked.

While visitors were never allowed to handle the larger birds of prey in Talon Hall, they could approach to within inches. This sense of closeness had a huge impact. Few people had ever seen a golden eagle from any distance, let alone one only inches away.

As Susan's fame slowly spread, revenues from Featherland increased. But at the same time, the Hyndmans had to spend more money on the property. Talon Hall needed improving to disguise its humble origins as a poultry barn. The interior was upgraded, with new reflector lighting to focus attention on the individual birds. As the tours often started, and sometimes ended, in the cottage, Cecil and Adele refurbished its spartan decor with "some faintly Oriental touches using bamboo curtains and rush matting."

Along with the physical improvements, Featherland extended its hours until 9:00 p.m. six days a week. This move necessitated stringing expensive outdoor lights. At the same time, the number of family members at Featherland continued to swell as Featherland became known as a sanctuary that accepted both injured and abandoned birds. Most of the orphaned birds were set free, but many others with permanent injuries remained with the Hyndmans the rest of their lives. They never turned away an injured bird, and often operated to save those that had been severely hurt.

The Hyndmans did more than just passively *receive* injured birds brought to their door. If a call came through about an injured bird, they would interrupt their busy schedule to drive miles and retrieve it. Sometimes this meant climbing trees. Few other wildlife rescue organizations went to such extremes. "People thought we were nuts," Cecil confessed.

Late in 1956 Cecil suffered a recurrence of the heart trouble that had plagued him most of his life. This flare-up worried Cecil, who had not experienced any heart problems in some years.

"Cec, look at this. They want to seize Susan!" Adele burst into the bedroom where Cecil was recuperating that fall.

She showed him a notice from the provincial wildlife authority

threatening to seize Susan. Cecil's agitation increased when he realized that confiscation notice was based on an error made by a still
photographer who had photographed Susan after her arrival in 1955.
The caption under the photo said that Susan came from northern
British Columbia, when in fact she had been hatched in the Yukon.

What doubly annoyed Cecil was the fact he had contacted the
newspaper at the time to demand a correction, since he knew any
eagle captured within British Columbia required a special permit.
But the newspaper had ignored his request.

Leaving his sick bed, Cecil traveled to the mainland to sort out
the problem. Although he was easily able to prove that Susan
had come from outside the province, it ultimately took two more
trips before he successfully got the wildlife authorities to rescind
their threat.

By now Susan was maturing physically. The greenish-yellow tint
high up on her upper mandible was changing to a bright yellow.
Some of her buff nape feathers were turning into the beautiful
golden brown so distinctive of adult golden eagles. Cecil wondered
about the next phase of Susan's life. As she reached full maturity,
would she calm down enough to accept him? Or would her aggres-
siveness toward him increase as her physical powers reached
their peak?

Cecil had his answer in a few weeks. One day near the end of the
season, after seeing a group of visitors off, he thought he heard a
wooden crashing coming from Talon Hall. Suspecting a door was
banging in the breeze, he returned up Huff and Puff Hill.

The violent thrashing increased in volume when Cecil entered
Talon Hall. The noise came from Susan's pen. He rushed down the
long hall to find Susan suspended upside down, her wings bashing
against the mesh. The huge bird had caught one foot in the wire

mesh. Every time she tried to free herself, she reared back, flapping her wings fiercely.

Fearing that Susan could break a leg in her panic, Cecil had no time to put on the heavy welder's gloves. Instead he grabbed a pair of ordinary working gloves and set to extricating Susan's talons.

Quickly Cecil managed to pry one of Susan's talons free. But as he worked on loosening the others, "Susan saw the chance she had been waiting for." She struck at him with her free foot. At such close range, there was no chance of missing. Cecil recalled seeing a "technicolor blur" when he looked down at his hand.

The force of the blow had driven her longest front talon completely through his gloved hand and out the other side. The four-inch-long talon, with the diameter of a fountain pen, impaled Cecil's hand. Bleeding profusely, he could do nothing but wait until Susan decided to retract her talon. The almost minute-long wait was sheer agony. The pain was like "being stung to the quick by an army of hornets." Finally Susan withdrew the skewer and flew back to her stand.

Cecil stumbled out of Talon Hall. His hand began to swell before he reached the cottage, eventually ballooning to the size of a baseball. The damage was compounded by the fact the end of her curved claw was blunt, not pointed. The blow had mashed tissue and nerve. The wound required antibiotics, and for a week after the attack the throbbing pain kept him awake at night. Eventually the wound closed, leaving an ugly scar.

This incident marked a turning point in the turbulent relationship between Cecil and Susan. Cecil likened it to "Susan declaring war — all-out war."

six

A Brush with Death

Late in the fall of 1957, the Hyndmans noticed that Susan seemed to be suffering from an allergic reaction. Cecil, who had studied veterinary science at agricultural college and pre-medicine at university, wondered if female eagles, like human females entering puberty, sometimes developed allergies as a result of hormonal change.

By trial and error, the Hyndmans discovered the straw used as litter on Susan's floor caused her to "sneeze with the irritation and experience all the nose-running annoyances common to human hay fever sufferers the world over."

Once they had isolated the cause, they worked on a cure. The removal of the straw and a daily wet cleaning ended Susan's sneezing, although the daily scrubbing added to the Hyndmans' heavy workload.

Only weeks after this minor health crisis, something much more serious happened. Susan developed a head cold. Her illness was no doubt brought on in part by cold weather and her evening bath routine. She often bathed her head in the large pan of water in her pen, then stood near the open window with her head still wet. That fall, however, a cold autumn breeze blew through the bars.

At first the Hyndmans were not alarmed. If anything, the sight of a golden eagle with a runny beak brought laughter. But as the days progressed, "instead of remaining localized and then clearing up, the infection gained a firm hold, spreading deeper into her eyes, throat, tongue, and finally deeply down into the breathing passages. Susan wheezed and drooped in a misery that left little room for her venom toward me," Cecil wrote.

The Hyndmans administered penicillin in her food, but Susan's condition worsened. "It might take a few days for the antibiotics to kick in," Cecil warned Adele.

The antibiotics failed to stem the spread of the infection. Now the Hyndmans were desperate. Although it was still autumn according to the calendar, the bone-chilling weather made it seem like mid-winter. The cold, wet air and unheated pen were a far cry from the dry atmosphere of the high plateaus where golden eagles live. Wild eagles migrated south during the winter — Susan could not.

"It was with alarm one night that we recognized the symptoms of acute pneumonia taking hold. We knew that the only possible hope for saving Susan's life lay in getting her immediately into a draft-free seventy-degree temperature, and beginning a whole series of local treatments as well as determining the specific organism involved," Cecil wrote in his journal. Unfortunately, their tiny cottage only had one closed area — their bedroom. With no other alternative and no time to construct a new pen, they decided to move her there.

By midnight they had cleared their bedroom. Quickly they constructed a makeshift grille from floor to ceiling over the curved archway leading to the bedroom. The last task was covering the window with bars so Susan could not break the glass and cut herself.

Now they had to get Susan into the padded box so she could be carried the 100 yards down the hill from Talon Hall to their cottage.

"Perhaps she might not remember it," Cecil hoped, knowing from experience that Susan had an excellent memory.

This conjecture brought a tired laugh from Adele. "I'm just hoping she's too sick to fight being confined."

Susan's immediate and hostile reaction to the sight of the box made it obvious that she did remember. The trauma of that earlier confinement outweighed her weakened condition. She raised her hackle feathers aggressively.

Adele and Cecil entered her pen, Cecil carrying the blanket from their bed to serve as a straightjacket if necessary.

"Ill as she was, Sue momentarily roused herself to put up a terrific struggle of resistance, but we succeeded at length in getting her boxed and started down the icy hill with her in the darkness," Cecil later wrote in his journal. He also admitted that, in their overtired and stressed condition, "the exchanges between Adele and I were inclined to be sharp and argumentative."

Halfway to their cottage, they almost slipped on the slick slope, wet from the rain. Adele spoke quietly to Susan as they stopped to rest and adjusted their hand positions. They waited a moment, expecting Susan to react. When she didn't, they continued on their crosshill journey, the weight of the huge box slowing their pace.

Despite their care, eventually Susan burst into action inside the box. Her frantic wing flaps generated enough power to knock nails loose; some she knocked right out. Wrote Cecil, "We had to hastily resort to tying ropes around to hold the top down. We made it to the new room somehow, just in time. There, before our eyes, she literally split the box apart in being freed."

By now dawn was approaching. Only one chore remained: to turn up the heat in Susan's new quarters. This resulted in the rest of their small cottage becoming as hot as a sauna. Exhausted and sweating, the Hyndmans collapsed into their bed, now situated in one corner of their living room, which they called the Bird Room as so many birds lived in the room.

The next morning saw no improvement in Susan's condition. Cecil set out to somehow convince a pathology lab to examine throat swabs to determine the exact cause of Susan's infection. He called the lab at Victoria's Jubilee Hospital. The startled officials brushed aside his request, telling him to contact a vet. Cecil attempted to explain that only a large lab like the Jubilee's had the advanced technology to isolate the germ.

His pleading brought no change in the official's response. "They said 'sorry but no,'" Cecil told Adele as he hung up the phone.

Few who knew Cecil Hyndman would describe him as being aggressive or pushy. But neither could he be considered a quitter. Cecil reacted to the lab authorities like any father would when faced with obstacles in obtaining medical help for a dying child. He did not take "no" for an answer.

Together Cecil and Adele began leafing through their address book, calling every doctor, scientist, or official they thought might bring pressure on the lab. This indirect route took time, but eventually it paid off. Finally the lab agreed to make an exception.

Once he had the official go-ahead, Cecil used a sterile swab to take a smear from Susan's throat. He rushed the smear to the hospital's lab, where the bacteria present on the swab was grown. The last step involved testing various antibiotics on the cultivated bacteria to see if any could kill the microorganism.

When Cecil asked how long the process would take, no one at the lab could give him a firm answer. Finding a suitable antibiotic often took days. Would Susan live that long?

While the lab worked on identifying the bacteria, the Hyndmans sought other medical assistance. They explained their predicament to a sympathetic ear, nose, and throat specialist, who declined to examine Susan, but did prescribe a new form of sulfa for her encrusted eyes. He warned that the application was critical, for if the sulfa reached her mouth, it could poison Susan. He also instructed them to "paint" Susan's throat every four hours with another medication he provided to reduce the swelling.

The Hyndmans nervously discussed how they would administer the sulfa drops on Susan's encrusted eyes, keeping in mind the doctor's warning about the liquid becoming poisonous if any reached her mouth. They resorted to the "blanket wrap" method: Cecil wrapped and held Susan while Adele administered the medicine. The first time, Susan objected to the sting of the chemical, but she soon took the medicine stoically.

Adele also took on the delicate task of administering the medicine the doctor prescribed for Susan's inflamed throat, using her bare fingers when the thick welding gloves proved too clumsy. While Cecil held Susan, Adele spoke quietly to the golden eagle, who responded by voluntarily opening her mouth at Adele's request. Susan scarcely flinched as Adele painted her extremely tender throat.

Cecil marveled to Adele at how amazingly patient and understanding Susan was about these treatments.

"I'm sure she realizes what we're doing," Adele replied.

The Hyndmans treated Susan every few hours around the clock, but still she became weaker and weaker. Cecil almost wished her fierceness would return, as her uncharacteristic meekness suggested she had given up her will to live. And still there was no progress from the pathology lab.

By now Susan's throat had swollen so badly she could no longer swallow food. The only way to maintain her little remaining strength was to hand-feed her bits of meat. Forcing an eagle's powerful jaw open was no easy task, especially as Adele had to use her bare fingers. Although she could have badly injured Adele's bare fingers and hands with her sharp beak, Susan never bit, despite the indignity of meat being pressed down her throat.

As the days passed, her condition deteriorated. Her fever rose and she barely had the strength to stand. Cecil recalled taking her pulse by pressing "the blood vessels in her neck. Her heart contractions could be directly felt by my finger pressed against the chest wall. The action of her great heart was much affected, its beat terrific, fluttery and feeble. The irregular rate was between 180 and 200 per minute. My own heart thumped in agitation. I shed tears."

Cecil and Adele watched helplessly as Susan's life drained away before their eyes. "Despite every measure we took, the violence of inflammation spread throughout head, gullet and respiratory system. It intensified to a point that brought her very near death. Susan could make no sound beyond feeble, lung-drowned gasps. Those brown eyes of hers, now shrunken and dulled, looked up into mine and Adele's — imploring us to save her."

Adele and Cecil realized Susan's fate lay in the hands of the lab. Cecil worried that even if the lab finally isolated the microorganism, Susan might be too far wasted to recover. In all his years of tending to sick birds, Cecil had never seen a bird in such critical condition survive.

The Hyndmans had no staff or help at Featherland. Susan's illness forced them to temporarily close the sanctuary to the public.

Their night and day vigil beside Susan produced a nervous anxiety that began to cloud their thinking. Even when they spelled one another off, sleep proved difficult in the sweltering cottage.

Adele was close to collapse from the strain and fatigue. Cecil noticed how she clenched her hands "until the knuckles went white" as she paced late at night, unable to sleep. "But she would not for a single moment admit defeat," he wrote proudly in his journal.

At last the lab called with news. The tests had identified two microorganisms that caused the pneumonia; the lab recommended a specific course of antibiotics to cure the infection. The Hyndmans immediately began to administer the medicine. The antibiotics had to be given every six hours for a week, then repeated after a short interval. Would they work a miracle?

At first the antibiotics made no difference in Susan's condition. Cecil, who had studied both animal and human anatomy, had successfully undertaken major surgery on injured birds. And many residents of Featherland had been cured of infections by antibiotics. Reluctantly, he concluded that they had exhausted all the avenues of conventional medicine, and that Susan's end was near.

"From a purely physical, pathological treatment standpoint, there was now no ghost of a chance of recovery at all. The infection had overwhelmed the body's forces of defence," Cecil wrote in his journal late one night as he tried to summon up the courage to tell Adele the truth.

The next morning he stopped Adele outside as she returned from feeding the rest of their feathered family in Talon Hall. "You have to prepare yourself. There's no hope of saving Susan," he told his wife.

Adele's already pale complexion turned white and she began to tremble. At first she said nothing, but just stared past Cecil into the cottage. Finally she said, quietly but with conviction, "Susan must live. I simply refuse to let her die."

Without another word, Adele stormed past Cecil toward the cottage. He followed her in to see Susan, who lay on the wooden floor of their former bedroom. In her pitifully weakened condition, Susan could barely move or speak. Cecil watched from the door as Adele talked quietly to the gaunt eagle lying listlessly on the floor. Her inflamed throat was still discolored and swollen, her eyes glazed and lifeless.

Cecil could hear Adele whisper to Susan, encouraging her, willing her to live. As he eavesdropped, he realized that behind this renewed attempt to revive Susan was one of Adele's deepest beliefs — namely that no matter how difficult or overwhelming the challenge, people were never defeated unless they gave up. Since Cecil had given up, she would carry on.

The strength of Adele's inner conviction shamed Cecil. He still doubted Adele could make Susan live by willpower alone, but he felt the least he could do was try. And Cecil knew Adele had intuitive abilities that defied any rational explanation. Her extraordinary ability training birds to speak offered proof of this. She also had established a close rapport with Susan that eluded Cecil.

They had already thrown everything modern medicine could offer at Susan; maybe addressing her psychological makeup could effect the miracle it would take to cure her.

Cecil joined Adele and Susan on the bedroom floor. The two Hyndmans kept a constant vigil beside the eagle, doing all in their power to encourage her. Adele continued to speak quietly to Susan, telling her over and over she must will herself to live.

Cecil later recalled Adele's quiet but fierce determination that long day and night. "Adele has a power of mind she seems to be able to project, a will to be reckoned with — one she can infuse into another being in some manner not possible to clearly analyze."

Neither Adele nor Cecil slept that night as they tended to Susan, administering the antibiotics and the antiseptic eye drops. Susan was so weak Cecil did not have to wrap her in the blanket. And even though her mouth was extremely sensitive from the infection, Susan did not object when Adele opened her beak and used her bare hands to paint her dry throat with the glycerine preparation.

As the sun broke early the next morning, Adele noticed a change in Susan. Her mucous-filled eyes shone for the first time in over a week. Had the crisis passed?

With a flutter of her nearly eight-foot wings, Susan rose from the floor. She managed to stand unsteadily for a moment. Although the signs were encouraging, the Hyndmans monitored her progress closely for another few hours before admitting the tide had turned. Hour by hour Susan's condition gradually improved.

In the pages of his journal, Cecil speculated about the dramatic turnaround, pleased but at the same time deeply puzzled. "Somehow Adele's psychological therapy, added to the medical treatment, had provided a miracle."

Over the next few days, Cecil recorded the improvements in Susan's symptoms. Her discolored throat, which had been so dry at one point the membranes seemed ready to crack, gradually regained its pinkness. Her mucous-encrusted eyes cleared and once again began to shine. Soon Susan could eat by herself. Each ounce she put on gave her the energy to stand a few minutes longer. "From a gaunt and wasted state, she began to regain flesh," Cecil wrote.

As her health improved, Susan began to take an interest in her new quarters. She inspected every square inch of the room with her eyes, and occasionally took short walks, stopping to examine certain spots.

As she regained her strength, Susan began to show interest in grooming herself again. Her lengthy and near-fatal illness had left her ordinarily glossy plumage rumpled and soiled. She began to spend hours preening, and soon her plumage regained its luster. As yet Susan had not attempted to fly, although she sometimes flapped her wings as if to test them.

Adele and Cecil were able to catch up on their sleep as best they could in the noisy Bird Room. They discussed whether to move Susan out of their bedroom now that her recovery looked certain. In the end, the Hyndmans decided to keep Susan in their bedroom at least until spring. They simply could not take the chance of Susan catching another cold.

Within a few days, Susan had recovered enough to fly to Cecil's arm as he entered the room. He was delighted that she had regained enough strength to fly, but declared that Adele could no longer safely enter the room. At first she protested, but Cecil refused to change his mind.

Cecil noticed something else over the next few days — a change so subtle he had trouble believing it. As he put it, "Susan's harrowing experience had noticeably softened her attitude toward me. It had partly washed hate from her brain. Now was my great opportunity and I grasped it."

The intimacy they had achieved during the eagle's long sickness promised a new and closer relationship. Now that Susan had given him a chance, Cecil decided to proceed gradually, as he feared "a single error could bring her original attitude of hostility rushing back." He outlined a plan to change her bad habits one by one, each change leading in incremental steps to the next.

The first step was the hardest. Although he had tried before and failed, Cecil was determined to finally break Susan of the habit, ingrained in her youth by her falconer owner, of flying to the arm.

Patiently, Cecil began to decondition Susan:

[I used] the greatest possible care not to arouse her temper unnecessarily. I blocked her as adroitly as I could, forcing her back with crowding action each time she prepared to leap. This was a tricky business. Just a second of impatience could trigger a wing swing forceful enough to literally decapitate me. If she so acted, I had no defence.

After blocking her leaps, he provided positive reinforcement by praising her. Like all golden eagles, Susan had excellent hearing. She was able to distinguish both words and the tone in which the words were delivered — much like the ability of a dog to recognize "command" words and whether an owner expresses them in anger or pleasure.

By now Susan was approaching the mature stage of her life. Perhaps her new inner calm and outward contentment merely reflected the gradual loss of youthful exuberance. Whatever the reason, Susan at last lost the impulse to fly to whoever entered her room.

The next step in deconditioning Susan involved the removal of the leather leg jesses used in falconry. The jesses were knotted in an ingenious manner, which had taken falconers centuries to develop.

The traditional method used thick ties that do not tighten on a bird's leg and cut off the circulation of blood. Carefully Cecil planned how to remove them.

He ruled out the most obvious method of catching and restraining Susan. She had given him her trust, and he feared that if he physically held her he could trigger an angry outburst. He had come too far to risk that.

During the daily hand feeding, he took in a pair of small clippers. Each day, while Susan was eating, he snipped at the tough rawhide knots to weaken them. Each nip was surreptitious and careful. If he cut too deeply, he risked slicing Susan's feet. If she discovered what he was doing, she might attack; eagles will not put up with anyone interfering with their feet. Cecil never pushed his luck to attempt more than his goal of "one nip a day."

As he had hoped, the knots weakened and eventually fell off. Susan did not seem to notice that the jesses she had worn since her capture in the Yukon were missing.

Next, Cecil set out to dispose of his welder's gloves. Adele chided him that they were so thick they were next to useless. Cecil agreed, thinking back to the terrible attack that had resulted from his fumbling attempt to grab the jesses. Although he knew it was time to remove the gloves, he again encountered a psychological barrier. Yet he was too embarrassed to admit his fear to Adele.

Even falconers, who controlled their falcons as masters, wore gloves. Was Cecil tempting fate? He had deliberately given up what little physical control he had over Susan by cutting her jesses. Discarding his protective clothing, while promising rewards, also posed considerable risks. Only by freeing Susan and rendering himself vulnerable could their relationship progress to the depth he wanted it to. This meant neither party could hold an advantage over the other.

While this train of logic made sense intellectually, Cecil still found it difficult to walk into Susan's new quarters unprotected. It didn't take Adele long to notice that Cecil seemed to be delaying.

"When do you plan to go in?" she pointedly asked him one morning over coffee.

"Today," he replied, "after the morning feeding in Talon Hall."

"Why not right now? I have her food sliced," Adele suggested. "Then I can watch."

Cecil was out of excuses. He entered Susan's new quarters for the first time without gloves. Susan seemed puzzled by the long, thin fingers that held out meat to her. She took a long time inspecting his hands. Cecil made a habit of always talking to Susan when in her pen. Today he reminded her of the time she had punched her talon right through the palm of his hand. *Could she possibly remember?* Cecil wondered, as Susan seemed to take special interest in examining his scar.

Although Adele had successfully fed Susan with her fingers during her extreme illness, attempting this feat now that the eagle had regained all her considerable strength was another matter. As he held out the strips of beef, Cecil's fears at first seemed justified as Susan's razor-sharp beak nipped him. Cecil braced himself, but the eagle did not follow through with an attack.

As the blood flowed down Cecil's hand, a remarkable change came over Susan. Her fierce expression softened as she noticed the blood. Cecil described her reaction as being "clearly apologetic, with a worried expression showing in her face when she hurt me. She looked up into my eyes seeking forgiveness."

Adele bandaged Cecil's hand when he left the room. Cecil could barely contain his delight. He had bared himself to her, and she had not taken advantage of his weakness.

After three years, a near-fatal illness, and several attacks, Cecil at last had achieved the breakthrough he had sought in getting close to Susan. Where this new phase in their relationship would take them, he didn't know. But he was determined to find out.

seven

A LOVE AFFAIR

On a warm spring day in 1958 Cecil and Adele hiked the rocky highland rising behind their cottage. This rite of spring had turned into an annual event. They said little as they climbed the slope, instead enjoying the sight of masses of colorful miniature flowers that resembled a Persian carpet. On their hike, as they often did, they looked for ferns to transplant to the maze of pathways below. Burble Creek still flowed, but the volume of water flowing down this "winter creek" was already slowing to a trickle.

On that dreamy spring day, Adele and Cecil discussed Susan's future. Up until now, they had both assumed that when the warm weather arrived, Susan would move back to Talon Hall. But the remarkable progress she had made since her move indoors prompted Cecil to surprise Adele with a radical suggestion.

"I think Susan should remain in the cottage," he said.

"Yes," she agreed.

"There's one problem — if Sue takes over our bedroom permanently, we'll have to build a new bedroom for ourselves."

Adele nodded. For the past few months, they had shared living quarters with some thirty to forty birds in the Bird Room, the main area of their cottage. In the summer, when Featherland was open to the public, the Bird Room was part of the tour. If Susan was to remain in what had become "her" room, they needed another bedroom for themselves. But where would they find the money to finance the addition to their small cottage?

While Susan's fame continued to attract more and more visitors to Featherland, the Hyndmans' financial position remained precarious. They were behind on their mortgage payments, and Cecil worried his father, Judge Hyndman, was growing weary of supporting Featherland.

Cecil had tried a number of projects to make money. After noticing that most visitors who toured Featherland were amazed at the "talking birds," he put together a series of audio tapes. But sorting through the thousands of feet of audio tape had proved an enormous job, and the few sales barely covered the time involved.

When conducting tours, Adele and Cecil also noticed that people delighted in their whimsical approach. One of the monkeys riding on their dog, or a bird wearing a hat, always brought laughter. Cecil took thousands of photographs and set up a darkroom in an attempt to put together a book featuring humorous animal photographs with amusing captions. But no publisher seemed interested.

As they sat surveying the landscape that spring afternoon, Cecil explained that he had a solution. Back in 1946, the eighteen acres they purchased was divided into two equal long, narrow lots. Both the cottage and Talon Hall were on the west lot; the eastern lot was a "buffer" area that they had never used; they had all the land they needed on the western half of the property.

"No, I won't discuss selling Featherland," Adele said as Cecil began outlining his plan.

"It's only a possibility at this stage. And it's only the buffer lot," Cecil protested as Adele rose to leave.

In front of them, in clear view, lay the land in question, covered in trees. It struck them that the buffer lot could be logged, and the money from the lumber, if not the lumber itself, could be used for the addition. They spent the rest of the evening drawing up plans for their bed-sitting quarters.

Spring gave way to summer and construction began on the addition. Susan accepted the noise and confusion of the work calmly. Cecil noticed other improvements in her disposition. Cleaning their ex-bedroom was a chore, since Susan's allergies meant no litter could be used. So the wooden floor needed regular wet mopping. At first Cecil had had to hold Susan in a blanket while Adele cleaned, since her new quarters were not divided into two sections as her pen in Talon Hall had been.

But as the rapport between Cecil and Susan deepened, he was able to sweep and mop the room while Susan was free. Cecil wrote:

She reveled in this housekeeping business. Sometimes she tore the mop or broom from hands with a grasping flick of a foot, but she could understand when I remonstrated with her and would give it up on request.

While the change from deadly enemies to friendly playmates seemed to strengthen the more Cecil exposed himself to Susan, occasionally she still forgot her manners. But Cecil accepted the risks involved in playing with a powerful bird of prey armed with curved talons and a razor-sharp mouth. Even while playing, Susan was capable of inflicting injury. Cecil's journal recounts one such incident as follows:

*Once when playful gusto took the upper hand, she forgot herself and
threw a "hook" into my toe — but unlike times of old, there was no
malice behind it. When she realized what she had done and saw my
blood ooze, she was visibly upset as if self accusing, and it took some
doing to communicate to her "think nothing of it."*

Susan's unexpected takeover of the Hyndmans' former bedroom
did create some problems. The telephone, installed in 1950, connected to their cottage through the bedroom. The line joining the
connection ran out of the room into the adjoining bathroom,
and Susan's keen eyes found the snake-like line attractive. At first
she merely played with the thin line, accidentally severing the
connection. Cecil managed to repair the line — a necessity, as they
depended on this voice link to the outside world.

When Susan cut the telephone line a second time, Cecil spliced the
wire and covered the line. This attempt at camouflage did not fool
Susan, who decided to attack the connection in earnest. No longer
content to cut through the line, she used her sharp bill to strip away
the insulation and short-circuited the line. Cecil cursed while Adele
laughed; this time he could not repair the damage.

After a long drive to reach a pay phone, Cecil contacted the telephone company's service department. When he confessed what
had happened, the amused operator promised to send out someone. Soon a telephone truck pulled up and the brawny repairman
laughed as Cecil repeated the story.

"The only safe approach is to work from under the cottage," Cecil
suggested as he guided the repairman to the cottage.

"No way," the repairman answered.

He refused to crawl under the cottage on his hands and knees.
Brushing aside Cecil's objection, he demanded to be shown the
connection inside. At the door leading to Susan's room, Cecil tried
again to explain that the reception might not be pleasant.

"Hey, no bird is going to stop me," the repairman insisted.

Adele and Cecil exchanged looks, then winks. "OK," Cecil said.

He opened the door a crack and nodded to the rugged-looking repairman, who peered into the room. Susan responded with an airborne attack. The repairman jumped backward, slamming into Cecil.

Grumbling loudly, the man crawled under the cottage. Even then Susan made his job difficult, refusing to release the line through the floor. The game of tug of war continued for some minutes with the sweating repairman wedged under Susan's room. Susan's strength impressed him — as did her talons. With his face pressed so close to the small hole in the floorboards, the talons appeared especially large. Adele and Cecil could barely suppress their laughter as they watched from the side of the house.

Finally, grunting mightily, the repairman wrenched the line free. Or so he thought. But Susan had one more surprise in store. She had released her grip so she could use her talons. As the repairman looked up through the hole, he saw the tip of a talon coming straight at him. The resounding "whack" as it hit the wood sounded like an explosion. The repairman scrambled out from under the cottage and finished the new connection without another word.

The Hyndmans had barely crossed "reroute the phone line" off their "to do" list when another problem developed a few days later.

"Come see this," Adele called to Cecil when he returned from the night feeding at Talon Hall.

He heard a wooden creaking sound coming from their former bedroom. "What's that noise?" he asked.

Other, even stranger, sounds followed in quick succession — ripping and rending noises. In their abrupt move to the main Bird Room, the Hyndmans had left all their clothes in a closet with sliding doors. Susan had learned how to open the wood-paneled doors. Now she was having fun shredding their clothes.

"We don't get to town much any more," Adele said as they surveyed the pile of ruined clothing.

Talon Hall, the two-storey building that housed many of Featherland's residents. The House of Max, the enclosure of the Hyndmans' great horned owl Max, is in the foreground.

Cecil and Adele Hyndman at their favorite spot high up on the rocky slope overlooking Featherland.

The young couple outside their newly built cottage outside Victoria in 1947. Adele and Cecil helped with the construction; Cecil laid the water line by hand. The cottage wasn't hooked up to phone service until the early 1950s.

Cecil's favorite photo of Susan, the "golden glamour girl," taken inside the Hyndmans' cottage after Susan took over their bedroom following her near-fatal bout with pneumonia.

Susan's eight-foot wings churn the air. Many experts stated that Susan was the largest golden eagle they had ever seen. Her talons measured ten inches from front to hind talon.

Adele had a special affinity with all creatures. Here, she poses with Toon, a raccoon.

Adele with Senator Snort, the first nine-banded armadillo brought into Canada, in 1962.

Coco, a Capuchin monkey, rides Jackie, their three-legged dog, in 1949. Coco and Jackie often performed for visitors who toured Featherland.

A real-life Dr. Dolittle, Cecil taught several birds, who many considered untrainable, to speak. Itchy the gull became the world's first gull to speak words. Her voice was broadcast over the radio, and she starred in a television commercial and appeared in a number of articles.

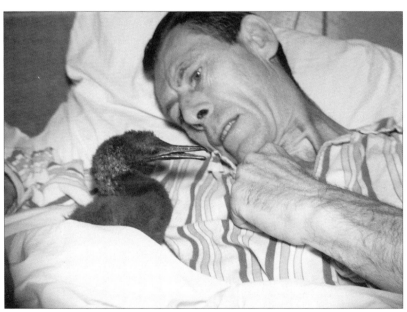

Cecil in bed with Snorkel the baby cormorant, who was incubated from an egg the Hyndmans collected.

Cecil with Goliath the raven, whose voice was broadcast on the CBC and was featured on an audio tape that Cecil produced.

Adele holds Horrible Horace the screech owl. Horace was one of forty screech owls at Featherland over the years.

Cecil stroking Kluane, a male golden eagle who was brought to Featherland with an injured wing. Kluane was much smaller and less violent than Susan.

Cecil treats Susan for an allergic reaction to straw bedding during her time in Talon Hall.

Cecil cautiously strokes Susan's feathers, attempting to win her trust.

Susan could be violent, and attacked Cecil on a number of occasions. But Cecil believed that to win a bird of prey's affection a person must make oneself vulnerable.

Susan finally accepts Cecil, and allows him to kiss her. During this period, Cecil often spent his evenings in intimate face-to-face contact with the Queen of Featherland.

As the trust between himself and Susan deepened, Cecil decided to test how far he could push the limits of their relationship. Cautiously he began a series of experiments to test how Susan would react — using himself as bait.

During their usual playtime, while cleaning the room, Cecil deliberately waited until Susan became very excited. Then he dropped to his hands and knees on the floor. He knew this vulnerable position would tempt Susan's natural instinct to pounce on prey. Cecil reasoned that if Susan could overcome such ingrained behavior, it would prove she had the ability to make conscious decisions. But if he was wrong, he would pay a terrible price, since he no longer wore any protective clothing.

As Cecil watched Susan out of the corner of his eye, she seemed unsure what to do. The tension increased as she extended her wings. Cecil's heart beat so loudly he was sure Susan could hear it pounding. For a few anxious moments she hovered, but she did not attack. Finally she flew to her "box" stand in the middle of the room.

Over the next few weeks, Cecil repeatedly placed himself in vulnerable positions to provoke Susan. At one point he lay beneath her as she stood on the edge of her stand. Each time she did not attack, their relationship grew deeper and closer, in a very real physical sense. Gradually, over the next few months, Cecil edged closer toward another breakthrough: to try pressing his face next to Susan's.

When conducting tours at Featherland, the Hyndmans often rubbed beaks with their large birds of prey, including great horned owls. Many visitors treated this as part of the show, some sort of "circus" trick designed to entertain them. Other bird experts, unable to explain the closeness the Hyndmans achieved, accused them of some form of hypnotism. Whatever the explanation, both Cecil and Adele were able to perform this feat even under the harsh glare of lights and the flashing of cameras.

To Adele and Cecil, putting the beak of a hawk, owl, or eagle next to their eyes represented the supreme act of trust between two creatures. Cecil explained:

long ago, many years before this, I discovered the immense value of presenting one's face to any bird under cultivation. It is a singularly disarmed and disarming gesture with which the hand can never compare.

As the day approached, Cecil confided his intentions to Adele. "Tomorrow's the big day — I plan on playing 'kissy face' with Sue." "Are you sure that's safe?" Adele said.

The fact that Adele, who was so fearless with their birds, was alarmed about this plan did not help Cecil's insomnia that night. He paced inside, then outside in the moonlight. Adele could not help but notice his nervousness, but said nothing.

The next morning, after an extra cup of coffee, Cecil steeled himself and entered Susan's room. Adele waited by the door in case of trouble.

As usual, Cecil talked to Susan as he approached her. He cautiously inched closer and closer until he summoned up enough courage to make face-to-face contact. He described the encounter as follows:

I pressed my face against her warm bill, waiting with heart in mouth. This deep confidence in her simply had to be offered. She opened her mouth and closed it on my nose — as gently as though those four razor edges and two points were velvet, as we stared into one another's eyes bang on. Adele was quietly watching from the Bird Room.

These acts of physical closeness became part of their daily ritual. They were always preceded by a mutual exchange of stares.

Although Cecil never claimed any scientific rationale for this method, he found with all the birds that trust could be established through a visual exchange. To Cecil, this was an important part of communicating with birds.

Like a pair of young lovers, Cecil and Susan began spending more and more time together. At night, Cecil would quietly leave his bed so as not to disturb Adele, and tiptoe into Susan's room.

Once inside their former bedroom, Cecil, wearing his pyjamas, would sit or kneel next to Susan. These intimate encounters usually began with a whispered greeting on his part, as he often left the light off. Susan would respond with her own greeting, which he described as being a "barely audible yet high-pitched twitter, feminine and happy." They would rub faces, Cecil now completely confident that Susan would not attack.

Cecil was no longer content to merely talk to her. He began to lightly stroke her feathers. This combination of Cecil's soothing voice and gentle stroking pleased Susan. She responded by stroking him, using her hooked beak. Only when contented do eagles groom their feathers; grooming another eagle is a sign of acceptance. Susan, who preened herself regally each day, seemed to take special delight in these nightly mutual grooming sessions.

Often Cecil blew gently on Susan's neck feathers as they engaged in rubbing beaks. Her golden neck feathers, when parted, revealed her pink skin underneath. The satiny texture of Susan's skin, much less coarse than human skin, surprised Cecil. He discovered that if he blew in a certain direction on her neck, Susan opened her mouth wide in response, revealing her bright pink tongue and throat — almost as a human might laugh when tickled. Cecil named this her "laughing yawn." Falconers call this action "gaping." This was one of many conditioned responses Cecil discovered and taught Susan to perform on command.

Cecil found Susan's fragrance unique and very pleasant. He wrote of her delicate scent, "very faint and subtle, [it] registered itself permanently in the storehouse of my memory." Cecil found he could recognize Susan, and most of the other birds at Featherland, by their scents.

Cecil tested the limits of their new physical closeness by deliberately running his fingers down, then between, the razor-sharp cutting edges of Susan's curved beak. Although Susan could have cut his fingers to the bone, she accepted his touch. Soon Cecil was able to run his fingers down her feathered legs and even polish her talons. A year earlier, any such gesture would have provoked Susan to attack.

During these nightly sessions, Cecil discovered something remarkable about Susan's sleep habits. Contrary to the information about golden eagles in most ornithological texts, Susan did not always sleep on her perch or box stand. Sometimes, he wrote, "Susan drowsed on her feet, or on one foot, the other drawn up out of sight under her breast feathering and her toes closed like a fist." But on other occasions she slept in a prone position like any human lying in a bed. Her sleep positions varied enormously:

Sometimes she naps lying on her "divan" or on the floor on her stomach, her wings lazily outstretched in utter relaxation. Time and again she will shift positions to lie on one side or the other just as you and I do.

Eagles cannot close their eyes; they have no eyelids. Instead, they have a nictitating membrane, a thin covering that unfolds over the top of the eyeball. Humans have a rudimentary form of this membrane in the inner corner of their eyes. Often when Susan was asleep, the nictitating membranes covered her eyes as her head slumped. She slept so soundly that on occasion she did not hear Cecil's approach, and would startle when he came up to her. Never did Susan snore, although other birds did, including a duck and a seagull who shared the cottage with the Hyndmans.

In the mornings, when shafts of early morning sunlight came

in through the window, Susan loved sunbathing. Many times Cecil saw her

drowsily luxuriating in the sun's cozy rays beaming through her south window. She lay flat out with wings flung wide like any sun worshipper on a briny beach — and equally well equipped with sunglasses, those semi-opaque membranes that automatically slide over her eyeballs. Sunbathing at those times with glinting head and hackles, she really was the golden glamor girl.

Now that Susan was contentedly settled into their former bedroom, Cecil began to devise games to play with her. These served both to amuse and to exercise Susan. Designing these games was easy, but putting them into practice was difficult. He decided to use lacrosse balls, which are extremely hard and can stand up to a lot of abuse. The incredible strength in Susan's talons would easily crush any softer type of ball.

Susan immediately became interested the first time Cecil rolled a lacrosse ball across the floor. She flicked out a talon and seized the ball. Now came the hard part: convincing her to give it back. Cecil held out his hand, but Susan refused to release the ball. He waited until she tired and dropped the ball. He then picked it up and rolled it across the floor.

Like teaching a dog to bring back a stick, Cecil patiently waited until Susan dropped the ball near him, then rolled it back toward her. After a few times, Susan learned to drop the ball near him. Eventually she would release it into his outstretched bare hand. As the training progressed, Cecil noticed how Susan carefully observed him, as if waiting for a signal. Indeed, soon she learned to respond on command.

The game of "catch the ball" demonstrated Susan's playful streak as well as her intelligence. Over the next few weeks, Cecil cultivated these natural traits little by little until he was not rolling but tossing the ball toward Susan. She liked this new game even better, literally rising to the occasion.

In the next stage, he began bouncing the ball, gradually increasing its height to force Susan to leap higher and higher to catch it. She used her stand to launch herself, flying up to the height of the ceiling. Often she twisted herself upside down, easily making the mid-air catch. Rarely did she miss anything thrown at her. Her excited chirping signaled her delight in these daily games.

To amuse Susan between games, Adele would roll up newspapers and toss them into the room. Or sometimes she sewed up a small sack or large sock with shredded material inside. Susan spent hours tearing apart these sticks and sacks. She delighted in using her talons, although she would sometimes rip apart the toys with her sharp bill.

Susan's love of games not only provided her with exercise, but also with an outlet for some of her natural aggression. Cecil noted in his journal how this "displacement activity" is common in birds of prey. Instead of flying into a rage and attacking him as before, Susan now vented her fury on the rolled-up newspaper sticks. While shredding one of these sticks, her whole posture became compressed and her eyes took on a wild look.

But if Cecil entered the room, her expression would immediately soften, as if by magic. As her erect feathers flattened, the fierceness left her eyes. Often a high twitter would signal that her transformation was complete.

As 1958 came to a close, Cecil looked back at his journal account of the year, the first in which Susan had shared Ookpik Cottage with them. He had discovered that she was much more than a killing machine. Susan was both intelligent and observant, with a good, even remarkable, memory. Her mastery of games like "fetch the ball" and her ability to perform on command proved she was capable of learning.

Tests on other golden eagles have demonstrated their memories — for example, they can remember which container their food is hidden under. Susan showed she also had a fun-loving nature, as well as an ability to be very gentle and loving. And her acceptance of Cecil, after her initial rejection, suggested she was capable of change based on life experiences. Susan had a unique personality, capable of developing.

Much as he had learned about Susan, Cecil speculated she was equally curious and appraising of him. He wrote, "If I put her figuratively on the psychiatrist's couch, she took her turn at the same game." He summed up Susan's first year in their cottage thus: "A year with an eagle in your bedroom gives you more insight into its nature than fifty years of seeing the same bird outside."

Susan's plumage gradually lost its darker coloration and contrasting pattern as she matured. As a young eagle, she had had a white tail, fringed with a broad black band at the end. As she approached the end of the three-to-five-year period it takes a golden eagle to mature, her tail became more mottled.

At the same time, Susan was acquiring her species' distinctive golden coloration. Cecil noted in 1959 how

> *the gold that in early youth merely lightly tips certain head and neck feathers, eventually extends to cover more of each of these particular feathers. So it is time, measured in years, that greatly enhances the impressiveness of this metallic feature.*

The Hyndmans also discovered that once golden eagles reach maturity, they shed their feathers almost continuously. But some feathers remain for up to two years, and therefore appear much lighter, bleached by weathering as they age. New feathers, by contrast, appear much darker. Another peculiarity Cecil noted in his journal was how the adult feathering in both bald and golden eagles seemed to hold tighter to the body, thus making adult birds seem smaller than juveniles.

Cecil kept a number of Susan's feathers, especially the sizeable flight feathers, for display. But the greatest prizes were the fluffy undertail feathers, which he described as

possibly the most exquisitely delicate and cloud-like known to the avian world. Dreamy white plumes, so mistily insubstantial that one's fingers cannot feel them at all, are the greatest rarities. We have only been able to collect six of these from Susan.

The love affair between Cecil and Susan continued over the next few years. As Susan came to accept him totally, Cecil began to photograph her. This task would have been fairly simple for most professional photographers, who carry an assortment of cameras and lenses. But Cecil simply could not afford such equipment. He had to make do with an old but reliable camera.

If he wanted to take a close-up of Susan, Cecil had to do just that — position the camera very close, within twelve inches. Susan never completely accepted the presence of a camera. Any new object brought into her room aroused her curiosity, sometimes causing an excited reaction if she thought it might be a new toy. But even though Cecil sensed she had reservations about the strange dark box, she now trusted Cecil, and this acceptance included the foreign object he carried. So he was able to take a number of photographs.

As Susan entered the beginning of her mature years, her behavior became calmer. Adele began calling Susan "the Queen of Featherland" — she seemed so sure of herself and her world. Her fierceness still remained, but hidden under her regal surface and firmly under control.

Cecil often painted portraits of the birds of Featherland. He mainly used watercolors, often producing life-sized portraits and always working with the subject in front of him. The Hyndman family, known for producing jurists and politicians, also had an artistic streak. Cecil's mother, the daughter of Sir Louis Davies, Chief Justice of Canada, painted in watercolors, and Cecil's younger brother Robert was a professional painter who specialized in portraits during one period of his career. Robert once accepted a commission to paint the Queen of England.

After deciding the Queen of Featherland deserved better than watercolors, Cecil attempted an oil painting of Susan. The sight of the painting gear in her room aroused Susan's curiosity. She closely examined the strange objects one by one: paints, brushes, and board. She seemed so fascinated that Cecil wondered how he could get her to pose.

But she turned out to be surprisingly co-operative — as if she were a model trained to hold a position. As the painting took shape, Cecil occasionally stopped to show Susan her likeness. Susan seemed fascinated by it.

She never, however, exhibited much interest in the other birds that were visible through the protective grille, covered with a decorative bamboo screen, that separated her boudoir from the Bird Room. Even though she could sometimes see various hawks and owls through the grille, she never exhibited any hostility. Nor did exotic birds such as the colorful scarlet macaw seem to arouse her. Adele and Cecil often speculated that perhaps Susan, having been raised with humans, identified herself with humans instead of eagles.

An incident late in the 1950s put this theory to the test. One of the smaller birds outside Susan's room decided to venture in. "Ferd the bird was an irrepressible small scamp," Cecil wrote in his journal, "whose life we had saved when he was brought to us as a baby suffering pneumonia." The robin flew toward Susan's room when the bamboo screen outside the grille was partially raised.

Adele and Cecil raced after Ferdy. They arrived at the bamboo barrier to see a talon shoot out and "with a lightning motion she picked him from the air." Cecil feared the worst as he raced around to the rear door of the room. Inside, he found Susan quietly examining her mid-air catch.

As I reached out to snatch Ferd, or what I anticipated would be left of him, Susan gave a startled surprise and the red-breasted detainee slipped loose and made a fast getaway through the door I had left open behind me. Susan, having turned her eyes to me when I popped in, never noticed the escape. When she looked again at her empty hand, there was such genuine puzzlement in her expression that I laughed.

Ferdy suffered nothing more from the encounter than a few missing tail feathers — pretty minimal damage for a creature seized by a golden eagle. The trouble-prone robin lived for thirteen-and-a-half years with the Hyndmans; at that time, his was the longest lifespan of any robin recorded by the Canadian Wildlife Service. During the last two years of his life at Featherland, Ferdy lost all the feathers on his head; his glistening dome reminded Cecil of a Buddhist monk.

As he shuffled toward bed the night of Ferdy's "close encounter," Cecil heard Susan call out. He tried to ignore her, but the pathetic sound of her pacing the wooden floor touched him. "I could hear her heavy talons clacking and dragging as she clumped along." Like Cecil, Susan often suffered from insomnia. He peeked into her room and saw her pacing back and forth with her loose, ambling gait, which had a slight roll to it. She suddenly stopped, turned, and looked up at Cecil.

Unable to avoid her stare, Cecil entered her room. He sat on the floor next to her and stroked her neck feathers. She responded by putting her bill next to his face, twittering softly. The moment lengthened, and before he knew it, Cecil had fallen asleep on the hard wooden floor.

Mid-summer of 1959 saw a housing crisis develop at Featherland. They were hand-rearing a number of baby birds, including screech owls, gulls, and ravens. The number of orphaned and injured birds that year strained the Hyndmans' resources of both money and space. They were so desperate for extra space that they resorted to using their new bedroom as a hospital zone for birds recovering from accidents or injuries.

One day, after conducting a tour for two carloads of visitors, Cecil returned to the cottage to make himself some coffee while Adele did the daily cleaning in Talon Hall. He was about to brew a pot in their tiny kitchenette, which was barely big enough for one person to turn around in, when he sensed something was wrong. Their bedroom opened into the kitchenette; ordinarily, his presence brought a response from the various birds that were housed in it. The unusual silence puzzled Cecil and he quietly crept toward the bedroom.

At that time, the bedroom residents included two mynas and one young gull named Poo, who had a sprained foot. Poo liked to lie on the soft mat on the bedroom floor. When Cecil craned his neck around the doorway, he saw "four long black talons gleaming in a shaft of sunlight encircling Poo. The little gull was voiceless with fear."

Susan was also silent. To Cecil, she seemed "deeply absorbed in savoring to the full this suspended moment of anticipation before applying the crushing squeeze that would snuff out the life and make a bloody pulp of that terrified little gull."

For a moment Cecil stood completely still, as if mesmerized by the frozen tableau in front of him. Neither bird had seen him. Poo's eyes widened as Susan began to fan her wings, a gesture that signaled her intent to kill.

Without thinking, Cecil made a flying tackle toward Susan. He managed, in one continuous swooping action, to grab her. Before she had a chance to react, he raced down the short passageway toward the open door of her bedroom and threw her in. Poo's excited calls signaled that she had not been injured. As Cecil heaved Susan into her room, the full realization of what he had done dawned on him.

Most people, encountering a golden eagle for the first time, remark on its "majesty, dignity, or regal bearing." Cecil had spent years trying to gain Susan's respect — making himself physically vulnerable in order to gain her trust. Even when she had attacked him, piercing his thigh and, later, his hand, with her talons, he had never struck back. Now he had committed a grievous bodily insult against her, unceremoniously grabbing and throwing her.

Her response to this indignity was immediate and violent. Cecil wrote,

Susan spun around like a taxiing aircraft, her hackles standing straight on end, anger written all over her as she made her own literally flying tackle back at me in revenge. As I took a swift step backward and slammed the door, she crashed against her side of it with a resounding thud that shook the walls and left talon marks in the wood.

As he stopped to catch his breath, Cecil faced another puzzle. How had Susan gotten out of her bedroom and into theirs? He checked the lock and realized that the door had been left unlocked. Susan, as she used to do in Talon Hall, must have simply reached up with her powerful legs and turned the doorknob.

Cecil returned to his own bedroom to find Poo ruffled but uninjured. Although in shock, the little gull quickly recovered, minus a few feathers. When he had finished attending to Poo, Cecil realized that his own hands were shaking. As he sat on the bed, trying to control his trembling, he worried that his tackling of Susan, while it had saved the baby gull, might have ended the relationship he had spent years establishing with the eagle. He could hear her talons scraping on the floor as she paced her bedroom.

As the coffee began to perk, he decided he needed a nip of something stronger and reached into the cupboard for a drink, his hands now shaking so badly he was barely able to pour. He decided it was best to let Susan cool down for the rest of the day — or days, depending on how long she bore a grudge.

That night sleep did not come easily to Cecil. After an hour of tossing and turning in bed, he got up — careful not to wake Poo, who was sleeping soundly in a cardboard box at the foot of the bed. Cecil could not wait any longer. He simply had to resolve the tense situation. Wearing only his pyjamas, he paid Susan a visit.

Nervously he inched open Susan's door, peering into the blackness, his senses alert for any signs of anger. Susan made no menacing sounds or threatening moves as he spoke softly to her, cautiously opening the door wider. For what seemed like an eternity, she remained silent. Finally Susan made a soft chirping sound that Cecil recognized as an invitation to enter.

He went in and touched Susan's head. Again she responded vocally, and Cecil knelt to rub faces with her. Relief flooded over him as Susan responded by rubbing her curved beak ever so gently over Cecil's face. Later he described that night as being "among the tenderest moments in my memory." If Susan had been angry, she now displayed no residual hostility. She had shown an ability to forgive and forget.

When Cecil returned to his bed hours later, he lay awake in a state of barely contained bliss. He realized he had truly won the love of Susan. Even after he had physically manhandled her, she had not turned against him. Few if any men had experienced or would ever experience what he had: the love of a proud and fierce golden eagle. The future seemed to stretch out before him. Susan had shown him her loving and tender nature. Her love made up for all the hardship, doubt, worry, and hard work that had gone into Featherland.

Cecil became so excited he reached over to wake Adele to share this breakthrough with her. But he stopped himself, and almost laughed out loud at the irony of the situation: a married man wanting to wake his wife in the middle of the night to express his love for another female. Even more odd, his wife also was in love with the same female. Although Adele accepted that Susan had chosen Cecil as her mate, lately Cecil sensed discomfort on Adele's part when he talked to her about how close he was becoming to Susan. This had created a curious emotional gulf between them. As Cecil tossed in bed, another troubling emotion swept over him — guilt. He felt as if he was cheating on his wife. But he truly did love both of the women in his life.

In the spring of 1960 the Hyndmans held a private party to mark Susan's fifth anniversary at Featherland. They had much to celebrate. Susan was now fully mature, and all the experts who visited her remarked that she was the biggest female golden eagle they had ever seen. She was the Queen, the star attraction at Featherland. A series of amazing photographs showing Cecil rubbing beaks with Susan had helped create even more interest in the sanctuary. This increased popularity meant increased revenue, which helped fuel Featherland's expansion.

The attachment Susan had formed for Cecil after her near-fatal illness had extended into her maturity, and, although built on a shaky foundation, seemed strong.

But shortly after the anniversary celebration, an oddity of the golden eagle's physical make-up threatened to end their love affair.

"Have you noticed Sue's bill recently?" Cecil asked.

"Yes," Adele answered.

"Are you thinking what I'm thinking?"

"We're going to have to trim it," Adele said.

"It's not something I'm looking forward to."

The two most lethal weapons a golden eagle possesses are its bill and its talons. Neither stops growing over the lifetime of the creature. The eagle's bill is made of material somewhat similar to that in human fingernails. A wild eagle naturally grinds down its bill by tearing away at the bones of animals. But a captive eagle's bill has to be cut back on occasion, just as humans continually trim their nails.

The operation of cutting back the bill on a bird of prey is called "coping," a term from falconry. Although most people use the term "beak," the more correct term is "bill." An eagle has an upper bill, also called an upper mandible, and a lower bill, or jaw. The upper bill curves downward in a dagger shape while the lower bill juts more or less straight out. If not cut back, the curved upper bill will continue to grow until it curves back up and prevents the bill from working. In this pathetic condition, the eagle slowly dies of starvation.

Cecil and Adele had coped Susan's bill before. It had been a difficult operation and Cecil knew that they could no longer count on surprise. Carefully they planned the two-person chore.

The first step involved Cecil catching Susan in a thick blanket. This offended Susan's dignity but there was no option. Adele simply did not have the strength to handle Susan. Another young and fit male falconer, Kent Durden, had written about helping his father cope the bill and talons of their golden eagle. Kent admitted he was barely able to hold the eagle's feet, so strong was she and so adept at twisting her feet.

Now that Susan associated a blanket with copings, Cecil had trouble catching her with it. Hiding the thick blanket proved difficult and Cecil had to rely on agility alone. He especially worried about making a clean catch. He had to grab Susan and pin her wings to her chest, so she could not flap free and injure herself or Cecil. At the same time, he had to somehow ensure her talons remained wrapped inside the blanket.

After blanketing Susan, Cecil held her as Adele entered with coping tools: a sturdy pair of wire cutters and a file. Adele worked quickly with the skill of a professional manicurist, clipping the usual sixteenth to an eighth of a inch. Knowing that precision was important — cutting too deep could badly injure Susan — Adele always worked with bare hands. But that meant that if she made a mistake, Susan's sharp bill could easily slice Adele's hands.

Next, Adele filed the upper and lower bill. The Hyndmans had soon finished off the tense and tiring chore successfully. Only Susan's fierce pride was injured.

The day after the trimming, Cecil opened Susan's door. Often she took a day to calm down after being riled. This time Susan's anger had not subsided. Cecil dared not enter her room all day. The next day he ventured in and Susan leapt at him.

But on the third day, Cecil wrote,

her hackles did not rise. While not rolling out the welcome mat, she allowed me to enter her room and all was reasonably well again except she began showing a slight suggestion of testiness at times.

Cecil noted a number of signs pointing to a subtle change in Susan's attitude toward him. Her greetings cooled and her eyes no longer shone as brightly when he entered the room. A chill had descended on their warm friendship. He found himself glancing up nervously while washing the floor, no longer completely confident of the bond between them. Once or twice, while in a vulnerable position cleaning, he caught Susan eying him with her hackles partially erect.

Although he continued to show Susan when they opened Featherland that summer, Cecil noted other signs of the strain in their relationship. Susan never attacked him, but the uneasy tension continued to trouble him. She seemed to be always watching him, sizing him up, as if to warn him *don't ever try to trim my bill again.*

eight

THE RIFT

The wind picked up as the pilot brought the small power boat toward the necklace of rock outcroppings in the often turbulent Strait of Juan de Fuca. For the two passengers, this morning in June 1960 was a moment to savor. The bright sun reflected off the brilliant blue water, matching the nearly cloudless sky above. Pale glaucous-winged gulls floated overhead. The stiffening breeze carried a salty tang as they neared the first in a series of low islands off Oak Bay called the Chain Islets. The pilot, Roger, nudged Cecil and Adele, pointing ahead to a rock ledge. Cecil rose, but found it difficult to maintain his balance in the tossing boat as it swung toward the rocks.

When Cecil had first approached Roger at the Oak Bay Marina, the pilot had warned him that landing on the bare, uninhabited, low-lying islands might prove difficult — perhaps impossible.

Undeterred, Cecil had hired the boat and Roger's services. Now, as Roger maneuvered the launch close to the sloping rock edge, Cecil realized he would have to time his jump as the bow rose, to avoid slipping on the ledge carpeted with wet seaweed.

The breezy chop caught the bow and banged it hard against the rocks. Roger gunned the engine and tried again as Cecil crouched in the bow. Timing his leap, Cecil landed safely on the rock ledge.

Now it was Adele's turn. Roger motioned to Adele to stand as he eased the launch towards the rocks. This time the launch's approach and the crash of waves synchronized perfectly, and Adele stepped ashore effortlessly.

The Hyndmans' arrival in this seabird colony caused an uproar of noise and movement. Hundreds of gulls and other birds that resided on the desolate island shrieked into the sky.

This visit to the Chain Islets was no idyllic summer outing. It was the first step in a pioneering study into sea- and shorebirds that would extend over the next eighteen summers. Over that span of years, Cecil and Adele observed a wild fluctuation in the number of nests on the islets, from over 2,000 to under 100.

In the mid-1950s, a few biologists studied flight movement, migration, and breeding behavior in sea- and shorebirds, but next to nothing was known beyond observations taken in the wild. A few years before this first visit to the islets, Cecil had made contact with Dr. D. A. Munro at the University of B.C. to pass on information about injured seabirds they treated at Featherland. After Dr. Munro became chief ornithologist of the Canadian Wildlife Service in Ottawa, Cecil corresponded with him, proposing to incubate gull eggs and hand-rear chicks. The department issued a permit to allow the Hyndmans to collect birds; in return, they provided the wildlife service with data.

After allowing the airborne seabird colony to resettle, Cecil and Adele slowly made their way up the rock ledge, trying not to disturb the many recently hatched chicks on the island. They soon discovered they had timed their visit perfectly. The remote and desolate island gave gulls, cormorants, and other seabirds refuge from their enemies. The relatively shallow water provided abundant fish in summer. Gulls and other seabirds coordinate their breeding, producing eggs that hatch within a day or so of one another. The emergence of so many chicks together gives the gulls a better chance of surviving.

In a rocky hollow softened by patches of sun-bleached, matted grass, they found a number of gull nests. "Hear that?" Cecil said to Adele, stopping among the closely packed nests.

"What is it?" Adele asked.

Cecil bent down and pointed to a chick struggling to break through its shell. Another egg rocked back and forth in front of them. Ten feet farther, they spotted a tiny downy chick emerging. They felt no guilt picking up eggs and chicks. Some bird experts estimate that over 90 percent of seabirds never reach adulthood; seabird chicks are probably more vulnerable than any other animal. Closely compacted on a few acres of low rock, they face being trampled by adult seabirds, being eaten by neighbors, falling into pools of water, or catching cold from a combination of rain, driving wind, and spray from heavy seas.

As the Hyndmans ventured inland, the wind died. The day turned fiery hot, and the sickening sound of rotting eggs exploding punctuated the air. Ahead, a glaucous-winged gull used its wide wings — about four feet — to launch itself airborne, tucking its webbed pink feet underneath. The high-pitched "keer, keer" sound would become all too familiar to the Hyndmans over the next two decades.

As the gull gracefully balanced in an updraft, Cecil marveled at how gulls, with seemingly no special skill, had adapted so well. They occupy a dominant position where land and water meet, having successfully evolved into some forty-seven species. Five of these species are native to the Pacific coast of North America. The ubiquitous glaucous-winged gull does well, evolutionarily speaking, because it is a generalist. This large gull is capable of eating almost anything, from marine life to garbage — although the Hyndmans were to find out that, given the opportunity, some of the gulls they raised could be very fussy eaters.

Moving farther inland, the two humans scrambled over slippery rocks, with Cecil almost stumbling into a crevice. As he stopped to catch his breath in the blast furnace heat, he noticed "a very tiny and fluffy infant still moistly matted by a mottled egg shell." He wrote,

I was about to ignore it as just another gull hatchling when something prompted me to look more closely. The feet told the story — no hind toes at all and hardly a suggestion of any webbing. That unique squarish head. Yes, the only black oystercatcher baby I would probably ever encounter, for breeding adults are relatively few and scattered and they purportedly hatch only a single chick.

With their time almost up, the Hyndmans retraced their steps to where the rented boat and operator waited, carrying a collection of chicks and eggs with care. The wind had died and the gentler ocean swells made the boarding much easier. Once on board, they closely examined their prize find, the three-toed black oystercatcher. Then they wrapped the chicks in blankets and put the eggs next to a hot-water bottle to protect them from any wind.

Roger took a different route back, pointing out a better landing spot for their next trip, which was scheduled for the following week. Cecil brushed aside Roger's concerns for their safety, sharing one of his NFB stories about an English cameraman who had misjudged his jump from a freighter while filming a wartime convoy off Halifax:

John Davidson was a stiff and clipped Brit — a master of understatement. He'd been in the Royal Navy. We went out on the largest

tanker in the world, which was part of this huge convoy. John Davidson was at the rail after we'd gone out forty miles filming the convoy. The pilot boat came alongside to take us back to Halifax. The seas were rough and each time the pilot boat approached, it bashed up against the tanker. Davidson became exasperated, leaned over too far and fell.

It was ten below zero and no one could survive in the frigid water more than a few minutes. Davidson was a true Royal Navy officer — he had never learned to swim. He went under the pilot boat and the captain turned off the propeller just in time so he wasn't cut in half. He bobbed up and a deckhand on the stern of the tanker threw a life preserver that hit Davidson in the face and he grabbed it.

The next day the press visited Davidson in hospital and said no one has ever survived such a fall before. When they asked for his reaction, all he said was "very inconvenient, very."

Windburnt and sunburnt, the Hyndmans drove back to Featherland with their new young charges. They had little time to recover from their tiring trip; it was feeding time for Susan and the rest of their furred and feathered family.

Susan seemed upset when Cecil did not stay after feeding her. She had grown accustomed to a nightly visit. Cecil felt awkward as he backed out the door, excusing himself with a lengthy explanation. He promised to visit her later that night.

"The Queen's upset," Cecil said to Adele.

"No more than these hungry chicks," Adele said. "I hope this works."

To Cecil's knowledge, no one had attempted to feed gull chicks or incubate their eggs before. The Hyndmans were pioneering the raising of sea- and shorebirds. While Cecil warmed up the incubator, Adele ground up lean raw beef, tinned sardines, bread soaked in milk, and cod liver oil. The chicks greedily accepted the mixture, although Cecil worried about the ingredients. "In the wild," he wrote, "the parents regurgitate food into the mouths of their chicks — food that has been partially mixed or processed by digestive fluids."

Meanwhile Cecil removed the eggs from their temporary incubator, a blanket wrapped around a hot-water bottle. The next hurdle involved setting up the incubator for the gull eggs. There were no temperature guidelines to follow, but if there was one thing Cecil could claim to be an expert in, it was incubating eggs. His experience stretched back to the day when, as a curly-haired boy of five in Edmonton, he had bought his first hen.

Cecil examined the mottled gull eggs before placing them in the incubator in their cottage. What temperature was best? When did the eggs need turning?

As he puzzled over these critical factors, a tiny noise caught his attention. It took a moment before Cecil realized the sound came from inside the eggs. He almost dropped them in his excitement. For the moment, all his worries about temperature vanished.

Part of Cecil's agreement with the wildlife service was that he would record the vocalizations of sea- and shorebirds as they developed to adulthood. Now he had a unique chance to record the vocalizations chicks made from inside their shells. Cecil's tiredness was swept away in the rush of adrenaline. He knew from his contacts with the wildlife services that no one had recorded gull sounds from inside the eggs.

After rigging a microphone, he turned on the machine and waited. And waited. Midnight passed. Then morning. But finally, late in the morning, he managed to record the sound of a gull chick *inside* the shell. He played back the tape to check the recording; the magnetic coating on those early plastic tapes was often uneven. Sometimes the surface had holes on it and would not record sound. But the sound was there, as clear as possible given the barrier of the thin shell.

Delighted with, but exhausted by, the long day, Cecil put the eggs safely back inside the incubator. He noted the temperature: ninety degrees Fahrenheit. He was guessing, and he knew the temperature was critical. If it were only a few degrees too hot or too cold, the chicks would die. Cecil's guess turned out to be right; all the eggs hatched and one of the Hyndmans' glaucous-winged chicks, Itchy, was to become famous in her life.

By September of 1960, as the summer tourist season was coming to a close at Featherland, Susan's bill had again overgrown to the point where they could not put off trimming it any longer. Cecil discussed the approaching crisis with Adele.

"Maybe we should hire someone else to do the catching and trimming?" she suggested.

Cecil shook his head. "Who would do it? And what if Susan was accidentally injured? Or what if Susan attacked and injured the person? We can't put anyone at risk."

Much as he disliked the task, Cecil resolved that the Hyndmans must do it, and by themselves. Adele suggested as a safety measure that Cecil revert to wearing some protection for the coping, including heavy gloves and a leather coat. He reluctantly agreed, and they steeled themselves to the task.

After gearing up, Cecil entered Susan's room with a blanket. The first part went surprisingly easily; Cecil managed to grab Susan cleanly and wrap her in the blanket. Now all he had to do was hold her still while Adele trimmed her bill. But when Adele entered with the instruments, Susan reacted with shocking violence. As Cecil described it, "She erupted inside the blanket in what I can only describe as a volcano of wrath, which I had never witnessed before or believed possible even in the battling years of old."

Even the normally unflappable Adele was alarmed by this change. Cecil told her to work quickly, warning her that he did not have the strength to hold Susan, who continued to thrash desperately inside the thick blanket.

"Maybe she'll tire," Adele said. "She usually does."

On previous occasions, Susan had struggled mightily but eventually accepted the inevitable. Not this time. As he strained to hold Susan's squirming body, Cecil realized that Susan's anger was directed at him, not at Adele, who was the one actually trimming Susan's bill.

Although the process took only minutes, it felt like hours to Cecil. Holding Susan tightly took all his strength, and by the end every muscle shook from exhaustion. Cecil also noticed that, while on every previous coping operation, Susan had calmed down near the end as if realizing the worst was over, today she continued to struggle fiercely, even as Adele gathered up her trimming instruments.

Cecil's anxiety mounted as he realized that Susan was now so enraged she would undoubtedly attack him as soon as she was released. How would he get to the door safely?

Cecil's first impulse was to leave the blanket around Susan and flee while she struggled to free herself. But he feared she might injure herself by getting a talon caught in the blanket. He shouted to Adele to keep the door open a crack as she left. Adele turned, and as Cecil made eye contact with his wife he saw the panic spread across her face.

"Get out!" he shouted at her, not wanting to endanger her.

Adele hesitated, then left, leaving the door slightly ajar as Cecil struggled to contain Susan. Finally he released her and, holding the blanket as a shield, bolted for the safety beyond the door.

The dash was only a few yards, but it might as well have been miles. Before he had taken more than a few steps, Cecil heard Susan's wings churn the air. He looked up to see a brown blur on top of him. Two outstretched feet struck out at him. Instinctively, Cecil held up the blanket for protection and twisted his head. The taloned foot whizzed by so closely he could feel the air blast on his sweaty brow.

Susan's other foot did not miss. It sliced through the thick blanket and Cecil felt her talons grasping the padding of his coat. For a moment, he was caught, jammed in the doorway with Susan pulling him one way and Adele the other. He heaved himself toward Adele as Susan lifted her free foot up to strike. Time froze as he waited for the talons to hit. He described the outcome of this moment thus:

Finally I jerked free with a ripping sound, leaving part of my coat in her fist and most of the blanket still caught in the door crack two or three feet above the floor. Susan hung in the air locked into the fabric. In an attempt to try to draw it through to me, to get her loose from it, I worked the door open barely an inch wider. In a flash, her hand whacked me on the glove.

Susan's blow landed on a nerve, numbing Cecil's forearm, wrist, and fingers. Disentangling Susan from the coat and blanket proved difficult. Every effort to calm her only increased her fury. She screamed at them while they slowly worked the jacket free from her fists, leaving her with the much-hated blanket. She set upon it, slashing away with her talons, venting her anger on the thick cloth, leaving nothing but a shredded mound.

Within a few hours the tingling in Cecil's hand signaled that the feeling was slowly returning. The emotional damage to his relationship with Susan was much harder to gauge, however. Cecil slept little that night, replaying the encounter over and over in his mind, remembering how close Susan's talons had come to connecting with his face.

He knew he would never knowingly harm her, but he realized that she did not share his perspective. From her vantage point, the trimmings were cruel punishment from a person she respected. Her fierce pride simply refused to tolerate such treatment.

That September night in 1960 was one of the longest and darkest in Cecil's entire life. All his years of working to establish a bond with Susan had blown up in his face. The emotional wound affected him deeply. He told his journal, "I despaired. Only a bleak hope remained that by some slim chance, her anger would subside in a day or two and melt away as it had done on past occasions."

Cecil's worst fears were confirmed over the next week. Each day he visited Susan, and each day her response was the same: she whacked at the door with enough force to move it. Susan's anger had never lasted more than three days before. But this time, on the third day, she continued to rage. By the end of that week, her anger had hardened to the point where even the sound of Cecil's feet in the Bird Room set her off.

Cecil admitted defeat: "It was the bitter end between us. I was divorced and worse. I could not conceive of any maniacal fury to exceed Susan's. It cut me to the quick. The bond of years had broken — snapped at her end."

nine

A BUSY TIME

On a warm Sunday night in fall of 1960, Cecil walked up the sloping hill toward the small wooden cottage inhabited by the Hyndmans' other golden eagle, Kluane. The late evening trek had become part of his routine.

Badly stung by Susan's violent rejection, Cecil had started making regular evening visits with Kluane. These were much more than an attempt to seek solace with another golden eagle, or to soften the blow to his ego. The loss of Susan's affection threatened the already shaky financial future of Featherland. Cecil was grateful that the "divorce" had happened in autumn, when Featherland had closed after its summer season.

"In a desperate effort to find some retreat of peace and quiet, I set up a table and chair in the shingled cottage that is home to Kluane, our male golden eagle," Cecil wrote in his journal.

Kluane used to soar high over the Yukon Mountains — until a broken wing brought him to earth. He is sitting companionably on his log, only a couple of feet from me, his feathering fluffed out, turning every so often to give me the eye — as soft and caressing as any eye in the world can be and with enough warmth to heat the sometimes chilly cottage.

Cecil had brought two boxes with him. Their contents represented two projects he had been working on some time. The success of one or the other was vital to the survival of Featherland. But Cecil found it difficult to concentrate. His thoughts kept returning to Susan's rejection. The potential loss of tourist dollars if he could not "perform" with her next season could be devastating. To make matters worse, another commercial zoo was about to open in Victoria.

Years ago Cecil had heard rumors that Victoria city council might invite zookeeper Paul Hertel, from outside Nanaimo to open a zoo in Victoria. Recently a group of interested zoologists had thrown their support behind the Hertel zoo. The mayor appointed an alderman to visit Hertel's private zoo, which was located nine miles out of Alberni and had attracted 7,000 visitors the previous year.

When the alderman visited Featherland, Cecil showed him around their property, pointing out the many rare and unusual birds — all of which had been privately financed at a cost of about $30,000. He informed him, "There is hardly room for one zoo in Victoria, let alone two. We have had no help or encouragement and it is grossly unfair for any city to extend privileges to an outside commercial organization." Cecil was adamant he would not shift his Featherland to the proposed Thetis Lake Park. Nor would he consider amalgamating with Hertel's zoo.

The alderman reported that both zoos could operate successfully in Victoria. He recommended to Victoria city council that the Hertel operation bring only animals in order not to compete with Featherland. But the Victoria mayor objected to any restrictions on Hertel's zoo. "Nobody gets an exclusive in a free enterprise country," he proclaimed.

However, the Victoria city council did ask government and SPCA officials in Vancouver to report on the Alberni zoo. While the government officials reported the zoo's safety precautions "adequate," the SPCA executive director for B.C. called the game department inspection of zoos mere "whitewashings." The lion cages at Paul Hertel's zoo near Nanaimo used a wire that had been rejected by the SPCA as too light to hold dogs. Once a lioness escaped, killing a little girl. "They seemed more concerned with financing Hertel's zoo than public safety," Cecil protested.

But eventually Hertel's zoo opened. "You could smell the zoo a mile away," complained Cecil, "as he had skunks and raccoons and foxes. The thing became a horrible stinking mess, with all those animals on a small property. He'd get discarded food to feed to these different animals — deer, lions and dingo dogs from Australia."

Competition from Hertel's zoo was just one of many things that troubled Cecil as he sat by the small desk he had set up in Kluane's cottage. From one of the two boxes he took out the folder containing Featherland's financial records. The latest bank statement showed that less than $100 remained in their account.

Turning on the oil heater to cut through the damp cold, he let his thoughts drift from the depressing financial statements in front of him to his upcoming birthday. He would be forty-nine in October. His father was eighty-six and not well. His parents' financial assistance helped keep Featherland afloat. Without it, he simply could not maintain the sanctuary. Although he was not ordinarily given to melancholic reflection, Cecil knew time was running out.

The figures in front of him were no comfort. Cecil realized he had to find other income to get Featherland on firm financial footing.

The first answer to this dilemma sat on her perch in Ookpik Cottage. The fame of Susan, the Queen of Featherland, attracted thousands of visitors. The story of the Hyndmans' intimate life with Susan — as well as so many other birds, like Kluane, who perched in front of him, was unique. So why not share his experience, and his passion for birds, with others? Nature stories like Konrad Lorenz's famous *King Solomon's Ring* sold well, and Cecil was convinced he could write a book.

Although the answer seemed simple, time was a problem. They found that there never was enough of it. The summer tourist season kept Cecil and Adele busy escorting carloads of visitors around Featherland. Summer also meant tending to injured and abandoned baby birds.

So fall and winter offered the only chance to write. Over the years Cecil had kept "bird journals," filling these notebooks with factual, as well as fanciful, information about bird behavior. He had begun to try to convert these into a book; one of the boxes contained the beginnings of a manuscript.

Cecil's second potentially money-making project had suggested itself when he first began writing the book manuscript. Training birds to speak was a large part of their life at Featherland, and they had succeeded with many birds. Yet writing about a bird speaking paled in comparison with hearing the real voice. Could he somehow combine the two?

Over the past few years, Cecil had put together a number of tapes of birds. The thought occurred to him that if a sheet of plastic recording tape could be inserted in a book, a movable magnetic head could be used like a pen to scan the sheet. The idea was simple and elegant. Inserting a small playback head in a pen was easily accomplished. Without a record head, the device needed no motor, only a small battery to power it. Cecil worked on a prototype, using bits and pieces of old tape machines. Once he had a crude device rigged and operating, another idea suggested itself.

Why not adapt this concept to letter writing? Instead of exchanging letters containing sheets of paper, people could exchange sheets of magnetic plastic. These "Vocaletters," as he called them, could be scanned by pen and the voice of the correspondent heard instead of read. This meant adding a recording head to the pen device, but the unit could still be powered by battery.

Excited by both uses for this invention, Cecil had contacted a number of family members. His older brother Lou, a member of a large law firm in Edmonton, could provide legal advice and guidance for the long and complicated patent process. Younger brother Jim in Toronto was the natural to raise finances. A well-connected entrepreneur, Jim himself was involved with developing another invention — a new type of personal aircraft.

When he contacted Jim, Cecil mentioned both projects — his book on birds and his Vocaletter invention. Jim was especially enthusiastic about Cecil's book project and promised to try to arrange a meeting with book publisher Jack McClelland in Toronto. Cecil accepted Jim's offer and booked a trip east later in the fall.

Cecil put away the financial folder, convinced that the contents of the two cardboard boxes, one marked "Manuscript" and the other "Vocaletter," would solve Featherland's financial problems. He decided to work on the book project that night, and opened the manuscript box. He unwrapped the rubber band and began writing in longhand. Adele had volunteered to type it, although their finances were stretched so thin they could only afford to rent a typewriter. Cecil had projected that completing a first draft of the book would take another month.

In reality, the book took almost a decade, undergoing a number of complete rewrites and various revisions, and consuming thousands of hours of work. Numerous versions of it would pass through the hands of a number of editors, literary agents, and publishers in Canada, the United States, and Britain. If Cecil in that fall of 1960 had had any idea of the anguish and financial loss the book would cost him, he would have flung the sheaves of paper on the oil heater. "Almost nothing else in my life would cause so many headaches or so much heartache," he later wrote.

At 2:30 a.m., Cecil headed back down the slope toward the cottage, tired but pleased with the night's work. He enjoyed the process of writing, shaping words into phrases and seeing them grow into sentences, then paragraphs. Most of all he enjoyed seeing the blank sheets in front of him come alive with lives of his feathered family. But reliving their lives on paper left him emotionally drained — especially as he was working on the section of the book dealing with Susan's arrival.

Entering the cottage, Cecil hesitated by Susan's room. He could hear her taloned feet clunk on the wooden floor, and Cecil knew she must be having one of the bouts of insomnia they both suffered. He had to fight back the temptation to enter her room. To be so near to someone he loved, yet so far, hurt.

Despite his lofty intellectual goal of probing avian psychology and physiology, he had fallen deeply, emotionally, for Susan, and admitted in his journals to the extent of his passion:

I had gloried in Susan. As very much a part of me, an extension of myself, she made me feel more than I was without her. In losing Susan's affection, I lost a subtle lift of the spirit. It might be that the loss was simply ego but I feel it went far deeper, was more complex than that.

And like a parent whose wayward child has left home, he blamed himself, especially as Susan had forewarned him repeatedly that she hated the bill-trimming sessions. She simply could not accept such an affront to her dignity from the person closest to her. As Cecil silently stood next to Susan's room, he heard her shuffling stop. He pictured her in his mind as he froze on the spot, not wanting to cause Susan to react angrily.

"Come to bed," Adele whispered as she tiptoed over and tugged at Cecil's hand.

"How was Susan when you fed her?" Cecil asked.

When they got to bed, Adele explained that Susan had seemed calm when she fed her earlier that night through the grille. Lately her behavior seemed much calmer with Adele, as long as Cecil kept out of her sight. He wondered if this was because hunger modified her anger. Or would time heal all?

Finally Cecil drifted off. The last sound he heard was the low booming noise of Susan's feet as she restlessly paced across the wooden floor of her room.

Autumn passed quickly as Cecil prepared for his trip east to Toronto. His brother Jim had not only talked to publisher Jack McClelland about Cecil's book, but had arranged a tentative meeting. Now the pressure was on Cecil to complete a presentable sample of his manuscript. His late-night retreats to Kluane's cottage became exercises in endurance as Cecil exhausted himself writing until early in the morning.

The patent process with his Vocaletter invention consumed his free time during the day. He had to sketch out technical diagrams, sort through existing patents, and rewrite his patent proposal to satisfy the lawyer.

The passing weeks brought no change in Susan. She continued to explode into violent rages every time she spied or heard Cecil, but accepted Adele's feedings at night through the grille. Now the Hyndmans faced yet another crisis in their care of Susan. The wooden floor of her room badly needed cleaning.

"Why don't I try entering Susan's room?" Adele said.

"No, it's too dangerous." Cecil held up his hands.

Adele pointed out the obvious: "The job has to be done. If her room gets any dirtier, it could affect her health."

Cecil tried to put off Adele, but she continued to pressure him, reminding him of how, the night of Susan's arrival, Susan had raised her hackle feathers when Cecil first approached her, but softened when Adele introduced herself. If Adele could deepen her friendship with the eagle, she could take over the performances and carry on their avian research. Otherwise they had no choice but to give up on Susan, which meant shipping her off to a zoo.

Cecil wrestled with the decision, noting in his journal that any transfer to a zoo "would certainly kill her from causes physical, psychological, or by a combination of both. Her lofty spirit could not long survive." They even discussed returning her to the Yukon, but releasing her back into the wild presented other enormous problems:

Sue knew nothing of the wilderness and without hunting skills, she would certainly starve. She also faced being shot, as she would undoubtedly fly toward any human she saw outdoors as the human world was the only one she had any experience with.

Cecil was sure of one thing: Adele's bravery. Time and again, she had proved her fearlessness with birds, even large birds of prey. During the tours of Featherland, Adele handled two other eagles — Kluane and Lightning the bald eagle — as well as other birds of prey residing in Talon Hall.

Despite that proven but indefinable attribute Cecil referred to as "Adele's magic way with birds," he hesitated. The question was not whether Adele was capable of accomplishing what he had tried but failed to do. Cecil's pride did not figure strongly in his determination of what course of action to take. His main concern was what might happen if Susan became excited or angry. Could Adele, much smaller and weaker, fend her off?

He wrote in his journal,

It was one thing for me to have taken the chances I did. But could I in a clear conscience allow Adele to do so, however willing and even anxious she was to put her life on the line to save Susan's future and try to keep intact our Featherland?

In the end, Cecil simply ran out of time before he could make a decision. During the last few days before his departure, he scrambled to complete his manuscript and assemble an improved prototype for his Vocaletter pen invention (Jim Hyndman had also arranged a meeting in Toronto with electronic experts).

The morning of his departure east, Adele calmly packed Cecil's bag while Cecil anxiously completed a last-minute modification of his Vocaletter prototype. He worried about leaving Adele alone. While she could cope under ordinary circumstances, what if the power lines went down? Or the telephone line — its failure was a common occurrence during Victoria's windy autumns. Each year the gusts snapped branches overhanging their line, cutting off contact with the outside, sometimes for days. Cecil quietly cursed the fact that they never had the money to hire help.

After calling the taxi, he told Adele that no attempt should be made to enter Susan's room in his absence. He was adamant that the solution to the problem of Susan would have to await his return.

Before heading outside, Cecil stepped toward the grille in Susan's room to say goodbye. Her wings snapped open as she launched herself violently at the grille. Then Adele stepped forward to speak to Susan, and immediately her bristling feathers softened and her mood calmed.

"Take good care of Sue," Cecil said as he kissed his wife goodbye.

Running Featherland was a two-person operation, and without Cecil, Adele struggled through her first day alone at Featherland. On the second day, Adele strained a muscle in her hand, which made opening tins and preparing the feed difficult. Although tired, Adele made a point of quietly talking to Susan as she fed the golden eagle through the bars of her grille. Susan responded with gentleness, taking the thin strips of beef delicately and remaining at the grille after Adele left.

Adele finally got to bed around 2:00 a.m. Although she was exhausted, Susan's restless pacing in the bedroom next door kept her awake. Occasionally Susan would twitter softly, her high voice clear as crystal in the silence. A rash and potentially dangerous idea formed as Adele tried to fall asleep. She struggled to push it to the back of her mind, but the thought persisted: she could not shake it.

All the next day the idea preoccupied her. Adele resisted, dismissing the notion as too risky. Or was it? The positive benefits would be enormous, if she could overcome her fear. On the third night after Cecil left, Adele again had trouble falling asleep. The autumn rains had begun, and the steady patter on the roof matched the rhythm of Susan's taloned feet scraping across the wooden floor. Only a few minutes earlier, Adele had fed Susan, barely able to look at the messy condition of the floor.

Sitting up in bed, Adele decided to act. Making the decision seemed to calm her nerves. Quietly she walked toward Susan's door, opened it, and stepped inside.

"Hello Sue," she said, trying to control the tremor in her small voice. "Having trouble sleeping? So am I."

The first leg of Cecil's whirlwind ten-day trip east passed in a blur. Using his younger brother Jim's house in Toronto as a base, Cecil met with a number of publishers about his manuscript, and with several electronic and technical experts about his Vocaletter invention. In the evenings, Jim took Cecil to cocktail and supper parties, using these social affairs to introduce his brother to his wide collection of friends and business associates — including publisher Jack McClelland.

Encountering the dynamic Mr. McClelland in his office left Cecil with the impression of "running into a one-man hurricane, with chaos swirling around him." In his earlier years and travels with the NFB, Cecil had met a wide variety of people ranging from royalty, military leaders, and foreign ambassadors to international business leaders. He knew a number of Canadian prime ministers by their first names, including R. B. Bennett and Mackenzie King. Few had impressed him as Jack McClelland did during that initial meeting.

McClelland summed up his personal credo to Cecil thus: "I publish authors, not books." He took pride in pointing out important Canadian authors he published, including Pierre Berton, Irving Layton, Peter C. Newman, and Margaret Laurence. His aggressive policy of seeking out new writers appealed to Cecil as much as his innovative and brilliant marketing.

Unfortunately, Cecil had little time to discuss his book project as their meeting was constantly interrupted by phone calls and staff bringing in papers and artwork for McClelland's approval. His behavior with his employees showed another side of McClelland's dynamic nature. Cecil noted:

He struck me as a fiery sort. Oaths poured forth when anyone brought something he was displeased with. A woman came in with a cover proposal for a book. He blew up and his language was really blue. He had a bad temper when under stress.

McClelland invited Cecil to stay after the staff left for the day. Another, warmer side of the publisher emerged as the two men shared a vodka, McClelland unwinding as he sipped his favorite drink. Their session "extended from mid-afternoon long into the evening." Cecil seized the opportunity, animatedly outlining his work at Featherland. As McClelland's enthusiasm grew, so did

Cecil's. Instead of dealing with a reader or editor at a publishing house, he was pitching his story to a man who could not only promote his and Adele's work with birds, but also solve Featherland's ever-worsening financial state.

Although he did not expect, nor receive, any definite commitment, Cecil wrote of McClelland's interest in his life and work: "[It] was a promising start and I left a copy of a few things I had written and he promised to go over it." As the evening was getting late, McClelland arranged a taxi to take Cecil back to Jim's place.

In the taxi, Cecil allowed himself to relax for the first time since arriving in Toronto. The trip east, which had been undertaken with a desperation arising out of necessity, had gone much better than he had dared to hope. The reaction to both his projects — the book and the invention — had been entirely positive. The personal contact with Jack McClelland and the drinks they had shared left him basking in a warm afterglow. He looked forward to driving to Ottawa with Jim the next day, and seeing his parents. As a surprise, he had "voiced" a letter to them using the prototype of his Vocaletter device.

As he indulged himself with thoughts of all these promising developments, one concern marred his buoyant mood. He worried about Susan, isolated in her room thousands of miles away at Featherland. Some breakthrough had to be achieved if she was to remain at Featherland. Yet he knew the decision was not his to make — it was Susan's.

On a damp and windy autumn day, a taxi swung off Burnside Road onto the long gravel driveway leading to Featherland. Leaves fluttered from the tall stand of Lombardy poplars beside the driveway. Cecil sat in the back seat of the taxi, and for once he did not mind the dismal, gray, "wet coast" weather. A smile broke across his face. His ten-day trip to the East was over. At last he was home.

As Cecil stepped from the cab, the glaucous-winged seagull Itchy flew forward to greet him. The taxi driver jumped back as Itchy landed on Cecil's back, then used her sharp beak to peck at his face. Cecil explained to the startled driver that Itchy was not attacking him, but merely welcoming him home. The driver remained unconvinced, especially when a number of geese began waddling toward the taxi, honking noisily.

Other birds outside the cottage joined the chorus. The driver shook his head — he had seen enough of this crazy place. He tossed Cecil's bags on the driveway, jumped back in his car, and sped off, leaving a rooster tail of gravel in his wake.

For a moment Cecil stood in the light drizzle, savoring the familiar sights and smells of Featherland. At his feet massed the outdoor members of his feathered family, including the little mallard, Toddles, who banged away at his shoes, expecting Cecil to carry him around as he usually did.

"It felt good to be home at last. Compared to the urban world of instant dishwater coffee and wrist watch fever, Featherland was Eden itself," he later wrote in his journal.

A panicked thought snapped Cecil's blissful reverie. Where was Adele? The noise the birds made should have alerted her.

"Adele! Adele!" he shouted.

When he received no response, Cecil pushed through the gaggle of waterfowl at his feet, ignoring their honks and quacks as he rushed to Ookpik Cottage. The moment he stepped inside the front door and put his bags down, Susan reacted aggressively.

"Her haughty response showed she was still riled at me. She raised her feathers and flew violently at the bars, edgy — almost thirsting for slaughter."

Cecil had hoped his absence might have dulled her anger, maybe even allowed for a fresh start. Now he had his answer — not the one he had secretly hoped for. Susan's hostile reaction deflated him. All the encouraging news he brought back from his trip east suddenly seemed empty. He would have traded the promise of a book for the return of Susan's affection.

Adele burst through the back door and dropped her feeding pails to embrace Cecil. Susan erupted again — if anything, she was even more enraged.

"Better get out of her sight," Adele told Cecil as she led him away. "I'm afraid she might injure herself by whacking at the grille."

Before Cecil could bring up the subject of Susan's future, Adele blandly announced she had taken the opportunity to test whether Susan's anger was specifically directed at Cecil or also included her.

"What do you mean?" Cecil spluttered, not quite comprehending what Adele was telling him.

"You see, the third night after you left I was looking through the grille here at the dirt on Susan's floor. I said to myself: 'My goodness this is really bad. It's not right for her health. It can't go on. I'll just have to go in and clean Sue's floor and that's that.'"

She calmly continued to fill Cecil in on what she had done during his absence. Although years later Cecil was able to laugh at the incident, at the time the shock of the incredible risk Adele had taken made his knees shake. He had to sit down, recalling all his close calls with Susan, from their first encounter, when she had nearly tagged his eye with a talon, to the many other times she had connected and left him bruised and bleeding.

"So I went in, closed the door behind me and said to myself, this is it. I started to clean up Sue's dirty floor," Adele continued, her usually quiet voice rising higher. She admitted she had been afraid but managed to override her natural impulse to run for the door.

Cecil was too overwhelmed to speak. This moment represented an unusual twist in their relationship. Ordinarily, Cecil was more talkative than Adele, although she was known to carry on animated conversations with their feathered family.

Adele became so concerned about Cecil's lengthy silence that she asked him if he was alright. Cecil nodded, trying to absorb the full impact of what Adele had accomplished. A mixture of awe and anger swept over him. He confided his reaction to his journal:

A quarter of a mile from the nearest source of help and physically defenceless, Adele entered Susan's room, closed the door, and proceeded to take over her care — with impunity. Had Susan turned on her out of any stormy mixture of feelings, within seconds Adele would have been no more than a gruesome statistic.

Adele was not the type to take unnecessary risks for the thrill involved. Her decision to enter Susan's room, while it could be called impulsive, was based on clear signs from Susan. From the moment of her uncrating, the golden eagle had shown a preference for Adele, and over her years at Featherland she had reaffirmed her affection for her. Adele's confidence sprang from conviction, which allowed her to overcome her fear. She knew the risks involved; as Cecil later said, "she had staked her life on her personal judgment and had won."

Finally the full impact of what Adele had done sunk in. Cecil's anger subsided, replaced by guilt as he blamed himself for not putting two and two together and realizing that Adele would do:

After living with the little dame all those years, I should have known how she thinks. What I could not do that must be done, she would do if it killed her. As simple as that. Perhaps it is that some strengths owe much to simplicity.

"Now tell me all about your trip," Adele brightened, offering Cecil a cup of coffee the way he liked it — strong and thick enough to stand a spoon straight up in. He badly needed it to steady his nerves.

Cecil thoroughly enjoyed the rest of his homecoming day. He took over the feeding, delighted to be reunited with his feathered family. He had missed them almost as much as he had missed Adele. Most of the birds responded with equal affection.

Between chores, Cecil recounted his trip, beginning with his private session with Jack McClelland. Cecil also updated her about Jim Hyndman's progress in building a prototype of a new aircraft. Not only had his younger brother become excited about the Vocaletter, but he had passed the diagrams along to an engineer for professional evaluation.

They talked throughout the day and into the evening. While Cecil admitted he felt energized pitching his projects, being reacquainted with the hectic pace of city life reaffirmed his decision to live away from the coldness of urban existence. Even if he still had "some people skills, and wasn't viewed as some country bumpkin," Cecil confessed he was no longer temperamentally suited for "life on some treadmill, fighting to keep ahead." All the glitter and frenzied activity of urban life simply paled compared to their Eden, Featherland.

Aware that Adele was by nature always supportive, to the point of being overly optimistic, Cecil cautioned that his trip had merely opened some doors. As the long day ended, they both found sleep difficult as they shared the same sense of elation.

Unable to fall asleep, Cecil wandered outside, walking up the hill to visit the small cottage of Kluane, then the great horned owl Max in his own separate cottage, and finally the birds in Talon Hall. All seemed right with the world. Even the clouds had partially cleared, revealing a mass of twinkling stars overhead.

"We're poised on the edge of a golden phase at Featherland," Adele said later when Cecil returned to bed. "I can sense it." Cecil agreed — for the first time in years their future seemed bright and promising.

ten

Progress

The autumn days shortened and the foliage came alive with fiery colors — reds, oranges, and golds. Cecil had little time to enjoy the last few warm days before the wet winter arrived. Early fall was never a leisure period at Featherland. The roof of their cottage, Talon Hall, and the numerous other small buildings and stalls needed repairing. Rotting fenceposts and loose barbed wire needed mending. Branches overhanging the overhead lines snaking to the outbuildings needed trimming.

Cecil took on these maintenance tasks with a vigor that surprised Adele. The trip east had done more than open a few doors. The experience seemed to revitalize Cecil. He threw himself into the outdoor repair work, not because he enjoyed it, but rather to have more time to complete the two projects he took east. His brief reacquaintance with hard and impersonal urban life had reconfirmed what a unique existence he and Adele had made for themselves at Featherland. He was determined to save the Eden they had acquired in 1946.

Although he occasionally cursed the place when he banged his thumb with a hammer, he wrote in his journal: "I knew I could never find such closeness, so much affection, with so many others if I returned to living in a cold, gray city."

As Cecil worked outdoors, one thought kept repeating itself in his mind, like a catchy lyric from a song: Adele's prediction of a "golden phase" for Featherland. Although he was not a man who relied on signs, Adele had been right so many times before that he relied on her powerful intuition.

The buoyant, expectant mood lasted through the next month, tempered by the amount of work they faced before the winter rains made outside work impossible. Life at Featherland seemed to take on a new beginning as new possibilities beckoned. With the outside fall prep work completed, Cecil entered an equally intense period working inside on the book and Vocaletter. If either one took off, their financial problems would end.

As the first of the autumn rains began their annual onslaught, Cecil set up his private retreat in Kluane's cottage. Meanwhile, inside Ookpik Cottage, Adele concentrated her energy on building her relationship with Susan. The next phase was the critical one. Adele had to improve and strengthen her bond with Susan — if Susan was willing. And as Cecil had found out, Susan could change her mind.

As Cecil began working on his manuscript, he knew he faced a time limit. While in Ottawa, Cecil had called another ex-NFBer about Jack McClelland, explaining how enthusiastic he was about Featherland. The friend warned Cecil, "McClelland is notorious for losing interest. He's got the attention span of a hummingbird and quickly loses interest if a project becomes stalled, moving on to the next promising project."

Progress

While Cecil worked, Adele made steady progress with Susan. Now that contact had been established, she gradually extended the time she spent in Susan's room each day, always carefully gauging the eagle's reaction. Susan showed no signs of hostility — unless she detected Cecil's presence in the Bird Room.

As the days grew into weeks, Adele progressed to the point of hand-feeding Susan inside her room. The golden eagle showered affection on Adele. Adele's relations with Cecil, on the other hand, became slightly distant and detached. She knew he was preoccupied with his writing and invention, but she also sensed his frustration. She knew he felt impotent, no longer able to visit Susan and only able to offer advice and moral encouragement to Adele.

In October Cecil's dreaded forty-ninth birthday loomed ominously. Adele became so preoccupied with Susan that she almost forgot about it. Cecil was disappointed, but not because he expected a big celebration. Secretly, he had hoped he might have some positive news about his two projects by then, "to lift the gloomy cloak from such a lifemark event." Although he had sent out follow-up letters, the passing weeks brought no response except a vague letter from Jack McClelland, saying he was assigning Cecil an editor.

Cecil became more and more anxious. By nature he was not a patient man — not because he could not wait, but rather because he was exceedingly sensitive to any slights, real or imaginary. The weather provided a suitable gray and dismal backdrop to complement his melancholic mood.

In early December an editor at McClelland & Stewart contacted Cecil, telling him, "Under certain conditions we feel that there may be material for a book." The editor noted the unique theme of Cecil's work — namely that "birds have a mental and emotional life usually disregarded by or generally unknown to scholars and recorders of bird facts." The editor acknowledged Cecil's ability to arouse an emotional response from birds. "Now, as a writer, the problem is to arouse interest and response in readers."

The editor suggested an outline, starting with a lively scene depicting life in Featherland to arouse the reader's interest. The second chapter would backtrack to the beginnings of Featherland, followed by a time line, detailing the arrival of each bird to Featherland. Subsequent chapters would focus on each of the main bird personalities at Featherland.

Each chapter would work up to a climax, ending with an element of surprise; for example, with a bird speaking its first word. Only then, the editor warned, after revealing their breakthroughs with specific birds, should Cecil delve into his philosophy.

"What do you make of all this?" Cecil asked Adele. By the tone of his voice, Adele knew Cecil's reaction to the long list of instructions was mixed.

"If they've appointed an editor to the project, they must be serious," Adele said.

While Cecil admitted the editor's suggested chapter breakdown gave the book a workable structure, the restrictons on expressing his personal philosophy seemed overly restrictive — almost a straightjacket.

"Now don't get pigheaded about this," Adele said, knowing only too well how stubborn Cecil could become.

Christmas at Featherland that year passed uneventfully, lacking the sense of closeness other Christmases had. Cecil and Adele were simply too busy and too preoccupied to spend more time together. Cecil focused his considerable energy on his book and invention. From his earliest days, he had shown the ability to immerse himself in a specific project. His experience at the CBC and NFB, where he worked long hours on one program, had reinforced this characteristic.

As the winter months passed, Adele continued to build on her closeness with Susan, which meant she had less time to spend with Cecil. He began to feel his emotional support fading — especially late at night when he wrote by himself in the outbuilding. On those lonely nights his thoughts drifted to Susan, whom he used to call his "second wife." Now Susan had found a new mate — his wife. So Cecil's loss doubled — he had lost Susan's affection, and now Adele spent so much time and lavished so much attention on Susan that she had little left for Cecil.

On those dark, cold winter nights in the chilly cottage, he remembered Susan's warmth during those moments of close contact. He recalled the many times he had entered her room completely unprotected, sometimes wearing only his swimming suit in summer. She would often greet him by rubbing her face on his as he blew on her head feathers. Now those two wonderful but brief years of contact were over.

Despite his keen sense of loss, Cecil pushed Adele to develop her relationship with Susan — with the ultimate goal being physical contact. But Adele still felt uncomfortable stroking Susan. Cecil noticed Adele's progress with Susan slow to a virtual stop. Cecil theorized that Adele "found it pretty nerve wracking to carry matters any further." While she would not admit it, Cecil suspected Adele was afraid.

New Year's of 1961 began with great promise. Cecil wrote to his brother Jim in Toronto, "What a sunny beginning to the year. I have the feeling and the bright hope of this being the year when the tide of prosperity turns and fulfills some ambitions for both of us."

A month later, the brief clear and warm spell changed back to the more typical gray and wet winter conditions. Cecil's tone also changed in his next letter to Jim as he wondered why his brother had not been in touch, nor even sent a Christmas card.

Finally a letter from Jim arrived in mid-February. He explained that he had married in January, then taken a much-needed honeymoon and vacation for almost a month. He was still involved in developing an aircraft, which was draining his financial resources.

Still, Jim shared Cecil's optimism regarding the future, "maybe some year I can give you an aircraft to tool about the island."

Jim still felt enthusiastic about the marketing potential of Vocaletter, but first the idea needed to be endorsed by a technical expert. While Cecil understood, the wait for an engineering and technical report effectively stalled the Vocaletter project.

In any case, writing the manuscript for McClelland consumed all of Cecil's limited free time.

One evening that winter, after an especially long writing session, Cecil returned to Ookpik Cottage. He quietly opened the back door so not to wake Adele. As he tiptoed across the floor, he heard Adele in Susan's room. Creeping as close to the grille as he dared, he saw how hesitant she was in her contact with Susan. "She simply could not quite muster the nerve to bend her face down into Sue's head feathering and face."

In bed that night, Cecil confronted Adele. She admitted that her relationship with Susan had "plateaued." While she felt confident enough to enter and clean Susan's room, and to hand-feed and occasionally stroke Susan, she could not bring herself to attempt the last step. She admitted the fear was irrational, yet it seemed as solid and unmovable as a concrete wall.

"It's silly, isn't it, Cec," Adele said.

"No, it's not," Cecil answered.

He felt partially responsible; he had cautioned Adele to "move in small steps," since any rash action with Susan might cause an attack.

"Whatever the reason, I simply cannot force myself to rub faces with Susan," Adele confessed.

"You have to — or your relationship won't grow."

"Maybe tomorrow," Adele said, as she rolled over and went to sleep.

After chores the next morning, Cecil caught up with Adele while she put the gulls outside for the day. He reminded her that "nothing short of physical cheek-to-cheek contact can set the stage for the fullest trust on both sides."

She promised she would break through the barrier — perhaps the next day. This same scene was repeated over the next few mornings, until Cecil realized his encouragement was not helping Adele overcome her hesitation.

At this stage he stopped being so supportive, and began, frankly, nagging at her instead. He wrote:

> *[I goaded] her to do one thing after another that I had been accustomed to doing. Adele became fussed and annoyed with my insistencies — but to prick her pride seemed the only way to force the issue.*

Over the next few weeks, Adele found Cecil's presence almost as intimidating as Susan's curved beak. She refused to attempt contact with Cecil hovering like some voyeur in the background. Cecil promised not to disturb Adele's sessions with Susan — if she promised to overcome her hesitancy.

Each evening, as Adele opened the door to Susan's room, she took an extra minute after cleaning to read Susan's face carefully. Although she was not sure what she was looking for, what the "sign" would be, she was confident she would recognize that special moment when it came.

The night finally came when Susan seemed in an especially affectionate mood. Her large golden eyes seemed unusually inviting when Adele fed her — as if she could read Adele's thoughts and was saying *touch me*.

After feeding Susan, Adele slowly bent forward, moving her face closer to Susan's — and to the golden eagle's razor-sharp bill. As the distance between the two closed, Adele could sense Susan tense slightly, as if caught offguard. Adele froze in mid-movement, only inches from the curved tip of Susan's bill. The female eagle twisted her head, riffled her feathers slightly, and inspected Adele with a quizzical stare.

As Susan's large beak opened slightly, Adele suddenly realized that they were at least an inch closer than they had been a moment ago when she had stopped moving. Adele almost laughed out loud as she realized *Susan* must have moved closer.

"So you want to rub faces?" she asked Susan as she bent forward to make contact.

The moment was one Adele treasured for the rest of her life. As she slowly rubbed Susan's face, the softness and warmth from her feathers brushed away her nervousness. Like Cecil before her, Adele found Susan's fragrance as intoxicating as any expensive perfume. Adele repeated the contact, then slowly withdrew her face a few inches from Susan's face to test the eagle's response.

Within moments Susan returned the physical contact, using her large beak to stroke Adele's face. Feeling the touch of that fierce-looking bill for the first time thrilled Adele. She had rubbed faces with other birds and had their beaks next to her eye. But Susan's bill was unlike any other; despite its deadly appearance, its touch was incredibly delicate.

The two women — one human, the other avian — embraced for minutes. While Cecil had warned her to move slowly, taking her time to establish contact, the emotional experience overwhelmed Adele. In her excitement she put her arms around Susan in a hug. But this impulsive action immediately caused Susan to stiffen; few birds of prey will endure being physically restrained.

Susan riffled her body feathers, as if announcing it was time for Adele to leave. After saying goodnight, Adele left Susan's room, went out the back door, and started up the hill to share the news of her breakthrough with Cecil. Atop the slope an orange glow shimmered from the window in Kluane's cottage where Cecil wrote every night.

Unable to contain her excitement, Adele spun in an impromptu dance to celebrate her accomplishment. Ignoring the light drizzle, she savored the experience, squeezing her arms tightly around herself as if the action could bring back the sensation of having her arms around Susan.

Embracing Susan had triggered a rare moment of ecstasy. She had fulfilled a desire she had suppressed for over five years. From the first moment she had seen Susan, she had wanted more than anything to hold her. She had achieved her dream, and the pleasure she felt overwhelmed her.

She spun until the surrounding landmarks became blurred and she fell to the ground. Not waiting for the dizziness to pass, she got up and ran up toward the small cottage, half-slipping on the wet slope but not caring. Adele knew her husband would welcome her interruption as much as he would delight in her news. Breaking through the barrier was an accomplishment, but far more important was the deeper implication of what had happened that evening. The intimate physical contact she and Susan had shared could only mean the love was mutual.

Over the next few months, Cecil pressured his younger brother Jim in Toronto for the engineer's report on his Vocaletter invention. In mid-April, it arrived. The technical expert had outlined his reservations in blunt language: "I feel it would be an error to proceed with the project. The reason for this is based on competitive products recently released on the market."

While Cecil had been developing his Vocaletter recorder, there were no small portable tape recorders available; only bulky and expensive reel-to-reel ones. Now the first Japanese miniaturized tape recorders were appearing in New York, selling for $14.95. The engineer's letter ended bleakly: "I am deliberately making this letter as discouraging as I feel it should be and sincerely feel that any further development along these lines would prove to be a financial error."

The unexpected news hit Cecil so hard he became very ill, reacting physically as he often did to emotional or personal setbacks. He stayed in bed for days, writing to his parents about an agonizing bursitis of the shoulder. Somehow, however, with Adele's support, he managed to keep up the work on the book throughout.

When he recovered, Cecil returned to sharing Kluane's chilly cottage, leaving Adele to bask in the warmth of Susan's friendship. He feared that his withdrawal from the scene might seem "melo-dramatic, like a rejected suitor sulking to draw attention." But there was a practical reason behind the move. Susan continued to exhibit extreme hostility toward him — often reacting to the mere sound of his footsteps in the cottage. In this volatile state, Cecil worried Susan might accidentally harm Adele when she entered. So he decided to limit his presence in the main cottage.

Cecil referred to the small wooden outbuilding that housed Kluane as his "private retreat." He kidded Adele that the cottage — in reality not much larger than a shed — was an all-male domain where females were not welcome. But there was some truth to the statement; Kluane had shown a definite preference for Cecil and now displayed a dislike for Adele.

The cottage Cecil shared with Kluane also had the benefit of providing peace and quiet to write in. Unfortunately, the writing progressed slowly. Cecil found it difficult to keep to the outline the editor at McClelland had provided. He confided to his journal his worry "that the book would turn out to be a fluffy, light-hearted look at two middle-aged eccentrics pursuing what only could be described as an offbeat if not decidedly oddball life."

Instead, he secretly dreamed of putting into words the essence of their avian research at Featherland. He believed, like Darwin, that humans and birds shared some faculties because of their common origin. But he knew McClelland wanted an entertaining book, not a controversial book full of unprovable theories written by someone without any scientific background.

As he struggled with how to best explain in words what they were attempting at Featherland, Cecil realized their unorthodox approach was easiest to define in terms of what it *wasn't*. Featherland was certainly not a research lab for birds. Most scientific labs caged birds to study them from a purely biological or zoological perspective, an approach that limited birds to mere data — how much they weighed, how much fat their muscles contained, etc.

Nor was Featherland a field research station. Wildlife naturalists who studied birds in the wild only recorded behavior; no field researcher ever interfered with a bird's behavior.

But to Cecil, birds weren't "just pieces of organic machinery." So, like pioneers who had no road map, they invented their own methods. Their aim was to study birds as living beings, not research subjects. This went against the grain of that era, since few scientists considered birds to have intelligence. Bird behavior was thought to derive from instinctual responses.

He summed up the current thinking about bird intelligence in the foreword of his manuscript:

Some may say at this point "Mind? What mind? A bird has no mind in the human sense of independent thought and reason and sensitivity. This bird, that bird, any bird has only a brain mechanism responding, reacting blindly to inborn or instinctive impulse and dictate."

Cecil intended to prove that theory wrong. He had observed that

many birds as individuals have brain powers and functions quite above and apart from mere instinct or inherited behavior patterns. Some can definitely possess true individualistic personality and some harbor within them portions, large and small, of completely human brain faculties.

At long last, he finished the handwritten version of the manuscript. He wrote to his parents:

This has been the hardest task by far of a single sort that I have ever attempted. It has been truly exhausting. It remains for the publisher to decide whether the effort has been successful, from their point of view.

His letter ended on a painfully embarrassing financial note:

We have been running the better part of a month behind since last fall and each time we deposit we only slightly cover the overdraft. In order to breach the gap, perhaps you could extend the loan a further $175 so we will not be continually in this situation. As you can see with the book and the invention, we are doing everything we humanly can to hasten the process of reaching some self-sufficient point.

Cecil's return to Ookpik Cottage from his months of writing in Kluane's cottage brought about a renewal of hostility from Susan. She flew into a rage, forcing Cecil to keep out of sight. He hid and watched as Adele entered Susan's room to calm her down. No longer was Adele tentative or anxious about Susan's reaction. As Cecil watched Adele put her face next to Susan's, he was amazed at how "Susan began to positively live for Adele, who had become to her the embodiment of all that mattered to her — not simply platonically, so to speak, but physically, sexually as well. She was now truly mated to Adele."

Delighted as he was with his wife's progress, Susan's violent outbursts toward himself continued to puzzle him. Adele and Cecil discussed this behavior, wondering how much of it was Susan's distinctive personality, and how much was based on her predator nature.

The Hyndmans knew that golden eagles mate for life and that this loyalty brings with it a drive to defend their territory against outsiders.

"She certainly shows a ferocity when it comes to her room — her territory," Cecil said.

Progress

They decided to curtain off Susan's room more completely. As they prepared the new screen, Cecil was not sure whether to laugh or cry at the thought that he now "was regarded as the enemy who had to be driven by force from the eagle's territory."

Cecil later expressed his feelings in his journal thus:

Over the years Susan has been in turn devil, saint and devil again in her relationship with me, whereas she has been saint all through with Adele. Whether she will ever again be my soft and loving Susan only time will tell.

Finally the bound and illustrated manuscript headed east. The accompanying letter revealed his anxieties:

My agonies as a bird man attempting to be writer are over in putting together the first rough draft of Behind the Feathered Curtain. *The text runs to 150 double-spaced pages plus illustrations. Some of the photos are unique: Goliath untying my shoelaces, Itchy with her bill next to me. Extreme close-ups of Joey, Max, and Susan will bring the personalities to life for the readers. In some cases the disturbing presence of a camera can mean extreme risk to life and limb, or rather eye. Many shots cannot be made by professional photographers from outside because the birds will not tolerate them.*

It seems simply impossible for me to string words together with ease and abandon. It is painful business. I have never before worked harder to do a good job and somehow on the whole I feel happy about it but at the same time am acutely aware that the real test is how you and Mr. McClelland and others assess it, apart from anything I may feel or say. I agree with Maxie, the great horned owl:

Thinking's harder than I thought
I'm exhausted am I not?

eleven

Ups And Downs

Throughout the spring of 1961, Adele's love affair with Susan continued to grow in richness and depth. Despite her earlier hesitancy to push the limits of intimacy, Adele amazed Cecil by her ability to embrace Susan. A human physically confining a golden eagle was a remarkable achievement. Cecil had never read or heard of anyone being able to hold a healthy eagle. Yet Susan allowed Adele to hold her.

The interaction between Adele and Susan involved more than just the nightly sessions of mutual grooming and embracing. Susan was now past her teenage years, but still retained her youthful energy and zest for life. Cecil encouraged Adele to stimulate "the highly active, exuberant side of the golden girl's many faceted nature." Often the overhead lamps in the cottage shook as Susan frolicked with Adele in an impromptu game of catch using lacrosse or tennis balls.

Sometimes they played tug-of-war, with Susan grabbing one end of a stick Adele held. When Adele raised the stick, Susan was thrown off balance. This in turn caused her to fan the air with her wings to maintain her balance. Adele worked on conditioning this natural behavior of Susan's, hoping to incorporate this into the performances Susan would give when visitors toured Featherland.

Susan understood both her name and some complicated commands. Adele would order her, "Sue, go and get a stick and take it up onto your box," and most times Susan would follow directions. She could differentiate between "fly to your low perch" and "now up to your stand." She especially enjoyed being encouraged to "bang your perch, Sue, punch holes in it," which allowed her to play rough.

Adele devised another game where she would toss objects to Susan, who picked them up with her talons. Adele also worked on Susan's aerobatic ability, stimulating her to leap into the air on command, then rewarding her with positive reinforcement. Soon Susan was not only flapping into the air on command, she was catching the two balls Adele threw toward her.

Cecil delighted in the progress Adele was making "training" Susan, reminding her she only had a few months before Featherland opened for the summer.

That spring saw an exchange of letters between an anxious Cecil and his editor in Toronto. While noting her pleasure at the manuscript's neat appearance and splendid photos, the editor informed Cecil that Jack McClelland was in England. Finally a letter from McClelland arrived in late April 1961. He wrote:

[it was] *an extremely difficult decision for us to reach. We have encouraged you to put a good deal of time on the manuscript but I am sorry to say the work has not come up to our expectations and our readers don't feel it is of a publishable standard.*

The rejection stung, and Cecil quickly wrote a reply, his desperation obvious:

Your letter not only puts me into financial distress but puts my whole future in jeopardy. That you have the right to reject my book is a fact but in view of the work and $600 in expenses of the photos I have taken for the purpose of the book, my trip to Toronto to see you and the months of intensive work I put in, I feel I have a moral right arising out of human decency for specific and adequate reasons for the rejection.

Jack McClelland's reply was measured and firm:

You ask for specific and adequate reasons for the rejection. If you will refer to the editor's letter, you will note "the problem is to arouse interest and response in readers." This is specifically what the manuscript fails to do. Accomplishing this is a matter of talent and technique. We made no commitment other than to read "with interest" the completed manuscript. It seems to us wholly unrealistic to feel we are somehow responsible for any of your own risks, decisions, or losses during the last three months.

The second rejection letter from McClelland bitterly disappointed Cecil, especially as it followed so closely on the engineer's discouraging report about his Vocaletter invention. Cecil was a complex man, driven by extreme emotionalism. The excesses of this trait were usually tempered by his more rational side. But often his passion led him to view different situations as either overly rosy or darkly bleak. In his mind, he had sold the book before he had even started writing it.

With the rejection, Cecil's emotional pendulum swung in the opposite direction, bringing him to a depression as intense as had been his enthusiasm for the book and Vocaletter projects. Adele kept an eye on her husband, afraid the stress building inside him like a pressure-cooker would blow.

Over the next few weeks Adele saw nothing that indicated Cecil had fully recovered from this double setback. He bore his burden physically, developing a slight stoop.

As spring gave way to summer, Featherland once again opened its gates to visitors. Although this was the first summer Adele "showed" Susan, her confidence increased with each exhibition. Foreign tourists and local visitors were equally intrigued with Susan. Even the rare visitor who had seen other eagles in zoos admitted to being thrilled when Susan fanned her wings on command from Adele. That impressive sight alone elated thousands of visitors.

Next, Adele would explain to the visitors how an eagle's feet worked, while Susan demonstrated her ability to turn objects using her feet and curved talons. Adele would then attempt to take an object out of Susan's talons, explaining the risks involved and stressing that this part of the performance was not rehearsed — the final decision was totally up to Susan.

At this stage of the tour, Cecil usually informed the visitors of Susan's previous attacks on him. His explanation added to the real-life drama unfolding before them as Adele cautiously approached Susan to ask her to release the object. The audience sensed the danger and watched silently as Adele checked Susan's facial expression. If Susan showed signs of agreeing, Adele would take back the object.

Toward the end of the performance, at Adele's command Susan would leap into the air and Adele would throw two balls toward Susan. The long hours Adele had spent training Susan paid off. Susan's impressive aerobatic skills never failed to astound visitors. Cecil wrote how "Susan's athletic performances thrilled us and visitors, with Susan making eight-foot-high snap catches of two balls simultaneously, her talons closing on the balls in mid-air."

To top this spectacular feat, Adele trained Susan to land on the tennis balls — not her talons:

The sight of Susan landing with a tennis ball in each foot on her box was accompanied by a double thudding clap. Then Susan would proceed to walk about on them in such a way that only the balls touched the floor. It should be rated as nothing less than a circus spectacular — an act of agility and timing believable only on seeing.

Conducting visitors around the grounds of their sloped property and showing their performing birds did more than keep Cecil occupied. Sharing his passion for birds with others began to re-energize him. The increase in the number of visitors over past seasons helped to ease Featherland's mounting debt, at least temporarily.

That summer, two representatives of a large American zoo toured Featherland. They were so impressed by the Hyndmans' approach that "they asked permission to copy certain aspects of the performance and incorporate these into their zoo's tours," Cecil wrote in his journal.

Later that summer another zoo manager arrived and commented on the interactive nature of Featherland. The manager candidly admitted that most zoos were little more than "steel bars and concrete cages." He alerted Cecil to a shift in public awareness. People were moving away from merely passively viewing wildlife. The manager praised the Hyndmans for the way they "performed" with Susan.

Adele and Cecil began to notice a change in the public's attitude toward eagles. Once regarded as vermin, now the eagle was more often seen as a victim. Laws were being enacted to protect this magnificent creature. Much of this radical shift in public opinion can be attributed to one book, Rachel Carson's *Silent Spring*, the first best-selling ecology book. Carson's book alerted the public to the widespread use of chemical insecticides, and of DDT in particular. She warned that birds of prey faced extinction caused by DDT contamination, which caused them to lay eggs with thin shells.

As July approached, Adele noted a physical change in Cecil. His slight stoop had straightened. The bounce returned to his step, as if the warm weather had somehow thawed him out. The next month they rented a boat for their annual seabird collecting trip to the Chain Islets. The invigorating sea air had never tasted better and was just the tonic Cecil needed. He returned almost a new man, refreshed and renewed.

The philosophical discussions with the zoo representatives and the improved public attitude toward eagles had reinforced his conviction that he was on the right track with the book. There was a growing demand for animal and bird stories — almost a need.

At last he felt ready to consider what he should do with the manuscript McClelland & Stewart had rejected. The Vocaletter invention also weighed heavily on his mind. Should he scrap the project after the engineer's discouraging report? In many ways, the decision about the invention was out of his hands. Cecil knew the patenting process could take another year. He could do nothing but wait until that hurdle was over before deciding whether to attempt to market his device.

The book was another matter. Cecil began to take long strolls at night up Burble Creek to his favorite "thinking spot" overlooking Victoria. Although attendance was up at Featherland, the increased revenue was still not sufficient to keep the Hyndmans afloat. As their overdraft continued to mount at the bank, the need to find an answer to their financial troubles became more pressing than ever. Cecil quietly resolved not to abandon either project. Alone on the rocky slope, he began to plan how to rewrite the book.

Raising Susan

On a bright summer Monday morning in July of 1961, the phone rang. At first Cecil tried to ignore the noise. He had been up until almost dawn, trying to save the life of a starving and dehydrated bald eagle two men had brought to Featherland the day before. Despite their attempts, the bird had died. Half asleep, Cecil staggered toward the phone. It was a local newspaperman, asking if he and a photographer could come out to do a story on the Hyndmans' gull, Itchy.

After Cecil hung up, the Hyndmans hurriedly prepared for the arrival of the news crew. A new batch of eggs from their recent seabird collecting trip lay in the incubator, and several chicks waited for their morning feeding. Cecil checked the temperature of the electric heating element, which was underneath the incubator. Adele put on a pot of coffee in the nearby kitchenette, then prepared the morning feed for the two downy gull chicks. To simulate food regurgitated from adult gull stomachs, they had devised a method involving raw oolicans soaked in hydrochloric acid for a half hour, then in pepsin solution. The final step involved moistening the feed in milk.

The coffee helped revive Cecil, and as he drank his second cup, he completed his notes on the bald eagle, which had been found near Sooke, almost forty miles away. The postmortem revealed that the eagle, a female, had died of old age, its ossified bill attesting to its long life. The shrunken stomach indicated it had not eaten in some time. Cecil quickly finished his writing as he heard the crunch of tires on their gravel driveway.

"Don't forget the tape of Itchy," Adele reminded Cecil, who threaded up the reel-to-reel recorder.

Cecil greeted the reporter and photographer outside, worried about how Itchy would react to all the photographic gear. Although she had flown to his back numerous times before, Itchy, according to Cecil, had an "inflated sense of self-importance. Ducks scatter and take wing when she chooses to throw her weight around. At other times she can be reasonably peaceful in a cool, rather snooty way." How would she behave today?

He needn't have worried. He wrote in his journal:

Despite the scary-looking electronic camera equipment, including bulky batteries and snaky coils of cord, Itchy posed on my back at my command for five perfect shots. She did exactly as I told the photographer ahead of time she would. I felt as proud of her as any father of a scholarship-winning daughter.

The newspaperman took notes as Cecil explained how he had trained Itchy to perform.

When Itchy was about one, I encouraged her to step on my leg while I lay on the grass. Gradually I got her to fly or jump on my body to play. This was difficult as a gull has no tendency to fly to an outstretched arm as a crow might. And a gull's feet are not well adapted to balancing on an unstable surface.

"Did you know she is the first gull to speak words in English?" Cecil asked as the newsman was about to leave.

The reporter wrote down the information, but was not interested in hearing the tape of Itchy speaking. As the black sedan roared down the gravel driveway, Cecil felt like shouting after the cloud of dust, "you missed the bigger story!"

Standing by the cottage, Itchy reached up with her bill and began to pick gently at Cecil's eyebrows. This was usually a sign of affection, although sometimes Itchy used her sharp bill as a weapon. Suddenly the gull's foot-wide wings flapped wildly and she raised her head. Cecil followed her eyes upward as another glaucous-winged gull passed overhead. Itchy's unfriendly "ka-ka-ka" vocalizations warned the other gull that this was her territory and that she meant to defend it. And often she did just that, flying to attack other gulls.

Although many people even now dismiss gulls as "common," they were a favorite of Cecil's, who prided himself on his maverick opinions. He wrote:

Gulls deserve to be ranked at or very near the top of the list in potential all-round mental stature. They have amazing reasoning powers, sharp sensitivities, and deep, strong emotions. In my view the gull's mental ability has much in common with the raven and crow.

Leaving Itchy outside, Cecil went back inside the cottage, where Adele was busy cleaning the incubator.

"Aren't they coming inside to hear the tape of Itchy?" she asked, disappointed.

Cecil shook his head. He knew the newsmen had been sent to get a quick "filler" photo of Itchy climbing on Cecil, with a cute story to accompany it. They hadn't been interested enough to learn about her real accomplishment. No one else had ever trained a gull to talk.

By 1961, Cecil and Adele had succeeded in training twenty-one birds of nine different species to speak at least a few English words. The list included five mynas, six budgies, four crows, three ravens, one magpie, one cockatoo, one cockatiel, one parrot, and one macaw — all members of either the crow or parrot family groups.

In his journal, Cecil wrote about avian speech:

no one had ever succeeded in demonstrating speech powers in any birds outside of these two feathered types — crow and parrot. It was considered impossible to do. After ten years of teaching birds to speak, I came to the personal conclusion that several of the so-called non-talking bird types did possess the necessary vocal mechanism to talk.

The challenge of upsetting the experts appealed to Cecil, although he was aware "it might take a lifetime of trial and error."

He started working on owls and robins, but to no avail. They attempted to work on the baby gulls they were raising in the cottage, finding them erratic but not completely unpromising pupils.

A remarkable utterance one day from a totally unexpected source encouraged their efforts with different birds. While Adele was teaching a baby myna called So So, Cecil overheard a tiny young swallow and an equally small purple finch respond "baby" after Adele spoke. Before they could start speech training, the purple finch died. The swallow showed progress for about three weeks, then his interest simply petered out.

Finally, Cecil began working with Itchy as she seemed a prime candidate, if for no other reason than her remarkable personality. When Itchy reached the feathered stage, she surprised Cecil by choosing him "as her beau." He recounts:

She viciously bit and picked at Adele or anyone else. Itchy lived for my company and attention and wanted no part of other wild gulls flying in from the ocean. If they approached her, she attacked them.

Itchy remained at Featherland of her own free will. She had her flight feathers and nothing prevented her from flying away. At nights she displayed her affectionate side:

Before the lights [went] out, she and I had long intimate sessions where she delicately massaged the skin around my eyes, preened my eyebrows and even my eyelashes. In this way, she was my little helper, repairing the daily damage that life too often does to one's spirits and ego.

As Itchy grew into adulthood, her vocal capabilities accompanied her physical maturing. In her third year, one evening in late June in 1961, Cecil succeeded in capturing Itchy on tape uttering the words "come here."

"And there it was," he later recorded in his journal, "a gull speaking two words of English. A bird unrelated to either parrot or crow family, which the experts considered an absolute barrier but one that I hurdled to fulfill an ambition of mine." The Hyndmans celebrated with a slip of scotch that evening, and for once, Cecil slept well. Eventually, Itchy added the words "Itchy" and "hello" to her vocabulary.

The photograph of Itchy climbing on Cecil's back appeared in the paper with a story that made reference to Itchy's remarkable feat of speaking. Soon the story was picked up by both Canadian and American wire services. Within weeks, radio stations began calling about the "world's first talking gull." A radio station in Auburn, Washington, broadcast Itchy's words in a fourteen-minute interview with Cecil that aired in August of that year. The following month a local radio station picked up the story. In October a CBC national radio program from Toronto interviewed Cecil and broadcast Itchy's voice across Canada.

All this publicity gave Adele an extra incentive to plan something special for Cecil's fiftieth birthday in October. While Cecil protested, saying he would rather forget than celebrate such a milestone, Adele went ahead with preparations, according Itchy guest-of-honor status. When the day came, the gull enjoyed more than one slice of cake with the Hyndmans.

The quiet celebration ended on another positive note: Cecil announced he would start the rewrite of his manuscript. He cautioned Adele that he dreaded the task as much as he had his fiftieth birthday. But the recent blitz of news items confirmed the public's and the media's growing interest in nature stories. Adele surprised Cecil by leading him up to Kluane's cottage and opening the door. Inside was his writing table, covered with an enormous red bow. On it lay a selection of pens and a stack of blank paper.

"How did you know?" Cecil asked.

"All I'll say is a little bird told me," Adele said as she kissed her husband. "It's all ready for you."

For the second autumn in a row, Cecil watched the trees change colors through the small window of Kluane's cottage. This second time around, he almost looked forward to being alone for the next few months. The experience also brought back memories from his boyhood years, when he had been so often shut off from others because of illness. Those early experiences had taught him to be self-reliant. And his completion of the first draft of his book the year before convinced him he could write — even if McClelland & Stewart did not share that opinion.

Cecil began his rewrite quietly and confidently, although he found his attention being diverted by Kluane. Often when frustrated in attempting to find the right phrase, Cecil would look up and see Kluane quietly staring at him, his expression quizzical, as if he too were searching for that phrase. Other times Kluane stood on his perch, watching as the soft and leafy crown of the oak forest outside fell to reveal the oaks' hard, gnarled silhouettes.

The male golden eagle was one of the blondest ever seen, his light feathering caused by long exposure to sunshine. Kluane was considerably smaller than Susan: almost all female birds of prey are larger and fiercer than males.

Cecil found that Kluane always had a certain reserve — perhaps because he was a wild eagle, and not hand-reared like Susan. His milder disposition and smaller size made him slightly easier to handle. Occasionally he became excited and, like Susan used to do, flew to the person bringing him his supper. But where Susan had flown to an arm, he insisted on landing on a person's back — Cecil called these "Kluane's hunchback landings." Although this habit unnerved Cecil the first few times it arose, especially as Kluane's wingspan was over six feet, the eagle never lashed out with his talons, despite having his "prey" at an obvious disadvantage.

The blond eagle's tranquil nature acted like a balm after the savaging Susan had shown Cecil. Not that Cecil lost any of his respect or affection for the Queen of Featherland. But he grew to crave the peace of Kluane's small quarters — to the point that Adele thought he was deliberately delaying the completion of the book. Cecil made steady progress, often working until 2:00 or 3:00 a.m., trying to meet his own deadline of completing the rewrite before the new year.

The exertion drained Cecil, and in January of 1962 he collapsed into bed, more exhausted than ill. He wrote in a letter to his dad that several members of his feathered family were also ill:

Mee Tu, one of our wonderful mynas, is being treated with antibiotics for a bronchial inflammation. Beeper, the black oystercatcher we brought back from the Chain Islets last summer, cut his toes months ago and picked up an infection in his feet. It's been a battle to prevent the infection from spreading and turning into blood poisoning. Then yesterday Max, our great horned owl, flew up on his wire door, got his curved bill caught and in getting him down, I got a talon in the thumb right through heavy gloves. He broke a talon at the base, which bled heavily and we had to catch him and dress the wound. In such a bird treating a wound is a real ordeal as their feet are tremendously powerful and they fight back hard against handling. We hope he will not develop any infection.

As if we did not have enough sick birds here to treat, we received a call about an injured bird on View Royal not far from Featherland. We drove out and found a sea duck — a surf scoter quite thin and obviously starving. A diet of beef brought the bird around and we have named her Little Girl.

Ups and Downs

As to his book, Cecil wrote in the same letter:

We finished it in total last weekend. Rewrote almost the entire book from start to finish. It has many new and good photos. Because of the way it is bound and prepared our reputation as eccentrics will be enhanced — we can only hope in the right direction.

The current March issue of Liberty *magazine carries an article, "Magic of Victoria," which features six pictures, one of which is of Itchy. I might add that this article, together with the newspaper syndicated items about Itchy and the network radio pieces about her, the United States release, etc., makes this bird the most publicized individual seagull in history.*

Cecil ended the letter by saying, "writing the book was problem enough but now the publishing problem will probably be equally as much of a headache." His words proved prophetic.

With the manuscript ready to be mailed off, Cecil paid one last visit to Kluane's cottage — partly out of habit and partly because they had decided to put Kluane in Talon Hall.

Back at Ookpik Cottage after his visit to Kluane, Cecil waited while Adele completed her nightly visit to Susan. The excited twittering that came from Susan's room both pleased and pained him. While he had enjoyed Kluane's companionship over the past months, the feelings he had toward the male golden eagle could never compare to the depth of his feelings for Susan, whom he always thought of as "the greatest lost love" of his life.

A few weeks after the new manuscript was posted, a car drove up the driveway to Featherland. The unannounced visitors ignored the "NO ENTRY" signs and walked into Talon Hall. The birds of prey reacted to these strangers by taking flight. Hearing the ruckus, Cecil rushed up to the hall, but arrived too late. The sedan raced off, its tires spinning gravel.

Cecil found Kluane, the newcomer to the hall, limping painfully. He had probably panicked or, provoked by the strangers, slammed hard against the wooden side of his enclosure.

"Dell, Kluane's hurt!" he shouted as he heard his wife's footsteps.

Later Cecil examined the enclosure more closely and found the ends of two nails protruding through the wall. These had apparently punctured Kluane's toes.

Within a week infection set in, swelling the toes and causing a fever. Now they had no recourse but to capture Kluane and treat the wounds. They decided to try to catch him at night while he rested on the tree stump that served as his perch. That evening Cecil put on his padded gear and entered the enclosure with a blanket.

The initial stage of the rescue operation went well. At Cecil's command, Adele flicked off the light switch, momentarily confusing Kluane. Cecil rushed in and used his "swoop and scoop" technique to capture Kluane in the blanket. When Adele entered, she switched the light back on, which caused Kluane to struggle so violently Cecil had to sit on the floor to subdue him.

Adele approached wearing thick gloves. Kluane reacted by lashing out with his feet, then clenching his talons so tightly that Adele could not open his fist. She discarded her clumsy gloves.

"What a powerhouse he was," Cecil later wrote. "It took everything I had to hold him although he had only a fraction of the muscle power of Susan. No human force could possibly open his clenched fist against his will."

The impasse lengthened, and as Cecil weakened, Kluane seemed to gain strength. When brute force failed, Adele tried a more compassionate method.

"Her eyes locked with the struggling eagle, and once she had his attention, she quietly asked him to open his foot." Although Cecil had often been surprised by some of the things that Adele had done with birds, what happened next he found unbelievable.

"At Adele's request, Kluane relaxed his feet. Encouraged by Adele's calm voice, he followed her next command to open his toes."

Adele reached across with her fingers to probe the eagle's toes. Although the swollen feet were undoubtedly painful, Kluane "accepted the sharp pain of a penetrating instrument inside a festering wound," Cecil wrote.

The Hyndmans continued their treatment of Kluane over the next few weeks. Each night the infected feet required soaking to draw out the infection, then dressing and the application of antibiotic preparations. While Adele worked gently on his wounds, Kluane watched and studied her face intently.

Kluane struggled less and less each night, as if he understood the treatments were necessary. Toward the end, he did not have to be caught. Instead, the Hyndmans found him standing quietly on his log, waiting willingly for the painful treatment. He never complained, even when Adele inserted tubes into his open wounds.

Incredibly, Kluane also seemed to realize the bandages were meant to stay on. Although an eagle's natural instinct is to remove anything on its legs, Kluane took extreme care not to allow his dressings to come loose, once rewrapping them around his own feet.

Finally the infection cleared. On the last night, the Hyndmans celebrated by posing Cecil holding Kluane. Even the flash didn't bother the eagle. Over the weeks, Cecil calculated he had held Kluane for over twenty hours total.

By late spring Cecil had crossed off the first name on the list of twelve publishing firms he had targeted for his manuscript, *Behind the Feathered Curtain*. The American publisher returned the manuscript with a short and blunt rejection letter.

The material collected by the author is certainly important enough to interest the amateur naturalist and original enough to intrigue the professional in the field. However, if the author availed himself of the services of a skilled writer the manuscript would be greatly improved, for at the present moment it lacks balance and the graceful continuity so important in a work of this kind.

This routine was repeated ten more times through May, June, and July as the manuscript circulated across Canada and the United States, then crossed the Atlantic. As Cecil crossed more names off his list of publishing firms, his anxiety increased.

All the rejections cited the same problem Jack McClelland had found with the previous draft: while the story was fascinating, the writing was poor. Cecil acknowledged the dilemma he faced in his journal.

Being primarily a bird man rather than a writer, I admit to being unequal to the task of giving this book the literary touches that might be expected from the pen of a professional writer.

By mid-July, the once-lengthy list had dwindled to one name: Lovat Dickson, best known as the publisher and promoter of Grey Owl. Cecil knew Lovat Dickson, who had been born in Victoria and had attended the University of Alberta with Cecil's brother Louis. In 1941 Dickson became a director at Macmillan & Company in London, England.

The family connection aside, Grey Owl's publisher seemed like a good bet for Cecil Hyndman, who had much in common with the more famous nature lover. They both had beak-like noses, high cheek bones, and gaunt faces. (As a child, Cecil had been taunted with Indian nicknames.) Both men wanted to share with the public their experiences and lives with wild creatures. Both wrote poetry, sketched, and loved the wilderness. Neither was really comfortable in society. And while a streak of romantic idealism ran through both men, the reality of commerce also lured them both. Both had a true passionate love for wild creatures and shared their homes with them.

Just as, in his books and lectures, Grey Owl argued for stopping the slaughter of animals, Cecil tried to change the public's attitude toward the killing of eagles as vermin.

In fact, a prominent Victoria businessman championed Cecil as "the new Grey Owl."

With the grim realization that Dickson was his last hope, Cecil air-mailed the manuscript to England. As the wait dragged on, Adele could only stand by and watch as Cecil checked the mailbox each day, the tension weighing heavily on his nerves.

July gave way to August, the most hectic part of the tourist season at Featherland. Two recent additions — the first armadillo in Canada and a caiman — created extra interest. On busy days anywhere from twenty-five to fifty visitors might arrive. Unfortunately, people often showed up in twos and threes at all times of day, ignoring the posted opening hours. Keeping any sort of a daily schedule was impossible, and often the Hyndmans went without meals.

Cecil and Adele would start the tours outside, showing off their grounds with the natural gardens. On hot days, the sight of all the geese and waterfowl frolicking in the outdoor pools delighted visitors. Other birds, including pheasants and quail, lived outside — many in protective enclosures covered with netting. During the summer some fifty cages stood outside, many containing abandoned birds the Hyndmans were caring for.

Toddles, the feisty mallard, would waddle down when Cecil called him and bang Cecil on the nose. A large Canada goose called Ulysses would evoke laughter as he entered into shouting matches with Cecil. After this Cecil would call the donkey, Antonio, who would charge through the paddock to the fence and rear up on his hind legs, braying wildly. He then picked up a tin pail in his teeth and banged it against a tree. This one-animal Calgary Stampede impressed and scared visitors at the same time.

Next stop was Talon Hall, where Cecil would rub faces with Talon, the great horned owl. People were encouraged to take photos of this unique event as Adele explained the great horned owl's reputation as one of the most feared birds of prey. Adele would then put on an act with the bald eagle, Lightning, directing him to fly to where she gestured. Sometimes he would defy her and fly at her. This aggression appeared quite dangerous, but Adele knew how to handle Lightning.

"Ladies and gentlemen, the king," Cecil would intone as the tour moved along to Pertino the vulture, next door to Lightning. Pertino wore a crown under the spotlight and had such a regal and arrogant presence that visitors often took off their hats. Then Adele would summon him down from his lofty perch. Adele and Cecil would go in and put their faces next to this fierce-looking creature's bill, causing gasps from the visitors. Pertino would march around on command, then fly back up to his perch to conclude the performance.

The tours ended back at Ookpik Cottage, where the little parakeet Blossom danced, spun, and sang on command. The blue-fronted Amazon parrot laughed and talked with a decidedly female voice and in an English accent. While the numerous other talking birds entertained guests with their speech, the raven would have a mock battle with Cecil. Sometimes Doctor Archibald, the little caiman who lived inside the cottage in his own heated pool, would splash visitors.

As if they were not busy enough with the heavy load of visitors that summer, the Hyndmans attempted to raise a baby rufus hummingbird that someone had brought them. Cecil and Adele marveled at the thimble-sized bird and the way that its long, tubular tongue flicked out of its delicate bill. The creature's high metabolism also amazed them: its heart beat 1,000 times a minute. The little hummer required feeding every twenty minutes.

"Have you been recording the number of injured birds this summer?" Adele's voice carried from outside their cottage early one August morning.

"Haven't had time, I've been too busy treating them," Cecil answered as he attempted to splint the broken wing of a robin in the main room of their cottage.

"Here's another," Adele entered the front door holding a box.

Often Adele found what she called "singing boxes" on their front doorstep in the mornings. As word spread about their avian refuge, more and more people put injured or abandoned birds in boxes and left the boxes by the Hyndmans' front door.

Finally an airmail letter arrived from Lovat Dickson in England. Adele raced back to the cottage with the letter in her hand, calling to Cecil, who was busy in Talon Hall. They sat in the Bird Room and Cecil opened the letter.

Dickson wrote, "I certainly remember your father and, of course, Louis was a great friend and contemporary of mine." He went on to say he had read the manuscript and had been "interested in all that you wrote about the work you have done with birds." But Dickson did not think he could successfully publish the manuscript.

Dickson's rejection hit Cecil hard, although he was determined not to show any emotion. Adele surprised Cecil with her reaction.

"The English always have a 'spot of tea' in times of difficulties, so why not we? Would some Red Rose tea cheer you up?"

Although he was used to Adele's sometimes enigmatic statements and behavior, this strange remark puzzled Cecil. Quickly she explained that a TV producer had phoned earlier about featuring Itchy in a commercial. She went on to say the TV ads were part of a promotion for Red Rose tea.

"It's not as exciting as getting the book published, but it is good news," Adele said.

Adele gave Cecil the producer's phone number. Despite Adele's optimism, Cecil had reservations, especially after his past experience with film crews upsetting the birds. Adele brushed these aside by telling him that filming would take place entirely outdoors. She added that Featherland needed the publicity.

Filming the ad took longer than expected. Cecil explained his mixed feelings about it in a letter to his brother thus:

> We lost a good deal of time with the filming of the commercial. The theme was "Featherland is famous for its wildlife and birds as Red Rose is famous for its bird picture series of cards in every package." The background of one scene featured our gull Itchy vocalizing into the mike. The ads were a huge success, running anywhere from four to seven times daily for six weeks.
>
> Itchy, our talking gull, is unquestionably the most widely publicized individual gull in history.

Not only had Itchy made numerous radio and newspaper appearances, but she now had a month's TV run on the coast.

The upbeat tone of his letter reflected Cecil's mood as the summer of 1962 ended. The recent media exposure reinforced Cecil's conviction that their work at Featherland was not only important, but unique enough to merit the world's notice. Being the center of the coverage helped rebuild Cecil's ego, which had been badly shaken by the rejections of his book.

He still had not given up on the Vocaletter invention, although it was progressing so slowly that Adele said it was "languishing on the back burner which wasn't even lit." Cecil resolved to rework some of the technical aspects, but was growing impatient with the convoluted process.

In late fall Featherland closed for the season: this year, Cecil had time for evening strolls. Not only did he like to observe the passing seasons, but these solitary walks also gave him time to think. Adele rarely joined him — she would rather spend her time with Susan. The eagle was another reason for Cecil's daily departure from their cottage. Even though Susan had grown less hostile toward him lately, Cecil worried that his presence in the cottage while Adele was with Susan might trigger an outburst.

The autumn sky one November afternoon reminded Cecil of a gray overcoat, spotted with shadows from the darker clouds under it. Cecil regarded autumn as the most somber, solemn season, almost funereal with its preoccupation with decay and death. A gusting wind from the west scattered the leaves on the ground and swept the few remaining red and yellow ones from the trees. The fitful wind bent the nearly naked branches as if they were lamenting the departed summer.

The thinning foliage enabled Cecil to do his seasonal tree count. During their first busy years at Featherland they had planted hundreds of trees, mainly native species. Any number of causes could kill them — a sudden freeze-up following a winter's rain, a summer's drought, insects, deer. . . . If a newly transplanted tree died, the Hyndmans replaced it the next spring. Over the years at Featherland, Cecil estimated they had dug up and replanted some 400 native trees.

He noted in his journal:

The shootings from the poplars, which I put in rows outside, are now nearly forty-five feet high. The other, more mature row in the lower field, some describe as one of the most beautiful fields around Victoria. Tourists tell us the winding rows of skyscraper poplar trees remind them of roads in France.

He neared Burble Creek, continuing up, past the "rock walls with green moss deeper than most living-room rugs. Ahead stood the old, large oaks that make you think of tough characters with big knuckles and hairy arms. In winter lichen blows in the breeze like a caveman's beard."

As usual, Cecil stopped to rest on a rock and lit up a cigarette after climbing "Phew Hill." At that time of year he barely heard Burble Creek, which was only a trickle, although he claimed it roared "like Niagara" when the winter pour was on.

Cecil continued along the path that wound uphill, arriving at his "private thinking spot." Few visitors had ever been taken up the rocky hillside to this scenic place, which Cecil wanted to keep both private and pristine. "Up here it's a different world of wild beauty. A world never touched by man except for my own footsteps. There's no sound, although we're close to the highway and ocean."

With the leafy arc of the woods now bare, Cecil could sense the year ebbing away. He thought with melancholy about his parents. His father, born in 1874, was now approaching ninety. Cecil worried more about his mother, especially after a letter he had received from his aunt, who had visited Ottawa recently:

It was very tragic to see how your mother has failed. There isn't much communication possible after fifteen minutes and the only person she really wants near her is your father. This is awfully difficult for him for she never wants him to leave her. It is a most difficult situation.

Cecil's first impulse was to fly east to be with his parents. Rationally, he knew this was impossible. He could not leave Adele alone at Featherland, nor could they afford to pay for outside help.

Cecil also faced a showdown with his brother Lou over his Vocaletter invention. He had not heard from Lou for over five weeks; he felt it was "make or break" time for the invention, which he had worked on for four years now.

With both his parents so old, Cecil could no longer count on their financial support. His book had failed to get published and the Vocaletter invention still had not been patented, let alone manufactured or marketed. In the meanwhile the Hyndmans' overdraft mounted at the bank. Featherland's assets were limited. A number of zoos had standing offers on the larger and rarer birds — including Susan and the bald eagle, Lightning. But Cecil was not prepared to sell any of their birds. "You don't sell family," he had stated on many occasions.

Featherland had only one other asset: the property itself. That November day, Cecil made the decision to sell a half-acre lot on the unused eastern end of Featherland. He and Adele had rejected this idea several years earlier, but now he had no choice. Even this was only a short-term solution to help pay down the overdraft.

As Cecil sat on a rock, he heard the crickets chirping and thought of his own shortening days. To Cecil on that November evening, autumn represented mortality.

The wind again began to gust and Cecil felt the first drops of rain. Shivering, he decided it was time to return to the warmth of the cottage.

Cecil entered through the back door. He heard a noisy clatter coming from Susan's room, followed by a series of thuds. It sounded like Adele and Susan were playing a game of catch. The noise faded and he heard Adele saying goodnight to Susan in her "bird voice — the unnaturally high voice she regularly spoke to the birds in."

Cecil got into bed, rubbing his calves, which ached from the climb. He heard Adele leave Susan's room and come into the darkened bedroom. Absently, she spoke to him in the same high-pitched voice she used on the birds. It took her a few moments before she caught herself and reverted back to her normal speaking voice.

This was not the first time Adele had forgotten whom she was talking to. On more than a few occasions lately she had talked to him in her "bird voice." And only a week ago a visitor had taken Cecil aside and hinted that Adele was slipping too deeply into the avian world. The remark had offended Cecil, who admired Adele's passionate commitment to birds. Now he wondered if she had crossed the line.

twelve

EAGLE SONG

"Take a vacation? And leave Susan?" Adele seemed stunned by Cecil's suggestion, even though she had not been away from her birds for any length of time since arriving in Victoria in 1946.

"You haven't seen your mother or family in years," Cecil said.

"This is my family," Adele said forcefully, ending the conversation.

The rest of the day passed in silence, except for the noise of the birds and the patter of rain on the roof. The tension continued over the next few days. Although Cecil and Adele had disagreed and occasionally argued in the past, their deep and convoluted relationship had suffered few ruptures.

Three days later, letters arrived from both Cecil's brother Lou and a patent lawyer Lou had recommended.

"After all these months — nothing has been done," Cecil muttered as he read them, becoming so angry he overturned a chair. Adele picked up the letters and scanned them as Cecil paced the room.

"You'll just have to go to Edmonton to sort things out," she finally said, ending the lengthy silence between the two.

The logic of Adele's snap decision impressed Cecil as much as her support. He smiled and held out his hands. The two hugged and hugged — until the scream of the scarlet macaw ripped through the room. The macaw had a truly ear-splitting voice, which he used rarely but always effectively, with an uncanny sense of timing. The other resident birds chirped in, and Adele and Cecil began to laugh. "Like children spontaneously 'oohing' when seeing their parents kissing," Cecil later wrote.

Although he could not really afford the trip, Cecil prepared to visit Edmonton to discuss the Vocaletter patent process with Lou. Before leaving, he wrote his father, hoping this would put pressure on Lou, who seemed decidedly unenthusiastic about the invention. Lou's help was vital. Without a patent to protect the invention, Cecil realized there was no chance of manufacturing and marketing the device.

Cecil's trip back to his birthplace took place late in the fall of 1962. He stayed at his brother's house, where he found Lou cordial, yet distant. After the demonstration of the advanced prototype of his Vocaletter invention, Lou and the patent lawyer raised a number of concerns, some related to the complicated patent process and others about the fidelity of the device.

Cecil remained convinced about the potential of his invention and assured Lou he could improve it, as well as complete the technical drawings necessary for the patent. He was more worried that Lou's objections masked his overall disinterest in the project. He pleaded with his brother, telling him the very future of Featherland depended on the invention.

On his return to Featherland, Cecil worked feverishly on improving the device. He was determined to overcome the obstacles his brother put in his path, not sure if they were real or imaginary ones. He was certain of one thing: few people were as uniquely qualified or had the extensive background in sound recording that he had.

His connection with the specialized field of recording machines extended back nearly twenty-five years, into the 1930s, when he had been a technician at the fledgling CBC. He had spent time with the radio engineer in charge of operating and maintaining one of the first magnetic recorders ever used. Later, he had worked with acetate disc recordings, and had operated the first wire recorder ever brought to Canada.

At Featherland, Cecil had used nearly a score of different makes and models to produce recordings of bird sounds that were played by radio stations.

To meet his Christmas deadline, Cecil struggled late each night to complete the diagrams and assemble the improved prototype. He noted in his journal one night the irony of his situation; to save Featherland, he had to withdraw from it to work on his invention. As he was unable to spend time with Adele, she had more time to spend with Susan. He could hear the two of them play as he worked.

As Christmas approached, Adele knew that Cecil was under extreme pressure, but felt powerless to do anything other than offer support. Besides, she had become so enraptured with Susan that she spent most of her free time and evenings with the now fully mature eagle.

Golden eagles have one of the longest maturation periods of any bird of prey. The physical signs of this maturity were now unmistakable in Susan. She had lost all of the white on her feathers and gained more of the gold coloration that characterizes her species. Now her head and neck shone with gold-tipped feathers.

With the visible signs of physical maturity came indications of an awakening of a different sort. The reproduction process in birds differs from that of mammals, as birds only have one ovary. When eagles mate, sperm travels up the oviduct to fertilize the egg. The egg then moves down the oviduct as the shell is formed. Finally the egg is laid and incubation begins. The ovulation process can occur without the bird mating, although any eggs laid in this case cannot be fertile.

Adele became aware of some subtle changes in Susan's behavior. Most nights Adele took in a wash cloth to touch up any soiled spots on Susan's plumage. She often called these night visits "the Queen's boudoir grooming." Like the Queen she was, Susan would extend a foot to her lady-in-waiting, expecting her to manicure her toes and talons.

Afterward, the golden eagle would close her eyes, or, more accurately, move the membranes that can slide across her eyeballs. Next she fell into what Adele called "an utterly limp collapse of love-making ecstasy," resting her body next to Adele, her curved beak touching Adele's cheek. Only Adele's arms around her, supporting her body, prevented Susan from falling down.

Not wanting to interrupt Cecil while he worked on his invention, Adele said little about the changes in Susan's behavior. She also wanted to wait to see if other signs might emerge, more clearly indicating a sexual awakening on Susan's part.

Before long, Susan astounded Adele by beginning to sing a new song. At first Adele was not sure what this meant. Could this song be evidence of her deepening attachment to Adele, or was it some biological outburst based on hormonal change?

Working until two in the morning, often much later, Cecil could not help but hear the notes of Susan's song flowing through the cottage. The first time he heard it, although he was struggling to balance the new flywheel in the prototype, he immediately stopped and listened.

"The song forming in Susan's heart began to assume a noticeably fresh, different expression in her vocal cords. This new high song, which had been in the past only rudimentary, began to fill Ookpik Cottage," he wrote in his journal.

As the notes of the beautiful song drifted through the cottage, he crept toward his favorite spot to quietly watch the two women in his life. Susan's attitude toward Cecil had softened somewhat, to the point where she no longer violently threw herself at the bamboo screen when she saw him. Still, he had no intention of interfering with the progress of her relationship with Adele.

Susan's "love serenade" continued, increasing in frequency and pitch, warming the cold winter night. He later described the song in his journal:

[Susan] puffs out her delicately elastic underthroat, lifts her voice in song imbued with high feeling and elation — music I have reason to believe our ears alone have ever had the privilege of hearing from the throat of a golden eagle. Up, up, up the notes rise as though into the sky. The love fervor is all there.

The holiday season of 1962 brought its usual annual presents — a blanket of snow to giftwrap Featherland for Christmas, and an illness for Cecil. Once again Cecil literally worked himself into a state of exhaustion and collapsed. He complained in a letter to his parents:

I've been in bed for two weeks with infection of some sort attacking my throat and chest. The glands in my neck are swollen at the moment.

We recently had a nightmarish cold spell and succession of snow falls so heavy that two days in a row Adele had to shovel the whole length of the walk to Talon Hall. The terrible storm caused serious damage, tearing off part of the roofing of Talon Hall. We also lost the outer storm covering off some of the windows in Ookpik Cottage. The roof nearly collapsed from the weight of the accumulated snow-falls. We couldn't get out of here, being snowbound.

Dell got some rolled roofing sent from Eatons and spent hours up on the roof of Talon Hall in the wind patching the big leaks which would have been ruinous. She looked after me and whole place — she's a wonderful person.

Cecil also brought his father up to date on his invention:

It is perhaps ironical that such a purposely simple device should require such a massive written and drawn presentation. I think I first wrote over 100 pages, revised it, re-revised it, boiled it in rough typing, and then rehashed this for the final typing in triplicate. The presentation was far from a picnic with the Quints when it had to be done in the midst of birds in a crowded bedroom, continually interrupted and largely on my bed to which I have been confined. My nerves became frayed and my digestion became paralysed in the tension of the process.

He also wrote his brother Lou, boasting that the improved device was "completely revolutionary as compared to Vocaletter demo earlier in the fall. The Vocapen is now six inches long and the entire voice recorder can be held and operated by one hand. The device is totally motorless and totally cordless." Despite Cecil's high hopes, Lou's reaction was muted and he made few comments on the improvements.

When Cecil recovered sufficiently to get out of bed, he made one last attempt to convince Lou. He again traveled to Edmonton, only to be told by Lou that it would take $5,000 to move the project forward — a sum Cecil did not have and could not raise, as he was already overdrawn at the bank. He had run out of options and time.

Cecil returned to Featherland defeated. He was angry and frustrated — angry at his brother Lou and his family for not having his vision and missing the opportunity his invention offered. He was also angry at himself for wasting the equivalent of almost a two full years on his two projects, with nothing to show in return. He had counted on the book and then the Vocaletter invention to pull Featherland out of its financial mess. Instead, they had only worsened the crisis.

He unwrapped the Vocaletter prototype he had spent so many years perfecting, placed it on the wooden floor, and jumped on it, smashing it into pieces.

"Let's have a proper wake," Cecil said after his destructive dance, "do we still have some scotch left?"

Adele got out the bottle and the two shared what little remained. In the background, Susan's song warmed the cottage.

"It looks like we might have to sell part of Featherland," Cecil said.

"We still have the birds — and Susan," Adele said.

Although he was despondent, the desperate financial state of Featherland did not allow Cecil any extended period to mope. The next morning, still lightheaded from the scotch, he called a realtor and told him they were ready to sell one small lot of Featherland.

Having cut his losses on his failed money-making schemes, Cecil turned his attention back to his beloved Featherland. To the list of overdue winter "fix-up" chores, he added another project: recording Susan's "love song" on tape. Susan's deepening infatuation with Adele presented a unique opportunity.

"Recording Susan turned out to be exasperatingly complex as it can never be exactly anticipated just when Susan will sing and if she starts, she is just as likely to end her session before I can set up to record," Cecil complained in his journal.

Unlike other bird singing, which often occurs at regular times, or in response to some specific stimulus, Susan's singing was not a reflex action. The eagle only sang when emotionally aroused. Not only did Susan have to be in the mood, but conditions had to be perfect before she would sing. Any new objects in her room put her off, which ruled out sticking a microphone in front of her.

Susan's hostility toward microphones was long-standing, dating back to the first camera crew that had filmed her years ago. The crew had deliberately upset her in order to film her in flight. Susan had an excellent memory and associated film equipment with unpleasantness. She tended to overreact to anything reminding her of film equipment — lights, cameras, and microphones.

Cecil tried disguising the microphone and placing it close to the wooden bars to overcome Susan's phobia. But her extraordinarily observant eyes easily spotted the hidden microphone. She attempted to get at it, striking out with her talons.

Meanwhile, Adele tried to acclimatize Susan to a concealed microphone by taking in a series of covered objects. Although she was now completely comfortable in Susan's presence, she always used caution when bringing in a new toy for Susan. In the wild, eagles must react instantaneously to avoid dangerous threats. Adele knew that all the love in the world could not counteract this "reflex startle reaction." If confronted with an unusual new object or action, Susan might panic and either "fight or take flight."

Slowly the suspicious side of Susan's nature relaxed and she accepted the microphone. After this breakthrough, Cecil spent two months patiently waiting by the recorder almost every night. But all he managed to capture were bits and pieces, never Susan's complete song. He wrote, "To record Susan's song free from the extraneous sounds of monkey, macaw, cockatoos, and other birds that are unavoidably in the near vicinity, has driven me to tear my hair out."

"We need to position the microphone closer — within ten to twenty-four inches," an exasperated Cecil told Adele over coffee one morning after they had spent the previous evening trying to get Susan to sing.

Adele sighed. It had been difficult enough to get Susan to accept the microphone. It would be even more difficult to accustom her to the microphone only a foot from her face. But Adele accepted the challenge, warning Cecil it could take weeks, if not months. "You'll just have to wait and be ready," she told Cecil.

Each night Adele moved the microphone a fraction of an inch closer. While Susan did not attack the strange object, its near presence seemed to put her off singing. Time was becoming a problem as the summer tourist season approached.

One May evening, Adele told Cecil over their evening coffee that Susan had been unusually affectionate the previous night. After their long and intimate relationship, Adele could accurately read Susan's moods swings.

"If she goes completely limp and remains that way tonight, she'll sing within a few days," Adele predicted.

Sure enough, that night Susan began to make the low noises that usually preceded her singing. Cecil hid out of Susan's sight, crouching and listening on his earphones connected to the tape recorder, which he almost forgot to turn on in his excitement. When he pressed RECORD, Susan's high-pitched singing set off the other birds.

"No sooner had a half-minute sequence been recorded than a myna named So So around the corner in the Bird Room spoke to ruin the passage. Then the next time, the beautiful notes of Susan's song were drowned out by Pedro the macaw, whose yells could rupture an eardrum," he wrote in his journal.

But eventually the long months of patience — the note-taking addict Cecil calculated at least 2,000 hours of waiting — paid off. On a bright May evening of 1963 Susan responded to Adele's physical preening of her feathers by running her beak tenderly over Adele's face. Like two lovers embracing passionately, they clung together. After Adele stopped gently rubbing Susan with the wet cloth, the eagle began to sing; her song began slowly, then the notes rose like a bird in flight.

This time Cecil managed to record Susan's love song cleanly and in its entirety. Adele's repositioning of the directional pick-up of the microphone enabled him to overcome the extraneous noise of the other birds. The Hyndmans celebrated that night.

"We have what is the only known recording of a love song of an unmated golden eagle reared in captivity. I doubt if this remarkable accomplishment is likely to ever again be duplicated," Cecil wrote with satisfaction in his journal.

thirteen

The Miracle

Twilight came early on November 10, 1964. The dull glow of the setting sun was barely noticeable in the overcast sky. Cecil rolled up the collar of his coat, shivering in the drizzle as he closed the double wooden doors to Talon Hall. He noted the icy wind had picked up, threatening a heavy downpour. Cecil could hear the gentle bubbling and foaming of Burble Creek in the distance. The creek had begun to flow earlier than usual that fall. Within a few weeks its sound would grow into a roar when it reached its heavy winter flow.

Few birds sang under the gunmetal-gray skies that darkened as night approached. Cecil clumped down the slippery pathway from Talon Hall, the dreary winter weather conditions matching his mood. Kluane had recently died of a virulent infection. His death saddened Cecil and brought back memories of the fall he had spent writing *Behind the Feathered Curtain* in Kluane's cabin.

Cecil heard a winter wren's liquid trilling in the distance over the incessant patter of rain. Although he had lived on the West Coast for eighteen years, he still found Victoria's cold and damp winters depressing. At least the shorter days gave the Hyndmans longer evenings to devote to training birds to speak. By the time Cecil arrived at the back door of his cottage, he was thoroughly chilled but looked forward to spending the evening working with the large Arctic raven, Goliath.

As Cecil entered the cottage, he heard a strange, off-key ringing sound. He shook the rain from his hat, took off his rubber boots, then stood and rubbed his ears, wondering if the wind could have frozen them. Adele breezed by, smiling strangely. She waved him over.

"Don't you hear it?" she asked.

Rubbing his ears, Cecil followed Adele as she tiptoed across the Bird Room. The "ringing" increased as they rounded the corner. On a high shelf by their bedroom door hung a set of old clock bells. Featherland's northwestern crow, Joey, head bent, was using his stout bill to ring the bells, "a surprisingly tonal performance, as the old clock bells had three different tones among them," Cecil later wrote.

Joey, according to Cecil's journal, had

always been peppery and full of mischief. Earlier in the evening, he put on his usual performance of warming his toes on the heater drum. When given his raw beef dinner, he spread it on a hot spot to heat or toast it, turning it over and over like a chef flipping hamburgers.

Like a child caught with a hand in the cookie jar, Joey flew off when the Hyndmans burst out laughing. The entertainment over, Adele began a speech lesson with a crested starling while Cecil spent the rest of the evening working with the raven Goliath.

Goliath had arrived at Featherland in 1958, "all mouth and appetite," from a nest on Vancouver Island. Cecil's fascination with ravens dated to his childhood, when he had read Edgar Allan Poe's famous poem. Although it was widely believed that ravens were capable of human speech, in reality few had achieved this feat.

Cecil's recording of Goliath was broadcast on a CBC network radio show in 1960 "to mark the first time that the English speaking voice of a raven was ever heard by a mass audience," Cecil noted.

Cecil regarded ravens as "perhaps the most intelligent of all birds, their extraordinary mental faculties matched by their ability to change moods radically in split seconds — from gurgling pleasure to biting anger — running the whole gamut in the space of a minute of two."

During the evening lesson, Goliath proved his usual changeable self, hopping onto Cecil's shoulder, flaring his majestic beard. Cecil discouraged this practice, as the still-growing raven had already reached two feet in length, with a wingspan twice that length.

Toward midnight, Goliath lost interest and, perched on Cecil's shoulder, gently stashed some excess food in Cecil's ear, as was his habit. The lesson ended a little past midnight. Cecil decided it was time to start to put the thirty-odd birds in the cottage to bed.

"Dell, it's bedtime for the birds," Cecil said as his wife finished her speech lesson with the crested starling.

"Could you put the birds to bed? I should see Sue, she hasn't eaten in the past few days."

Cecil agreed, not unduly concerned. Over the years they had noticed that many of the larger birds of prey seemed to lose their appetite during the winter. Cecil speculated this was because they built up their fat reserves earlier in the year.

Adele walked under the archway leading to Susan's room, carrying her cleaning gear. Susan immediately bobbed her head in an affectionate greeting. She fussed so lovingly that Adele could not even begin her nightly sweeping. As Adele rested the broom against the wall, Susan tried to snatch it out of her hand. Adele stopped to pay attention to the Queen.

"Alright, Sue, we'll talk first," Adele whispered to the female eagle.

Susan responded with an outpouring that both surprised and delighted Adele. As the notes of her love song soared higher and higher, they filled the cottage. Never had Susan's song seemed so vibrant to Adele.

The unusually fluid notes of Susan's song caused Cecil to stop in the middle of putting the three seagulls, Winkin, Blinkin, and Nod, in their cardboard carton beds for the night. (The trio shared the Hyndmans' bedroom at night, their boxes arranged at the foot of the couple's bed.) As Susan's singing continued, Cecil closed his eyes for a moment and imagined spring had come.

Goliath, who also shared the Hyndmans' bedroom, responded to the uplifting notes of Susan's song, hopping onto Cecil's shoulder. Goliath wiped his face against Cecil's, so moved that his "feather muscles at the skin set up a rapid, strong vibration all over his body like an electric massage machine." Together, Cecil and the raven listened to Susan's vocal outpouring as they sat on the bed.

The song stopped abruptly and Cecil heard a shriek from Adele. His first thought was that Susan had nipped Adele in her excited state. But before he could rush to Susan's room, he heard his wife's light, quick steps coming toward him.

"Come quickly and look in Susan's room — you won't believe what you see," Adele said, flushed and obviously agitated. She dragged Cecil by his sleeve, "you'll think you're dreaming." Cecil rushed with Adele to the archway outside Susan's room.

ꞏ   He recorded what he saw thus:

My eyes popped on looking where Adele pointed after moving aside the bamboo screen. There on the floor beside Susan's feet was a crushed whitish egg. Its almost cream-colored yoke streamed out

*around her. It had cracked as Susan laid it on the hard surface and
a touch of her heavy feet had then caved the shell in.*

For more than a few seconds, Cecil remained frozen to the spot,
thunderstruck by the event. Although he had raised egg-laying birds
since he was five, worked on a poultry farm, done original research
into the egg-laying process, and broken records at Featherland while
it was a poultry farm, this was the most unusual egg-laying event he
had ever encountered.

While Cecil stood in a state of disbelief, Adele hurriedly entered
the room.

"Susan's expression was maternally soft and gentle. She voiced
small thin notes and merely looked on interestingly without objection as the shell was carefully gathered up and the sticky contents
mopped away," Cecil later wrote.

Once the shock wore off the next morning, Cecil called the local
newspapers, explaining he knew of no other golden eagle raised
alone and in close human association that had ever produced an
egg. The Canadian Press picked up the story, and other wire services
passed on the news of this unique event. Over the next few days, the
phone rang incessantly as newspapers called from as far away as
England and New York.

The Hyndmans took pride in Susan's remarkable accomplishment, but became distressed when a number of local and international authorities tried to discredit the event. One ornithologist
stated the egg was probably a hen's egg that had accidentally rolled
into Susan's room. Cecil laughed at this suggestion, especially as
Featherland had gone out of the poultry business over fifteen
years ago and no hen had ever lived there since. A University
of British Columbia professor of zoology claimed Susan was "a
really mixed up bird. She is completely abnormal and her egg-
laying mechanism is completely out of order." He concluded by
dismissing the occurrence as "simply an oddity." Nevertheless,

congratulations continued to pour in over the next few days.

By November 17, the Hyndmans were just resuming their regular routine at Featherland. At 2:30 a.m., Cecil was up late tutoring Goliath, and Adele was feeding some of their feathered family nearby in the Bird Room, which they had recently renamed the Plume Room because of the collection of brilliantly colored tail feathers from the scarlet macaw it housed, as well as Susan's long flight feathers.

Just before retiring, Cecil followed Adele to the archway with the bamboo curtain to say goodnight to Susan. Quietly Adele peeked through the bamboo curtain, to gauge Susan's mood before allowing Cecil a look. Although Susan rarely became enraged at Cecil any longer, she often showed him hostility in other ways, especially if he accompanied Adele.

Susan stood at the far end of the room, away from the door, unusually quiet and preoccupied. Ordinarily her acute vision missed little, but that evening she did not seem to notice them. As he stood there, Cecil wondered to himself if Susan's continued refusal to eat was significant. She had eaten almost nothing since the "smashing event" of the week before. Cecil wrote later, "I had the flicker of an exciting thought but brushed it from my mind as probably absurd and too much to expect."

"Shhh," Adele whispered to Cecil, "I'll tempt her with a treat."

Adele went to the kitchenette to cut some raw beef into strips. Meanwhile, Cecil turned to the final step in their nightly ritual: putting the birds to bed.

Adele set aside the bamboo screen and entered Susan's room with the tasty treat. Adele sensed something was wrong. Ordinarily Susan roused herself when Adele entered; shook her feathers, and then spread her wings wide like a person throwing open their arms to greet another. Tonight she remained in an awkward position on the floor.

The thought crossed Adele's mind that Susan might be ill. Quickly she knelt down beside Susan. The golden eagle's body

Adele holds proudly the second egg Susan laid in November 1964. News of this remarkable event was carried in papers around the world.

After Susan "divorced" Cecil following an attack, she bonded with Adele. They became so close that Susan laid several of her eggs directly into Adele's hands.

Adele holding Kluane II. The Hyndmans captured the starving female golden eagle, who had got caught up in the netting outside their cottage during a gale, in 1969. Cecil spent many long hours with Kluane II after Susan rejected him in favor of Adele.

Susan died in 1978. She had lived almost 25 years with the Hyndmans. During that time, she laid 17 eggs, each one an "act of love," according to Cecil, and a feat likely never to be repeated.

Cecil Hyndman in 1996, a year before he died at the age of 85.

After Susan died, Adele was heartbroken. She was confined to a wheelchair after a series of strokes. She died in 1990.

stiffened at her touch and immediately Adele withdrew her hand, although Susan showed no sign of any aggressive intent. Her amber-gold eyes with their intense black pupils gave no indication of what could be wrong.

Slowly Adele ran her hands lightly over Susan's body. Again the golden eagle's body tensed. Adele found her abdominal muscles were straining. Susan twisted her head and half rose, as if in pain.

"Oh, Sue," Adele whispered, "you're not about to . . ."

Finally realizing what was happening, Adele put her hand under Susan. The female eagle crouched, her lower body contracting. Adele could feel the wet egg emerging. After a few more contractions, the warm, moist egg landed in Adele's hand, as if Susan had been waiting for Adele to arrive and catch it.

Her hands trembling, Adele excitedly showed Susan her egg. The eagle made a series of "little cooey sounds and a gesture unmistakeably 'you take it' in meaning," Adele said later. Overcome with emotion, Adele kissed Susan on the face. For a moment she wondered what the eagle would do if she took the egg away. But her previous gesture had been so clear to Adele that she hurried out to show the egg to Cecil.

Cecil heard Adele emerge from Susan's room, recalling how "she wore a strange expression on her face, preoccupied and almost entranced. Something glinted in her hand."

Adele held up the egg. "Sue laid this right into my hand so it never touched the floor. It's intact and perfect."

Carefully Cecil took the still-warm egg, just moments old. Wet and bluish-white, it was almost the size of a goose egg. Cecil became almost overcome with the importance of what he held. He wrote,

I was fearful of dropping the only newly laid egg of a golden eagle ever held between human fingers. It was less than sixty seconds old. As careful investigations have confirmed, no other eagle, either golden or bald, in any circumstances as these had ever been known

to produce even one egg, not to speak of two — and more than this, laying directly into a woman's hand.

Rolling that still-warm egg in their hands was a sensation neither Cecil nor Adele ever forgot. As they paused, passing the treasure back and forth, in the background they could hear Susan's voice twittering, then the whooshing sound of her winged leap onto her stand.

Susan's second egg promised to silence those critics who had dismissed her first as a freak occurrence. Although delighted, Cecil worried about the approaching tornado of publicity that would descend on Featherland.

The egg, laid by a golden eagle raised with humans, was a triumph of applied psychology. There was simply no parallel for what had happened. Few wild birds, especially unmated ones, had ever laid eggs outside their natural habitats. Even birds with mates rarely attempted reproduction in captivity. The fact that she had laid an egg indicated to Cecil that Susan regarded Adele as her mate. Love between a woman and a golden eagle had produced the eggs.

Cecil was convinced that "Adele, as the object of Susan's love," had "put into motion the whole complicated chain of internal bodily functions involved in the production of a clutch of two eggs."

Within days, the news of Susan's second egg caused a storm of publicity that far overshadowed that accompanying the first. The telephone rang all day and all night as newspapers from around the world called to check on the wire service story. Photographers began converging on Featherland to take photos of Susan and her egg. The coverage ranged from the local papers to the *London Daily Mirror* in England with a circulation of millions. A number of large

American newspapers phoned to verify details. Radio and television producers also pestered the Hyndmans.

The interest was not just in the scientific breakthrough. Most of the coverage centered on the unique relationship between Adele and Susan. The love affair that produced eggs added to the human drama of the story, and the newspaper articles stressed the one-of-a-kind nature of the event.

Although Cecil had personally photographed Adele with Susan and her egg, the various news agencies insisted on sending their own photography crews. Adele's patience began to wear thin after the first few sessions, especially after one photographer, while attempting a close-up of Susan's egg, almost allowed it to roll onto the floor.

There was another reason for Adele's hesitancy. Cecil wrote, "since I first met Adele, I have never known her to 'give a hoot' for personal public notice. It is not shyness. She sincerely doesn't care." But she did care about Susan. Adele's greatest fear was not that Susan might injure a photographer or reporter, but rather that she might injure herself if panicked or provoked to attack the interlopers.

Eventually, Cecil faced the tricky task of emptying the contents of Susan's unfertilized egg while keeping the shell intact. First he drilled two small holes in the egg. Next he used two plastic straws to blow out the yolk and white.

The final step in the exhaustive research into Susan's egg took place that morning at breakfast in the cottage.

"I wonder if we're the first to do this?" Adele asked as she cooked the contents of Susan's famous egg.

fourteen

An Eventful Winter

The winter of 1964 brought a series of crises to Featherland, culminating in another amazing event. On a surprisingly mild mid-December night, Cecil sat in the cottage bedroom looking through the south window at the gull and raven play area edging Burble Creek. In another part of the cottage, Adele was busy treating the feet of the magpie Checkers.

An assortment of papers lay scattered on the desk in front of Cecil: data for his mallard duck research project. After completing a rough draft of his report, he took out his journal to begin an entry.

The raven Goliath was perched nearby. As Cecil began writing, he felt his left eyelid being touched. A magical moment ensued:

With his great bill, Goliath lifted the lid with the sensitivity of an eye specialist, peered intently into my orb and then just as gently dropped the lid down and rubbed his face against mine. I have never felt more honored in my life — nor as scared!

As Cecil opened a drawer to put the papers away, he heard an unusual sound from outside. He thought it was probably deer who often browsed close to the cottage.

Adele passed Cecil at his desk and walked out the front door to bring in the gulls for the night. In the murky darkness, she noticed Gumption some distance from the house. She called his name but there was no response. As Gumption often strayed, she decided to bring the other birds into the cottage first.

Quickly she rounded up Winkin, Blinkin, and Nod. After carrying them inside, she went back out for the other two, Fraction and Gumption. Fraction came, but not Gumption.

She had grown especially close to Gumption. A native of Featherland by birth, Gumper had hatched out of a mottled egg on the Hyndmans' bed to become a member of the only group of hand-reared educated gulls in the world. A few days before, he had thrilled Cecil by speaking three entire words of English on tape. Growing more annoyed by the minute, Adele walked over to the shadowy outline where she had seen him earlier, some distance from the cottage. As she bent down to pick up Gumption, a blur of feathers erupted in her face.

Inside the cottage Cecil heard Adele's shriek and raced toward the front door, scattering his carefully sorted data sheets.

Faintly outlined in the light from the open door, Adele stood shaking, her blouse splattered with blood. As Cecil raced closer, a large and lightly colored form fluttered silently off into the night, as if Adele herself had given birth to this night creature.

When Cecil arrived beside Adele, she held what remained of Gumption in her hands.

"A gray-white great horned owl," she explained, her voice surprisingly calm but her trembling hands betraying her shock. "The way it was hunched over Gumption — in the darkness, the two forms seemed one."

Cecil took the bloody remains from Adele. Gumption's head and part of his neck were missing.

"We have to get the netting up," Cecil told Adele.

After putting the other birds inside, they strung up the overhead and side netting that protected the outdoor waterfowl from predators. Adele was still shaking and Cecil sent her inside, not sure if she was shivering from the cold or the tragic event.

A rustling noise distracted Cecil. He moved toward the source of the sound and watched as "the whitish form of a great horned owl rose at a steep angle through the leafless branches of a fallen clump of gnarled oaks." He wrote of this encounter:

I could have thrown myself on him just a second earlier. Although still angry in one sense, seeing that stealthy and beautiful killer fly in the dark made me think of Satan the Dusky, a great horned owl at Featherland. If I had caught this owl, I would have set him up in comfortable roomy quarters and delivered meals on a tray as an equal with any other citizen of Featherland. Owls too eat to live and in the wild this means they must kill. So does humanity.

With the approach of Christmas, the number of long distance calls about the eggs faded as the press moved on to more traditional nativity stories. The Hyndmans looked forward to a little peace after the hectic pace of the past few months.

In mid-December an unusually thick blanket of snow fell. The weight of the wet snow collapsed a number of the netted enclosures outside. Cecil and Adele scrambled to prop up the fallen posts, especially the shelter that protected the flock of wild mallards, part of an on-going project on determining the sex of ducklings.

They woke up the morning after the first night of extremely cold weather to discover some of their mallards frozen to death. The next two nights they stayed up, taking shifts to check on the birds outside. Whenever the straw outside froze, they spread fresh straw to keep the ducks' feet from freezing.

On the third night of frigid weather, they carried every one of their flock of over fifty waterfowl into one of the birdhouses.

The severe cold spell continued, the snowfall accumulating until the weight crushed the roofs of a number of smaller sheds and outbuildings. "Outdoor rooflet shelters of every sort were squashed flat or tipped to crazy angles. We fought a running battle night and day to keep our large research flock from disaster," Cecil wrote in his journal.

Finally the temperatures eased as Christmas approached, although the heavy snow remained. Cecil had barely tacked up the 1965 calendar when an illness forced him into the hospital. The problem got worse and he finally underwent a hernia operation. His stay in hospital stretched to two weeks.

Meanwhile, Adele struggled to run Featherland on her own. Each night she checked the outdoor thermometer as the temperature hovered close to freezing. The snowy conditions also made it difficult for her to visit Cecil at the hospital. As she did not drive, she had to find someone to take her, as well as someone to "bird-sit" their feathered family.

To add to her problems, Adele had to somehow cover the unexpected medical expenses. Despite the sale of one small lot and the revenue from logging trees, the financial condition at Featherland had continued to deteriorate. The recent cold spell threatened to double the usual winter heating bill to an amount they simply could not afford. The situation was so critical that Adele told Cecil not to write the hospital a cheque for $28, as she was not sure they had enough money in the bank to cover it.

Adele wrote to Judge Hyndman, outlining to him their financial difficulty and asking if he could cover the hospital expenses for his son. (He agreed.)

On January 27, Cecil wrote:

I arrived home in a taxi from the hospital, feeling weak and shaky. Despite the recent storm onslaughts, all was basically under control here by this time and the warmth of my reception from all my "family" was overwhelming. In Susan's case, she welcomed me with one of her most malevolent stares. I literally fell into bed and lay back thinking: Ah, home sweet home.

Adele offered to brew a pot of coffee while bringing him up to date. Her most important news concerned Susan, who had been singing her love song for the past week, but had stopped singing the day before. Cecil tried to pay attention, but lapsed into a deep sleep, as he had been troubled with insomnia while in hospital.

Barely an hour later, a ruckus woke him from his badly needed sleep. A loud flailing and splashing rose from the Plume Room. Adele rushed into the room, followed by Cecil. At first he wondered if he was experiencing a nightmare. The scene in front of him resembled some special effects show, with layers of steamy mist combined with smoke to create a curtain of gray. Geysers of water rose sporadically and the shrieks of over thirty birds added to the bedlam.

"Don't just stand there," Adele shouted at him.

She waved him over, pointing to the ten-year-old caiman, Doctor Archibald, who was writhing in convulsions in his large pan of water. The violent movements of his body, nearly three feet long, showered the surrounding area with water. Nearby birds fluttered their wings and cried out loudly, adding to the chaos. One of the electric heaters that kept the water in the caiman's pan heated had short-circuited, electrocuting Doctor Archibald and causing the steam and smoke. Cecil described the scene thus:

Doctor Archibald was twisted like a pretzel in agony, the diamond shaped pupils of his eyes hidden under the horny lids that were jammed shut. Adele grasped his thrashing form and deeply massaged his stomach and heart while water splashed in her face.

Cecil assisted Adele, listening to the caiman's weak heartbeat. Twice Doctor Archibald's heart stopped, and twice Adele's rhythmic massage restarted it. Finally the caiman recovered.

The Hyndmans were years ahead of their contemporaries in the use of therapeutic massage. Cecil had studied various techniques and taught them to Adele. Once she had revived a magpie with no heartbeat; another time the same technique had saved an owl.

Adele's hour-long massaging of Doctor Archibald had exhausted her, but she still had the rest of the regular nightly chores to do. Cecil offered to get her some coffee, but the pot had stood so long the coffee resembled black sludge. Adele and Cecil exchanged a laugh before Cecil again retired. He had barely closed his eyes when a series of high-pitched screams erupted from outside the bedroom.

After a moment he realized the panic-stricken shrieks came from the gull enclosure located outside. Clad in slippers and pyjamas, Cecil opened the door from the bedroom that led outside. Adele caught up to him and together they discovered the gate to the enclosure had been smashed open.

In the darkness they almost tripped over two thrashing forms on the ground. Had some predator broken into the gull enclosure? Feathers flew everywhere as Cecil blindly tried to intervene to separate the combatants. Finally he recognized Fraction, one of the beloved hand-reared gulls. She was being ripped open by one John "Fireball" Kennedy, a Muscovy drake. Of this duck, Cecil wrote:

[He] is a veritable delinquent, sadly failing to emulate his illustrious namesake. Built as low to the ground as a sausage dog, his tail

is so long and heavy that in waving from side to side as it does, it gives him a drunken weave.

Cecil managed to loosen Fireball's grip on Fraction. While Adele tended to the little gull, Cecil checked over Fireball, who was bloody but not injured. Fraction had not fared as well, with an ugly and bloody split running from skull to shoulder.

I felt sick to look at her. High strung in the extreme, she could die of shock alone. A gull even when wrapped in a cloth can be an escape artist at wriggling free. So we had a frantic time stopping the haemorrhage.

By now it was past midnight. Both Cecil and Adele fought off waves of fatigue as they struggled to save Fraction's life. The gull lapsed in and out of consciousness from the pain of the terrible injury. The complicated surgery to close the wound took a long time. Adele helped Cecil back to bed but could not join him — someone still had to put the other birds to bed.

Cecil closed his eyes. Never had the comforts of a bed felt as good. He fell immediately into a deep sleep, but his rest was broken again only a short while later by Adele.

"Cec, Cec — are you awake?"

Adele was standing by the bed. Her strange posture alarmed Cecil and he bolted up, afraid that Fraction's condition had taken a turn for the worse. Only then did Cecil notice Adele carried something.

"Susan just laid another egg. It will be the first in a clutch of two, you'll see."

Cecil was so disoriented all he could do was mutter "Is this a dream?"

Adele used one arm to help him up from bed, carrying the still-warm egg in her hand and chatting away. "She laid it only a few minutes before, at about 2:30. See how this one side is crushed as the egg was laid on the floor."

Despite his exhaustion, Cecil had to peek at Susan from behind the bamboo screen while Adele went in to visit the Queen. Susan welcomed her with a twitter and swished her tail happily.

A few minutes later Adele came out and told Cecil that the egg was a "welcome home" gift. When he did not react, she flicked on a light. Propped up by a wall, Cecil was snoring away while sleeping standing upright. She led him back to bed.

After the best night's sleep of his entire life, Cecil awoke very late next morning. By now he was an old hand at informing the press, having saved the names and numbers in one of his many note-books. Proud as any parent, he gave the details of Susan's third egg to the press wire services.

"You must tell them another is due — I'm sure of it," Adele told Cecil.

While Cecil did not feel totally comfortable predicting Susan would lay the second egg of the clutch very soon, Adele was so con-fident that she convinced him. Although her hunches were based on intuition, rarely were they wrong.

While not as many Canadian newspapers carried the news of Susan's egg laying as the first two times, news of this third egg spread around the world on the wire services, bringing extensive international coverage. One headline read, "SHE LAYS EGGS FOR KICKS — NOT CHICKS."

Although he was still recovering, Cecil spelled off Adele in keep-ing a close watch on Susan over the next few days. Not only did they want to witness the next laying, but Cecil wanted to make notes regarding Susan's behavior leading up to it. He observed:

Susan always had in her room a number of small branches and twigs. On the third morning while Adele was in with her, Sue began

carrying some of these over to Adele. She dropped several at her feet.
Others she held up for her to take from her bill. It was apparent she
wanted Adele to arrange them to form a nest on the floor.

Susan watched with interest as Adele made a stick nest on the floor, adding bundles of dried grasses to soften the middle.

What happened next surprised Cecil. He expected Susan to sit on the nest to check it out. Instead she "shuffled over to a far corner to pick up a lacrosse ball in her talons." For a brief moment, Cecil wondered if Susan wanted to play catch. But instead she dropped the ball in the nest, then went over and did the same with the other lacrosse ball in the room. The shape of the balls resembled eggs, and Susan sat on them for intervals into the night.

Adele was so sure Susan would lay that night that she went into Susan's room every few minutes to gently probe under her. After midnight Adele noticed Susan tense up, and stayed with her. Sure enough, around 1:00 a.m. Susan delivered an egg into her hands.

Cecil examined the egg, comparing it to the one laid a few days earlier. The second egg in the clutch was slightly longer and heavier than the first. Cecil carefully recorded the laying in a notebook set aside for Susan: "January 31st, 1965, Susan laid fourth egg."

After this fit of domesticity, Susan became boisterous again in February. Her buoyant mood matched Cecil's. As winter faded, he felt his vitality slowly returning after the operation.

The scientific critics who had poo-pooed Susan's previous egg laying remained strangely silent. No one could explain away this clutch of eggs. Cecil remarked to Adele that it was almost as if the skeptical scientists felt if they remained silent, Susan and her puzzling eggs would go away.

fifteen

Tough Going

As *his recovery progressed*, Cecil ventured outside in early February to start repairing the collapsed roofs and fallen posts caused by the heavy winter snowstorms. The deep snow had melted, revealing rows of fenceposts littering the ground like giant matchsticks. As Cecil stood surveying the damage, he reflected on all the difficulties with which 1965 had begun. Little did he know that the severe winter that began 1965 and devastated Featherland foreshadowed an entire year of upheaval in which, as he later wrote, "Survival turned out to be the theme." Cecil and Adele later looked back on 1965 as "the Year from Hell."

Cecil's first task was assessing the damage. The roofs of two of the older outbuildings were beyond repair. Another building had suffered so much damage it had to be demolished.

In the evenings, Cecil faced a chore he would rather avoid:

dealing with the mountain of bills stacked on his desk. The heating bills alone were staggering after the long cold spell. Most were already overdue. Cecil had no choice but to write his father once again for more money.

Cecil had another major worry: his father had written that his mother was getting progressively worse and could no longer be left alone even for short periods. Cecil was very close to his mother, whose temperament he shared. Cecil also claimed he had inherited his artistic talent from his mother, who was an accomplished water-color painter. (Cecil's younger brother Robert had spent years studying art in Europe and, after flying Spitfires in the war, had become a war artist for the RCAF. In his letter, Judge Hyndman told Cecil that Robert had had a one-man showing of sixty paintings at an Ottawa gallery.)

Adele joined Cecil in the Plume Room after she had been in to see Susan. His face looked so pale and gaunt that Adele was concerned he might have overexerted himself outside. He momentarily basked in the sympathy she rarely showered on him, as she ordinarily reserved most of her nurturing for the birds.

Finally, in a quiet voice, Cecil told Adele that he saw no way around their problem. He proposed what they had been postponing for years: the breakup of Featherland.

Adele immediately sat down. Cecil passed the stack of overdue bills to her, pointing out that they simply had no reserves to cover any sort of emergency such as the winter heating bills. Even with just ordinary expenditures to worry about, Featherland had been slipping deeper and deeper into financial trouble.

Cecil and Adele discussed their options. They had climbed up their sloping property the previous summer to investigate the possibility of building a new cottage higher up the slope to gain more revenue through the sale of the more valuable lower and flatter part of their property. Adele reminded Cecil that they had discounted that possibility, as building a cottage on the rocky uplands was simply too expensive. To run water uphill meant blasting through hundreds of yards of solid rock.

Cecil got out the map of their property, and pointed to the line that divided their eighteen acres into two long and narrow lots. They could keep the western nine-acre lot, which contained the cottage, Talon Hall, and outbuildings, and sell off the eastern lot.

Adele fidgeted uncomfortably at the prospect of losing half of her beloved Featherland. A few years earlier they had sold off a half-acre east of Talon Hall. Even the loss of that very small lot had deeply affected her. Up until now they had both always refused two things: selling any of their birds, and selling any large chunk of Featherland. But she knew that even if they had an excellent tourist season that year, there was no way they could make enough to pay off the overdraft.

"Dad's ninety and he won't be here forever," Cecil pressured Adele.

"There must be other options," Adele countered.

The discussion went late into the night. In a very real sense, their passion for birds had created a prison of their own choosing. Even if Cecil, at age 54, managed to find another job outside Featherland, Adele could not handle all the work by herself. So more money would be needed to pay for hired help. And bringing an assistant to Featherland would create more problems, as the Hyndmans' birds were bonded to them.

Cecil reluctantly explained what he called the "wild-card option": He could approach Jack McClelland again.

Adele immediately objected. She had seen what the rejection of *Behind the Feathered Curtain* had done to Cecil's pride and self-confidence.

They argued back and forth, Cecil explaining that this time the story would focus on Susan, beginning with her arrival at Feather-land. The tremendous press coverage demonstrated that the story had wide appeal. He also reasoned that the main objection to the previous attempt had been the quality of the prose. This time he would agree to work with an editor or other writer, as long as he had final control over the shape of the book.

The conversation went around and around in circles, always coming back to the central problem. To support their work with birds, they needed money. Discounting the distant possibility of selling a book, their only sellable resources were limited to the birds and Featherland itself. With a heavy heart, Adele agreed to put half of their property on the market. Neither Cecil nor Adele slept well that night.

Despite Adele's lack of enthusiasm for reviving the book project, Cecil resumed his nightly writing schedule. The late winter gave him a window of opportunity, as that period was always the least busy time at Featherland. He concentrated his energy on the book, setting himself a quota of words to produce each day. Soon he had progressed far enough to contact Jack McClelland.

He outlined the book he intended to write about Susan, which he tentatively titled *The Golden Affair*. Cecil included in his letters a number of newspaper and magazine articles written about the Queen of Featherland.

At the same time, Cecil contacted a local real estate agent, knowing that it would take weeks to survey the parcel of land and perhaps months before a buyer was found. Meanwhile, their debts continued to mount.

An uneasy mood of tension hung over Featherland that spring. The unrelenting pressure of writing, the impending land sale, and the continuing deterioration of his mother's health troubled Cecil. Judge Hyndman had written again about his wife's "frail and vague condition," and said she was "unable to communicate at all as she used to."

On a more encouraging note, Cecil was pleased that his father had liked a unique pen holder he had made from Susan's discarded talons, and had also complimented his poetry. Judge Hyndman hoped Cecil's book would "turn out to the satisfaction of some publisher."

Other family members also wrote Cecil about the declining health of his mother. Cecil became preoccupied with death, recording in his notebooks the unusual number of deaths at Featherland that year:

Jan. 12 – downy woodpecker, brought to us after being shot, died two days later.

Jan. 15 – Satan, our dusky great horned owl, died. Two years ago a great horned owl had attacked at night, killing five birds in one of our netted enclosures by the cottage. In its panic to escape when we arrived outside at the pen, the large owl became entangled in the netting. We captured the owl and added him to our feathered family, christening him with an appropriate name — Satan.

Jan. 24 – an injured red breasted sapsucker brought to Featherland died. A robin also died on same day.

Feb. 8 – greater scaup died.

Feb. 26 – a long-eared owl died.

Feb. 26 – cockatiel died from pneumonia.

March 6 – Pie, the magpie, died after long foot trouble.

March 18 – an injured flicker, Poker, brought to us by a woman living near a winery, died.

March 22 – the second long-eared owl died of no apparent reason.

The mounting losses at Featherland in 1965 were not confined to birds. Senator Snort, the nine-banded armadillo that had arrived from Texas as a baby in 1962, developed pneumonia. The armor-plated armadillo had lived in a special room in Talon Hall, where the Hyndmans had installed an electric heater underneath the boards to provide extra warmth. A nocturnal, burrowing animal, one night Senator Snort used his powerful legs to tear through the wooden floorboards and in the process short-circuited the wiring. The one night without heat proved Senator Snort's undoing, and within a few days the armadillo died.

The Hyndmans had grown quite attached to the unusual animal with an equally unusual personality. Cecil had dubbed him the "flying football":

> He would curl himself in a ball and even as a baby roll right out of our hands. Senator Snort was the first armadillo in Canada and had been trained by Adele to walk on his hind legs while Adele held him. . . . We'd describe him to visitors before showing him as "a creature with a pig's nose, a donkey's ears, and shaped like an armor-plated rugby ball."

In late spring Adele and Cecil accompanied a team of surveyors as they staked out the property they were subdividing. Watching the first stage in the partition of their land was too much for Adele. She felt overwhelmed with a sense of loss and had to return to the cottage. Cecil wrote,

> Driving wooden stakes into her beloved Eden proved painful for both of us, with Adele being especially affected. She experienced a reaction that was almost physical, as if the wooden stakes were being driven into her own flesh. Deep down, she feared this might be the beginning of the end of Featherland.

He tried to ease Adele's discomfort by pointing out that the remaining property was still substantial, and they were keeping all the buildings. But there was no denying the size of the loss — almost half of their present land. Secretly Cecil shared his wife's fear that once they began selling off chunks of Featherland, they would eventually be left with only a small piece where their cottage stood.

July of 1965 brought with it the usual summer rush of visitors. That month Cecil also completed his five-year project of determining the sex of mallard ducks at the time of hatching. Using their wild flock, Cecil carefully noted the visual characteristics of newly hatched chicks. He sent his report to both the Canadian and American wildlife services.

Later in July, Cecil received disturbing news. His mother was not expected to live much longer. Cecil's older brother, Louis, suggested they travel east together. On Monday, July 12, Cecil left for Ottawa.

Alone at Featherland with no help, Adele managed to cope with both her feathered family and the daily visitors who brought much-needed revenue. At nights, after putting their other birds to bed, Adele visited Susan's room for her routine "preening sessions" with the Queen of Featherland.

The first night after Cecil left, she entered Susan's room feeling tired after a long day. "Sue, I can only stay a few minutes," she said, using a soft, wet cloth to gently wash the golden eagle's feathers. But within minutes of entering, she felt the tension of the day fade. Being with Susan relaxed her, then revitalized her. Instead of staying minutes, she spent hours with Susan.

With Cecil away, Susan became the person she communicated with. "Best of all, Susan always agreed with me and never answered back," Adele said. The bond between the two women had deepened to the point where Adele could read Susan's moods as easily as a barometer. The way she bobbed her head, the crossing of her wings, a riffle of her feathers — all these little gestures that meant nothing to an outsider gave Adele a clear indication of Susan's feelings.

The communication between the two females went both ways. Over the years of their relationship, Susan had also grown accustomed to Adele, who had the distinct impression Susan could read her moods. That first night Susan seemed especially comforting, repeatedly stroking Adele's forehead with her beak as if she knew

Adele needed extra support with Cecil away.

Adele believed that, where humans depended on words in a relationship, birds responded on a deeper and stronger level. And birds' responses, unlike the changeability of humans, remained true and constant.

"With Susan, there was a kind of deep understanding that most people do not achieve even with others, including family," Adele said. A closeness that defied words, yet was rock solid.

One warm July evening, while Cecil was away, Adele decided to attempt something she had never done before. Without Cecil in the cottage to overhear her, Adele began to sing to Susan. In her high, slightly wavering voice, Adele broke into a love song. She kept her eye on Susan at all times, looking for clues indicating herresponse. Susan listened attentively, almost swaying her head with the song.

"I like your singing much better," Adele confided to Susan after she finished her song. The two caressed, Susan's sharp beak gently rubbing against Adele's face. It was moments such as this that kept Adele going that difficult year.

Cecil arrived in Ottawa on Friday, July 16, two days after the death of his mother. Missing the chance to say goodbye devastated him. After remaining in Ottawa for two days, Cecil accepted a ride back to Toronto with his brother Jim. Cecil planned to stay overnight at his brother's house before taking the train back to the West Coast.

On Monday morning Jim left for his office, leaving Cecil alone in the house. "It was around 10:00 a.m. I was sitting in the living room when I started to feel very strange," Cecil later wrote.

My mouth dried to dust and my chest tightened as my breathing became difficult. My skin also dried and I was amazed to see it change until it looked like parchment.

Slowly a paralysis began to spread over me. I knew I had to get help, but there was no one home. That meant I had to make it to the telephone. Unable to walk, I crawled on the floor. It seemed to take forever as I pulled myself, inch by inch, toward it. I managed to dial Jimmy's office. Even this simple task took forever as time had slowed, turning into slow motion. I asked my brother to call an ambulance and insisted he keep talking because I was afraid I'd die. By then, I could barely breathe with this paralysis tightening its hold on me.

When the ambulance arrived, the attendants found the front door locked. Inside, Cecil lay on the floor, unable to move and barely able to speak. He somehow made himself heard, and the attendants used crowbars to break open the front door. Convinced he was going to die, Cecil refused to be lifted onto the stretcher until the ambulance attendants put a call through to Adele. When they finally got through, although he had trouble speaking, Cecil managed to ask Adele to "will him to live." At first Adele wanted to know what was going on, but eventually she complied with her husband's request.

On the way to the emergency ward, Cecil lapsed in and out of consciousness. He could only recall bits and pieces of the almost surreal experience:

After blacking out, I suddenly found myself up in the sky — as though soaring high on eagle wings. Ahead huge puffy white clouds filled the blue sky. I flew toward one enormous white cloud, which drew me toward it like a magnet. But as I approached, something kept pulling me back. Then I'd go forward again toward this white wall of cloud. Three or four times, something kept pulling me back as I neared this formation of cloud.

After being admitted to the hospital, while he waited for a doctor, he could feel his paralysis fading. Cautiously he tried moving his legs, and found his strength returning. Finally a doctor arrived and examined him. Cecil was startled when the doctor opened his shirt and revealed a huge blue-black bruise on his chest over his heart. The doctor couldn't explain what caused the attack.

Lying in the hospital bed in Toronto, Cecil tried to make sense of what he had gone through. "The incredible near-death experience left me numb. I'd been to the 'other side,' and come back. Yet there was no fear, more an acceptance — accompanied by a sense of calm as I flew through the sky. Then something, someone pulled me back. I'm convinced Adele's willing me to live pulled me back." His deep conviction that Adele had this power was as unshakable as it was irrational. Years before, Susan had suffered a near-fatal infection. Cecil had given up hope that Susan could pull through, but Adele had refused to accept that Susan was fatally ill. She willed Susan to live, and she recovered.

After the results of several tests proved negative, Cecil spent a few days recovering at his brother Jim's house before catching the Dominion train west. He wrote Adele en route,

I have endured the ultimate — and lived through the experience. I'll never be afraid again. After this, everything else is the merest trifle. . . . I swear to God and you that by having you will me to live, I did live!

How I hope you have not felt so sick or worried since my phone call. Smile and relax. Everything is going to be alright — in fact better than in years. I saw Jack McClelland alone for three-quarters of an hour in Toronto. Tough guy and secretly, I think, a good guy. Felt free to "god damn" with him in perfect comfort. The book, as to content, "should be done" according to Jack. My writing as it stands is not good enough but The Golden Affair *can be done in collaboration with an able writer. I think we understand one another on all necessary issues and the personal meeting has been most valuable.*

Despite the upbeat tone of his letter, Cecil had not fully recovered from the bizarre out-of-body incident. Nor did it help when he realized his berth number on the train was the same as one he had during a horrific train crash in 1942. Although he was not a super-stitious person, he could not shake off the ominous coincidence. As the Dominion reached the Rockies and the train approached the spot of the crash almost a quarter of a century ago, vivid memories of the crash resurfaced.

In the spring of 1942, Cecil joined an American film crew from Paramount planning a series of documentary films on Canada. In the Rocky Mountains, a flood knocked out a rail bridge, forcing their train to stop. While they were stopped, Cecil and the film crew dined in the observation car — the last car of the train.

They heard a metallic scream. Cecil looked up in time to see a 400-passenger troop train split the car apart, killing the two engi-neers sitting at the end of the car. The locomotive continued toward them, ripping the steel floor as if opening a gigantic tin. With the huge steel-gray mass of the engine only feet away, Cecil dove through a thick glass window. He landed on his left shoulder, his momentum carrying him under another car and down into a slough filled with water.

Later, he was found, dazed from shock, and carried up the slope. Others weren't so lucky. Eight died in the wreck, and seventy-five people were injured. Cecil was moved by cattle car to Royal Inland Hospital in Kamloops. At first the doctors feared he had broken his back. Cecil's face had over fifty cuts and his left arm had shrivelled, leaving just enough muscle so he could move it slightly. Only weeks of intense therapy restored the muscles to somewhere near normal.

When Cecil arrived back in Victoria on July 24, 1965, his physical condition alarmed Adele. His gaunt face appeared more hollow than ever; he had lost weight. He was so weak he could barely carry his bag from the taxi. The emergency phone call from Cecil in Toronto had first panicked, then puzzled Adele. She wondered if his attack in Toronto had been more psychological than physical — until she saw the ugly purple-black bruise covering almost half his chest.

What was even more alarming, Cecil seemed emotionally strung out, and displayed signs of anxiety by his hyperactivity. Although he was ordinarily a man with intense emotions, Adele found him now "a complete and total nervous wreck."

She tactfully told Cecil he needed rest to recover his strength. When he started to object, Adele pointed out how his hands were shaking. As he often did when he had overextended himself, he collapsed into bed. Adele made an appointment for Cecil to see a specialist about his heart. The doctor ordered extensive tests, but none provided an explanation for the bruise across Cecil's chest.

After a few days in bed, Cecil could no longer stand the inactivity and he resumed his work with the birds. Adele noticed a remarkable change in Cecil.

"What's come over you?" Adele said to Cecil. "You're running around like you're in overdrive."

"I feel like I've been given another chance," he replied, "and it's all due to you. You brought me through — saved me."

The first bird Cecil had visited on his return was Susan. For once the Queen of Featherland did not display her usual hostility as he peeked through the bamboo barrier. Even Adele expressed surprise at the eagle's behavior toward Cecil.

Although he had no reason to believe she had mellowed since he left, Cecil decided to press the contact. He still felt imbued with a sense of a second chance after his near-death experience. Cecil hoped this might extend to his relations with Susan. Adele confirmed that the golden eagle had been somewhat more subdued that summer. Cecil wondered if her recent maternalism might have softened her toward him. He decided to test the waters, as he had nothing to lose and everything to gain.

One sunny summer day Cecil peeked through the wooden grille to check on Susan. The sunlight streaming into the room caught the eagle in a shaft of bright light. Susan looked every bit as regal as her nickname suggested. Her golden plumage glowed with an iridescent sheen and her amber eyes sparkled. She stretched her neck, flicking her wings wide as if to capture the warmth of the sun.

Hiding behind the grille, Cecil tried to take a mental snapshot of the scene. He wanted to capture every detail, imprinting Susan's regal beauty on his mind as she stood completely still with her wings spread. "Susan, with her eight-foot wings spread, reminded me of a Roman legion emblem, come to life, radiating the color gold," he wrote.

Cecil recalled how he used to blow gently on Susan's neck feathers. He closed his eyes as memories of being with her replayed in his mind: how she would respond to his gentle stroking with a twittering sound; her curved beak stroking his cheek; the unmistakable smell of her feathers as she ruffled them next to his nose.

Lost in the flood of recollections, a terrible sense of loss overwhelmed Cecil. His eyes filled with tears. Just then, he experienced a coldness so intense it caused him to shiver. Cecil opened his eyes. Clouds had moved in front of the sun.

Her sunbathing ended, Susan folded her wings to her body. She suddenly turned her head toward Cecil and for a moment their eyes locked. Although Cecil wanted to move, he was fixed to the spot by the intensity of the eagle's gaze. Slowly Susan moved her head from side to side in a motion characteristic of birds of prey about to attack.

Cecil often compared this hypnotic movement to a "cobra death dance, before the creature strikes." Susan crouched down into her pre-attack posture, wings snapping open with a cracking sound. Before she could take off and crash against the bars, Cecil stepped back out of her view. Her hostile response had answered his question about whether Susan's maternalism had changed her.

Before Cecil had fully recovered his strength, the real estate agent arrived with an offer on the eight-and-a-half-acre part of Featherland that was on the market. Adele was distressed. She felt she was giving up part of herself.

Cecil seemed more able to rise above the loss. He put a positive spin on the sale, saying, "we have to let go of the past, look ahead and not back."

The property was soon sold, and almost immediately, the purchaser started developing the land, with disastrous effects. Wrote Cecil,

> He had a huge power saw that he ran all day. We couldn't hear ourselves speak. Next he started blasting stumps and the blasts knocked our birds right off their perches. We simply couldn't safely show under those conditions.

Featherland was forced to close its doors in early August. A Victoria radio station, as well as some local newspapers, carried the story. Cecil was quoted as saying, "we have decided to devote the rest of the year entirely to research."

Cecil, who had a longstanding love-hate relationship with the local newspapers, could not help but take a backhanded swipe at what he perceived as local indifference to Featherland. He told a reporter interviewing him that he had never regarded the wildlife garden as a local tourist attraction in the normal sense. His biggest delight had been in receiving visitors "who had heard of our unique collection of 200 birds in scattered corners of the world — Cairo, Johannesburg, Bangkok, the Philippines."

Cecil had always been ambivalent about the tours at Featherland. On the one hand, he wanted to be taken seriously as a bird expert. At the same time, entertaining visitors brought in money to support his work. He justified these "bird performances" by saying his real intention was to educate the public in an entertaining manner. And the birds' performances — whether dancing on command or talking — proved that birds had intelligence.

In some ways, the Hyndmans fit in well in Victoria, which also suffered from a dual reputation in that era. It claimed the title of Canada's retirement city and was often referred to as "a cemetery with a shopping center." But there was another side to staid and tweedy Victoria. A visitor who parted the "tea and crumpets curtain" would encounter more weird and wonderful characters walking the streets than anywhere else in Canada. Small wonder Victoria was also called the oddball city of Canada.

So, to many locals, Cecil fit in as an eccentric bird man. He even looked like a bird, with his sharp beak. He was spoken of as living in a house that was more like a gigantic birdcage, with owls and eagles as roommates. Numerous things about Adele and Cecil, such as the fact that they had trained their Mexican donkey to pull railway spikes from fenceposts with his teeth, confirmed Featherland's reputation as tourist attraction, not a scientific research station. Even Susan's unprecedented egg laying was not viewed locally as a remarkable achievement in avian research but rather as an oddity.

Autumn gave way to fall, and 1965 ended as it had begun, with a severe winter snowstorm. Adele woke early on a Monday, only days after Christmas, to find Featherland transformed into what she called "a winter fairyland setting — an overdue white Christmas." Cecil viewed the blanket of white over a foot deep with less romanticism. Remembering the previous winter's disasters, he worried about the effect of the extra weight of the snow on the roofs of the outbuildings.

The snowfall did not let up, and soon tree limbs began to crash down. Within hours both the power and phone lines went dead. The power outage quickly chilled the cottage and Featherland's other buildings. The storm continued all day, breaking the old record for most snow recorded over a twenty-four-hour period.

The thick snow closed roads to traffic. In the early afternoon, Cecil managed to contact BC Hydro after splicing together his fallen phone line. Despite his desperate pleas about the cold killing the birds, the power company was unable to give Cecil any indication of when power would be restored.

Luckily Ookpik Cottage had an oil-fired space heater supplied by a tank outside the cottage. Adele used it to prepare warm baths for Doctor Archibald, heating pans of water on top of the oil heater. The caiman's tropical metabolism could not tolerate exposure to cold. Cecil tended to the birds in Talon Hall.

As night approached, Cecil and Adele began gathering their birds and bringing them into the cottage. Trudging back and forth through the deep snow to Talon Hall and the other outbuildings took hours. They were barely able to move in the cottage crowded with so many extra birds and birdcages. Over fifty of their two hundred birds were given the shelter of their home following the snowstorm.

Adele worried about Susan's reaction to the extra guests, but the Queen of Featherland did not react to the noise and unfamiliar birds crowding the cottage. Adele felt badly at not spending more time with Susan, especially as the golden eagle was in another egg-laying phase.

Only a few weeks earlier, on December 11, Susan had laid her fifth egg at 12:30 a.m. Cecil had noted in his journal how the Queen of Featherland followed this feat with "fantastic surges of her love song." He wrote that the singing was most intense on December 14 and 15.

Usually a second egg arrived within days of the first, but over two weeks had passed. Would there be another? With the unusual cold spell and the stress of the overcrowded cottage, Adele was convinced Susan would not produce another egg that year. As usual, Adele's prediction proved correct.

When Adele came into the bedroom late Monday night, she could hardly see the bed for the dozens of birds, many taking up space on the bed itself. Not that she expected to sleep much that night — the priority was caring for their birds. Adele found Cecil bundled up in two coats and attempting to make a pot of coffee on top of the space heater.

During the night they took turns checking the birds remaining in the other buildings, warming the caiman's water and changing straw to keep the waterfowl from freezing in the outdoor pens. Somehow they managed to cope without power that night.

The next morning Cecil went outside to check on his feathered and furred family. He found four waterfowl frozen to death, despite the extra straw. The day after the record-breaking dump, more flurries added to the total. The deep snow isolated Featherland and prevented BC Hydro crews from reconnecting electric power. The grim ordeal continued all day Tuesday.

Further complicating matters for the Hyndmans was the need for temporary repairs to the storm-damaged roof of Talon Hall. There was nowhere to move the many birds housed there if the roof collapsed.

Without electric power, the Hyndmans faced another sleepless night. The temperature dropped that night, forcing Cecil to go outside every two hours to the waterfowl pens, where he laid fresh straw down.

By midnight, Cecil realized he was losing the battle:

By then we were moving like zombies, after thirty-six hours without sleep. While outside, I could hear sharp cracking sounds as tree limbs snapped loose or exploded in the freezing conditions. It was like a war zone — the violent "snap, crackle, and pop" sounds echoing in the stillness of night.

Cecil went back inside and explained the situation to Adele. They bundled themselves against the biting cold, then carefully dismantled the pen entrances and transported the waterfowl to an unused outbuilding. It took hours, as each duck had to be individually carried through the deep snow up the slope.

Some of the larger and more aggressive geese had to be restrained in blankets. As the biggest geese weighed close to thirty pounds, this task required both of them. While Cecil carried the goose, Adele secured the neck and bill; the spring action of a goose's neck can deliver a blow powerful enough to stun a fox.

With the waterfowl finally safe and warm in the unused outbuilding, the Hyndmans tried to spell one another off. Daylight came all too soon and they began the morning feed routine, which was made even more difficult as all the water and food for the outdoor birds had to be heated. Even Tony, the ten-year-old Mexican donkey, insisted on hot water with his meals.

Finally, power was restored on Wednesday. A professional roofer also arrived to repair Talon Hall. Cecil and Adele spent the rest of the day and evening moving back all the temporary tenants of the cottage, then collapsed into bed, still clothed.

Cecil had barely fallen asleep when high-pitched screams erupted outside their bedroom window. Adele nudged him, and he stumbled outside to one of the waterfowl pens protected by a mesh. A gray form flapped violently, accompanied by loud quacking. In his exhausted state, it took Cecil a moment to realize the ghostly form was a starving goshawk attacking a duck next to the mesh.

Only a year ago a similar attack had occurred. Cecil speculated it might even be the same bird, driven to such a bold attack by the grim winter conditions. The bird of prey flew off, leaving the duck badly injured. Cecil repaired the torn mesh, patched up the duck's torn wing, and returned to the bedroom.

After two days and two nights without sleep, Cecil found himself close to a state of delirium. He tried to sleep, but shook so violently he woke Adele. Her nerves were also stretched taut after the snow-storm ordeal. Cecil wrote:

After all the activity and noisy conditions, the silence seemed unbearable. Lying in bed too tired to sleep, half expecting another crisis, we began to laugh. Why, I can't remember — but our laughter turned hysterical. If anyone had come in, we would have ended up committed to the nut house.

The outburst relieved some of the built-up tension, and soon Adele fell asleep. But Cecil found sleep impossible as his head kept spinning. Images from the year whirled by, as if thrown up by a film projector running out of control in reverse. The past twelve months had been traumatic, with his mother's death, the sale of a large part of Featherland, and the closure. Yet there had been positive signs, such as McClelland's interest in a book on Susan. And the near-death experience in Toronto had energized him, although the warm afterglow from the out-of-body experience was beginning to fade. As he lay there, New Year's Eve only a day away, Cecil wondered what the next year would bring.

sixteen

A New Era

The arrival of 1966 marked the twentieth anniversary of the establishment of Featherland. It also signaled the end of one era at Featherland and the beginning of another. Although Cecil and Adele discussed reopening Featherland, the gates to their property remained closed throughout the summer of 1966. In fact, the closure became permanent. Never again would cars or buses full of visitors be entertained by their feathered and furred family.

But as one door closed, another opened. Featherland was evolving once again, reinventing itself as it had so many times in the past. What had begun in 1946 as Featherland Farm, with thousands of egg-laying chickens, then become Featherland, the Land of the Talking Birds, was now envisaged as a private facility devoted to avian research. Cecil had a plan in mind, one he revealed to few as his goal seemed both impossible and too grandiose. He wanted to be the next Darwin.

Forty years earlier, when Cecil had been bedridden for a year, with no companions but his father's thousand-book library, the fifteen-year-old boy read and reread Darwin's *On the Origin of the Species*. The revolutionary book had deeply affected the precocious teenager. He found himself especially influenced by the concept that "people are animals."

At that early age, Cecil had already developed an eccentric outlook he would pursue for the rest of his life. He felt Darwin's concept could and should be reversed: "animals are people."

For forty years, Cecil had kept his goal secret. Now he felt poised to accomplish what he had only dreamed of as a young teenager isolated for a year. Although he was cut off from academic and scientific research, Cecil was in tune with the mid-1960s trends. The time was right, as Darwinism was not only being revisited, but revised. Austrian biologist Konrad Lorenz was recognized as one of the founding fathers of ethology, a "new science" that focused on animal behaviour.

Susan held the key to Cecil's bold ambitions. Even before she had begun her unprecedented egg laying, she had elevated Featherland from the status of another roadside attraction to something truly unique. Large metropolitan zoos across North America had sizable standing offers to purchase Susan — a clear indication of her rareness and value. Once she began to lay eggs, her value skyrocketed. No other golden eagle had laid eggs without being exposed to others of its own species. The hundreds of articles and photographs, the radio and TV shows — all reinforced Cecil's conviction that the general public was fascinated by the convoluted love story of a man, a woman, and a golden eagle.

Adele's prediction of over a decade earlier was coming to pass. "With us, Susan can be world famous," she had said when the letter arrived from the Yukon offering the Hyndmans a golden eagle.

Susan could be a means of combining their passion with profit.

Now Cecil intended to elevate his aim and make a name for himself in scientific circles. If he only could prove birds possessed some "human" qualities, he would make an enormous breakthrough. Teaching birds to speak suggested they shared intelligence with man, but Susan's egg laying seemed the most promising behavior to pursue. He decided to publish some original scientific research about Susan in academic journals to overcome his stigma as an eccentric amateur. This was the first step toward his long-range goal of being the "new Darwin."

But first he had the "commercial" book about Susan to complete. This time Cecil was determined not to let the publishing opportunity slip by. He had learned the hard way about the harsh demands of the publishing industry and had swallowed his pride, tentatively agreeing to a co-author. If he could not deliver a "salable" manuscript about Susan, Jack McClelland had offered to supply a writer to tell Susan's story. And this time around, Cecil would be free from the financial pressure that had driven his previous attempts to write a book.

The revenue from the sale of half of their property had not only provided relief from "that dark cloud that had hung over Featherland for most of its existence," it bought Cecil precious time to write and to explore his other projects. Cecil was convinced 1966 was going to be their "breakthrough year."

Both Hyndmans used their extra time wisely. Without the daily demands of showing visitors around Featherland, which had often taken up most of their afternoons and evenings, Adele devoted extra hours to being with Susan. The golden eagle responded positively to Adele's increased attention.

In mid-August Susan began singing her love song, the high notes filling Ookpik Cottage. Although the singing continued for some days, and in the past the song had preceded egg laying, Cecil was not convinced Susan was about to lay. All her previous eggs had arrived much later in the year, from mid-November to January. But Adele was certain the singing indicated that more eggs would soon be on their way. To test her intentions, Adele collected some twigs. Susan responded by attempting to construct a nest.

Susan's first egg arrived on August 30, at what had become her usual laying time of 12:15 a.m. The second of that clutch emerged a few days later, almost catching the Hyndmans off guard as Susan laid it at the unusually early hour of 7:00 p.m. Every one of her previous five eggs had been laid between midnight and 1 a.m.

A month later, Susan again surprised Adele by showing signs of laying. At first Adele was unsure. So, again, she brought in twigs and sticks as a test. And again, Susan immediately began lifting the pieces with her bill, indicating her intention of constructing a nest.

On October 18 Susan laid an egg, her eighth, and six days later she laid another. These eggs delighted Adele and vindicated their decision to close Featherland to the public. The extra attention Adele was able to devote to Susan had paid an incredible dividend — four eggs in a little under two months.

The Hyndmans were pleased with this truly remarkable achievement. But they worried that Susan seemed to take a very long time to recover after producing four eggs in the space of such a short period of time. Cecil was especially worried about the long-term implications of this feat. What if she should continue to produce at this rate? Would her body stand up to such a pace?

They celebrated Susan's accomplishment with a bottle of wine. Adele proposed a toast, to "Susan's record-breaking laying, which will add to the already unique story of her life." Although Cecil agreed, he wished Adele had not brought up the subject of the book. The manuscript was not going well.

Jack McClelland had sent his executive assistant, Jim Douglas, to Victoria to discuss the book. Douglas handled matters for McClelland on the West Coast.

Adele prepared the cottage for Douglas's arrival with high hopes, scrubbing both Susan's room and Susan. Cecil kidded Adele that she was going to rub the golden sheen off Susan's feathers. Adele was absolutely convinced that once Douglas viewed the majestic Queen of their feathered family, he would be so impressed that he would agree to publish Susan's story. Cecil cautioned Adele not to expect Douglas to arrive with a contract.

The initial meeting turned out to be disappointing. Cecil found Jim Douglas's speech "so strongly Scottish" that he "couldn't make out six words out of ten." Douglas was terribly offended by the fact that Cecil couldn't understand him.

The visit ended with no definite commitment, which surprised Adele. Cecil had the distinct impression that Jim Douglas was feeling them out, possibly to test how far Cecil was willing to bend. Douglas seemed unenthusiastic when they discussed using Cecil's photographs.

Douglas visited Featherland eight times that summer to discuss Cecil's *The Golden Affair*. Cecil found his visits exasperating, complaining, "the canny Scot would write notes on the ferry over from Vancouver that I didn't like. His ideas were as far apart from mine as the moon."

Cecil did not want to argue with Douglas, especially as he knew McClelland already regarded him as a difficult author. While he tried to remain calm, a nagging doubt began to eat away at him. His intuition told him something was not right.

On a chilly afternoon in late February 1967, Cecil went outside to warm up the car. He needed to drive Adele into Victoria for a doctor's appointment. When she did not emerge from the house, he went back inside to find his wife in Susan's room.

"Come quickly," she said. "Susan's just added fresh material to your book."

Cecil rushed to the grille. Susan had caught them off guard by laying her tenth egg at 3:00 that afternoon.

"There was no sign of any blood on the shell," Cecil later recorded in his journal. "Twenty-four hours earlier, she had been sick to her stomach and had some distress." Ordinarily, Susan's eggs were speckled with blood.

Quickly Cecil canceled Adele's appointment and contacted Canadian Press. After a photographer arrived to take some photos, Adele gave Susan back her egg to gauge her reaction. Although the golden eagle began to sit on it like any nesting mother bird, Cecil and Adele noticed she still seemed to be in some physical distress.

Their elation over this latest egg faded as Susan's condition worsened over the next few days. Adele grew concerned about the length of time it was taking her to recover.

After a week went by and there was no improvement, Cecil speculated the "bloodless" egg might be a clue to her condition. Susan did not lay a second egg, and her "weak and listless condition continued for some time."

Adele closely monitored Susan and noted that the inside of her mouth had changed to an unusual color. After conferring with Cecil, she started Susan on a course of erythromycin. Adele also painted Susan's mouth with an antifungal ointment. The medicine failed to bring a prompt improvement, and they were forced to continue the treatment well into March.

While Adele administered to Susan, Cecil kept up his writing. By now, relations with Jim Douglas had reached the crisis point. Finally Cecil completed the first draft of *The Golden Affair*. He called Douglas in Vancouver with the news, and in March gave him the finished manuscript.

Weeks passed. Since he had put enormous time and effort into telling Susan's story, he was becoming exasperated with the lack of a definite response. Finally Douglas told him McClelland was returning the manuscript with reluctance and "regret." The stumbling block, oddly enough, seemed to be the use of Cecil's photographs.

Cecil respected Jack McClelland as a tough but fair publisher, but now wondered if this trust was misplaced. He decided to test the "literary waters elsewhere, especially as time was ticking away." He contacted a few literary agents and publishers in the east to get a second opinion about his manuscript. He also wanted to gauge their reaction to the layout of the book as he envisaged it, with his own photographs accompanying the text.

The rest of 1967 sped by in fast motion. Cecil traveled to New York in the spring to talk to literary agents and publishers. When he returned, the Hyndmans went on their annual egg-collecting expedition in early July. It turned out to be one of the most successful trips they ever made to the barren islets off Oak Bay.

Later in July, Adele, who had never taken a proper holiday away from Featherland, left by train for Toronto, Ottawa, and Montreal, where Expo '67 was being held. It would be the last time she saw her mother. Cecil felt relieved; it had taken some years of gentle persuasion and the fever of Expo to entice Adele to take a holiday. Adele also made a number of side-trips to see publishers and agents.

Cecil's trip and Adele's follow-up calls paid off; a number of agents and publishers expressed interest in Susan's story. In the fall of 1967, Cecil mailed off the revised manuscript to a literary agent in New York. He had changed the name of the story to *The Grasp*. Although he had no firm offers, the sample pieces he sent off brought positive responses as winter came to Featherland.

McClelland, while rejecting the draft Cecil had written, still professed interest in the story and diplomatically suggested an editor look at it. The offer surprised Cecil, and the interest expressed in *The Grasp* by McClelland and other publishers buoyed up the Hyndmans' hopes. Perhaps, after all, 1968 would be the break-through year.

The beginning of 1968 saw little let-up in the hectic pace of life at Featherland. On Saturday, January 27, a Toronto-based editor from McClelland arrived for a visit. The Hyndmans took her on a tour of Featherland, starting with the birds in Talon Hall, then introducing her to Susan. The editor left after a few hours, impressed by the golden eagle's appearance but unimpressed with Susan's rather subdued behavior. Even Cecil was surprised at how "Susan seemed unusually quiet during the visit."

The reason for Susan's uncharacteristic behavior became obvious later that evening as the golden eagle showed signs that she was about to deliver an egg. Adele, convinced Susan was about to lay, spent time with Susan, gently stroking her. Her long vigil paid off at a few minutes before 3:00 a.m. on Sunday, when Susan laid an egg directly into Adele's hands.

Susan's eleventh egg turned out to be the largest she had laid to date. The excited Hyndmans, when they finally retired early that morning, remarked that had the editor stayed a few more hours, she would have witnessed an event few others had ever seen.

Over the years, Cecil had patiently recorded details of Susan's egg laying. Besides writing Susan's story for the general public, he hoped to produce a scientific paper for an ornithological journal. But professional science journals had exacting standards and rarely published papers by anyone without a number of degrees. Cecil, lacking the necessary expertise, was regarded as a self-taught amateur — if not an eccentric.

He took this egg to an independent professional to provide out-side documentation of his facts. The pharmacist recorded that the egg weighed just under 4.5 ounces.

As Susan usually laid clutches of two eggs, Adele spent extra time with her over the next few days. Her long wait was rewarded on Thursday, February 1, at 5:15 p.m. Susan's twelfth egg weighed just over 3.5 ounces. With both these eggs, Cecil noted, "Susan was physically ill at her stomach and in visible pain for a few hours previous to laying."

The busy pace of January and February set the tone for the year. Cecil deliberately devoted all his time and efforts to his goal of getting his book published. While he maintained his links with McClelland, his New York literary agent, Ruth Aley, circulated the manuscript among American publishing houses.

"This time it'll sell," Adele assured him, sensing Cecil's impatience and growing frustration as the rejections of his manuscript slowly came back from both sides of the border.

Ruth Aley passed on the following reaction from an editor with an American publishing house.

The story of Susan is remarkable, as is Mr. Hyndman's knowledge of and work with all sorts of birds. He writes excitingly but I was disappointed to find the book autobiographical, full of theorizing, and the material about Susan more gory and sensational than fascinating and illuminating.

The literary agent added:

And this was the most sympathetic editor I could think of — young, eager to find fresh material, creative in every way. This bears out my feeling your book as yet doesn't convey your intended message. It may be that you are too emotionally close to the situation to write of it in the most convincing way for others.

As the rejection folder grew, Cecil explored his fall-back plan of self-publishing, traveling to Vancouver to check out local printers. Cecil gave himself a specific target date. If no publisher expressed a firm commitment by that date, he was prepared to self-publish the book. Not only was this prospect financially risky, especially with their limited resources, but the work involved would be enormous.

By now Cecil was absolutely convinced his photographs of Susan should feature in the book. Susan's story, as envisaged by Cecil, would be a visual feast, with forty to fifty photographs documenting Susan's remarkable life with Adele and Cecil at Featherland.

While Cecil was juggling the difficult task of preparing the book and photographs for self-publication, he decided to give the commercial publishers one last chance. He pressured both his New York literary agent and McClelland in Toronto.

By mid-1968, Cecil had been trying to sell Susan's story to Jack McClelland for three years. During that period, he had talked to McClelland personally, his West Coast representative Jim Douglas, and to another editor. The tangled web left Cecil so frustrated that his misgivings darkened into a form of paranoia.

Cecil suspected his manuscript was being "shopped around," shown to different writers and editors without his permission. The final and puzzling last straw came late one night when Jack McClelland phoned Cecil from Toronto and offered Cecil $900 for all rights to the story of Susan. Cecil refused.

Only after Cecil decided to go ahead and publish the book himself, did Douglas made it clear to him that McClelland had wanted to turn the story over to Farley Mowat, who had always been close to McClelland. Cecil wrote, "That's why he didn't want my photos, he wanted an artist in Toronto to do it because he wanted to fictionalize the story."

At this stage Cecil's commercial publishing options for Susan's story had run out. He determined to self-publish. The cost would be substantial, so the Hyndmans went to the bank to make arrangements to take out a second mortgage. But as Cecil wrote in his journal, "From jacket to final word, this book is all my own."

By the fall of 1968, preparations for the book consumed almost all of the Hyndmans' time. A local printer had agreed to undertake the project in the summer. The work involved seemed endless as Cecil had to do a final edit of the text, supervise the typesetting, prepare the photos, proofread, consult with a graphic designer, and lay out the book. He even ordered the leatherette cover material from eastern Canada.

As always, Cecil worked flat out, often staying up until early morning to keep to their deadline. They planned on having the book out for Christmas — the best season for book sales.

"I hate to tell you, but it's bill trimming time," Adele announced one winter night after her evening session with Susan.

Once again, the curved upper mandible of Susan's bill had grown to the point where it interfered with the lower part of her mouth. Although Adele had taken on many of Cecil's tasks at Featherland, trimming the bills of the larger birds of prey was a two-person task. The bills of both Susan and LBJ, the bald eagle, needed trimming.

Although ordinarily this was a dreaded task, Cecil almost welcomed the opportunity this time. Anything to break the long nights spent editing and wrestling with the layout of his book.

"So, the experiment didn't work as well as expected," he said. He had deliberately placed sturdy branches and twigs in Susan's room in an effort to keep her bill ground down. In fact, the plan had succeeded to some extent, as it had been over a year since her bill last needed trimming.

Cecil could see from the safety of the grille that the upper portion of Susan's bill overhung a fraction of an inch. He estimated they could leave the trimming for another day, maybe two. But when he told Adele they could safely postpone the task, she protested.

"No, not tomorrow, right now. Let's have it over with right away and not have to think about it all night."

The prospect unnerved Cecil. He had problems focusing his eyes after concentrating on proofreading all day. But Adele was adamant that Susan was experiencing trouble closing her mouth already. Wearily Cecil agreed.

Neither spoke as they prepared for the ordeal. There was little need, as both of them knew the routine so well. Cecil found the thick blanket and put on his protective gear — padded coat, chaps, and heavy gloves. Meanwhile, Adele gathered up and sterilized the instruments — two pairs of cutters, and files to smooth off the edges after they were clipped back.

The initial phase of the "trim" went better than Cecil had feared. Perhaps because it had been so long since the last trim, he managed to catch Susan off guard, grabbing her in a fast, sure swoop of the blanket. Adele worked surely but slowly, careful not to clip too deep and cause bleeding, which could lead to an infection. Within a few minutes, she completed the dreaded task.

After Adele was safely out of the room, Cecil released Susan and ran for the door. For once the trimming operation had gone perfectly. Cecil wrote:

No fuss. The whole thing had been as smooth as oil. Pleased with ourselves, Adele and I elaborately bowed to one another and shook hands in horseplay of self-congratulation while I shed my trappings — heavy enough at house temperature to make one steam in no time. Then I went around to the bird room to look in at Sue through the grille.

The smile on Cecil's face vanished the moment he saw Susan. She was still having difficulty closing her bill. They had not cut far enough.

"Damn. All that for nothing," Cecil muttered.

He had good cause to swear. Susan was now both alerted and angry. He knew capturing her again would be extremely difficult. But there was no choice.

Cecil blamed himself for not checking the results more closely.

He put on his protective padded clothing for the second time that evening. As he feared, Susan immediately took to the air as he held the blanket in front of him, "looking like a silly caricature of a bull fighter" he later mused.

But at the time, the incident was anything but funny.

She wheeled around me in a menacing way, airborne part of the time and always just out of reach. Somehow I couldn't find the opportunity to pin and wrap her firmly with her wings folded.

A time or two she came uncomfortably close to wiping my own "beak" off — no aesthetic loss if she had. I descended on her clumsily. She flipped over on her back, left wing waving free and with insufficient cover over her legs and feet. If, I thought, I let her go at this point in order to try for a better catch, the situation could turn worse, so I lifted her flailing poundage to the box stand.

Adele quickly entered and attempted to trim Susan's bill back, but she had a difficult time as Susan struggled under the blanket. Both were concerned about Susan injuring herself. While Cecil tried to hold Susan steady, Adele tried to squeeze the cutters while holding Susan's bill. She found the previous trimming had sapped most of her strength. As they fumed and exchanged angry words, Susan managed to free a wing.

Before Cecil could warn Adele, the tip of the wing struck her cheek. The impact left a red welt, but could have been much worse had Susan been able to put all her strength behind the blow.

"Run out and get that wool tuque in the bedroom bureau," he instructed Adele. The plan was to pull the tuque over Susan's head in an effort to calm her.

Adele rushed out as Cecil continued to hold Susan, who squirmed mightily. The effort was draining Cecil and he wondered who would become exhausted first.

Adele returned and Susan briefly quit struggling long enough for

Adele to pull the tuque over her head. Quickly Adele widened the hole in the tuque to allow Susan's bill through.

Again Adele tried cutting the bill, but found the cutting pliers had become so dull with use that they "hardly dented the horn of a bill grown steel-hard in maturity." They couldn't afford high-quality instruments designed for bill cutting and were now paying the price.

Although blindfolded, Susan wriggled relentlessly until she worked loose one end of the blanket. Out of the fold flashed a foot.

"She's got me," Adele told Cecil in a flat voice, her face expressionless.

Cecil peered down and saw the talons of Susan's foot clamped around Adele's thin left wrist. Cecil dared not release Susan, for Adele, as always, had entered the room in a blouse and with bare hands.

For a moment Cecil came near to panic. His mind refused to work as his eyes locked on Susan's talons, squeezing tighter around Adele's wrist. Soon they would break through Adele's skin. Suddenly Cecil thought of a solution to resolve the impasse.

"Pull off the hood," he told Adele, "let her see which one of us she's got."

With her free hand, Adele drew back the tuque. Susan immediately saw whom she had in her grasp. Adele spoke softly to Susan and she opened her foot, releasing Adele's wrist and dropping her foot limply to the blanket. The risky move had paid off, and Adele somehow found the strength in her hand to finish the trimming operation.

After the exhausting struggle, the Hyndmans decided to postpone trimming the bill of LBJ. Although a bald eagle has a rougher bill and lack the control of a golden eagle, they were always less trouble, and never as dangerous as Susan.

Eventually, LBJ's bill was trimmed that October. But that success was overshadowed by the death of the ringtailed monkey, Coco. He died in Cecil's arms at twenty years of age. He had come to the Hyndmans from Ontario in the late 1940s when he was between one to two years old. Wrote Cecil, "Each night I would wrap him in his night blanket before putting him to bed and each night he always hugged me tightly."

In mid-November of 1968, Cecil registered *The Grasp* with the Canada Copyright office in Ottawa. He paid the first instalment of $400 to a Victoria printer. Although the original plan had been to have the book in stores for Christmas, this prospect now looked unlikely.

As if to celebrate the occasion of the book going to press, Susan provided the perfect present: another clutch of eggs. By now Adele recognized the signs. Susan began to sing with a passion, and, as Cecil noted, "she took Adele aside and tried to build a nest with her out of sticks."

Cecil duly recorded the event, noting that Susan's thirteenth egg was laid on November 14, exactly thirteen years and one month after her arrival at Featherland. Cecil was interviewed on the radio the next day.

The following Monday, November 18, Susan laid her fourteenth egg at 2:30 p.m. Again Cecil recorded the details in his journal:

Second of this clutch laid directly into Adele's hand. Adele had seen her straining and in pain at 2:25 and went in to see her. New blood on egg, which got on her hands, and she was able to wash off most of the blood under tap. Immediately drove to office lab of Dr. Algard at University of Victoria campus where explained matter to him.

Cecil had long believed that an eagle's egg was white. His theory ran contrary to the general scientific convention of the day, backed up by the fact most golden eagle eggs in museums had a splotchy or speckled appearance. Dr. Algard's tests confirmed Cecil's belief that the blood seen on the surface of the golden eagle's eggs was indeed from haemorrhage.

By now Cecil knew most of the local newspapers' city desk editors, as well as a number of radio reporters and TV stations. The reporters looked forward to his calls, as Susan's egg laying always added color to the usually drab winter stories and broadcasts. "RARE AS GOLD" read one headline, while another quoted Cecil: "EGGLAYING AN ACT OF LOVE."

The coverage was more sensational than factual, stressing the unusual aspects of the triangular relationship between Susan and the Hyndmans, who had "tried to live with her whims, bizarre love affairs, and ferocity for thirteen years." Susan was described as "the confused golden eagle" with "murder on her mind and love in her heart." The stories mentioned that she resided in "her own gilded bedroom after displacing the Hyndmans." Her egg laying at Featherland was termed as being "in defiance of all natural law."

The holiday season turned out to be a festive occasion, and not only because of Susan's early Christmas presents. Cecil took a much-needed break from preparing the book. He had little choice, as an extremely cold period brought over a foot of snow, and the frigid temperatures forced the Hyndmans to once again bring most of the birds who lived outside or in the outbuildings into Ookpik Cottage.

The "unexpected Christmas guests" included the huge vulture, Pertino. The King of Featherland had a five-foot wingspan and a colorful, if oddly shaped, head. The small, already overcrowded cottage became almost impassable, with only a narrow walkway between the stacked cages. The Hyndmans were forced to sleep in the main room, as the great horned owl Darwin and the gulls occupied their bedroom.

But even the freezing spell could not dampen their festive spirits. At New Year's, they quietly toasted the arrival of 1969. The prospects for the upcoming year looked bright indeed. The publication of *The Grasp*, although it was the biggest financial risk they had taken since purchasing Featherland, did not daunt them. They were convinced the book would sell. Adele made a special toast to Susan, "the Queen of Featherland and the upcoming star in a book about her life."

Despite these high hopes, the new year started poorly. In January, after paying the third instalment of the printing contract, Cecil found out why the local printer's bid had been so low. "Our manuscript was nearly clean, and in correcting the final proofs, the printer made other errors on the final plates."

Meanwhile, other costs kept escalating. Cecil had to hire a graphic artist to touch up some of the photos, pay for the white leatherette covers sent from Guelph, and also pay for the binding of the books. To finance the project, the Hyndmans had taken out a second mortgage on their property. They had set aside the considerable sum of $3000 to cover the production and promotion of the book, but the cost overruns left the budget almost $1000 short.

In March of 1969, 500 copies of *The Grasp* arrived from the printers. After their long struggle overseeing the printing process, the Hyndmans felt more relieved than elated. But they had little time to relax, as the arrival of the book meant more work. Cecil knew that getting favorable reviews was the first and most important step in publicizing *The Grasp*. Once the reviews came in, booksellers would buy the book. The Hyndmans worked almost non-stop, writing letters and mailing out dozens of copies of the book along with a promotional handout.

As the first few orders came in, Cecil and Adele's enthusiasm returned. Adele wrote in a letter to her relatives in the east: "A large bookstore in Vancouver bought fifteen but we haven't received a cheque from them yet. Also the Bay and Eaton's and library here bought books."

The early reviews were not yet in, and Adele's apprehension over the success of the book showed:

At the present moment we are pretty worried financially but we know in the long run the book will sell and bring us a return for many years. As soon as this first edition is sold we will have the second printing underway. We believe we will eventually be in a position to have an American publisher issue it in the States but these things will take better part of a year to do.

As part of their promotional plan, Cecil bought both print and radio ads in Victoria and Vancouver. Often Adele would go into Susan's room when the ads aired over the radio, turning up the volume on the radio outside the room beforehand. "Do you hear that, Sue? The book's all about you."

Finally the first reviews came in. "A golden eagle is the heroine of this unusual compilation, although the two subsidiary characters — the author and his wife — are unusual enough to command considerable attention," said the *Montreal Star*.

Over the years Mr. and Mrs. Hyndman have established an international reputation for their unique work with birds, particularly eagles, for "getting into their brains" to establish an understanding between the feathered creatures and human beings. The Grasp is the record of one of these, whose name is Susan, whose physical aspects are formidable, yet whose nature is compelling as described in the smooth prose of Mr. Hyndman. Susan dominates this thoughtful and beautifully produced volume, which contains some striking photographs.

The *Star* review, by David M. Legate, was typical. Other favorable reviews appeared in newspapers across the country, and on radio stations, including the CBC. Orders began to come in — not only from bookstores but also from a number of universities and libraries, including several in the United States.

On a bright day in May, the first cheque from book sales arrived from Duthie Books in Vancouver. Adele took it in to show Susan.

"It's really hers," she told Cecil.

The golden eagle responded by gently picking the cheque out of Adele's fingers. Susan kept it for a moment, moving her bill up and down, "as if weighing it," Adele said. When Adele asked for the cheque back, Susan returned it to her hand.

"We should use the money for a short holiday," Cecil suggested to Adele.

But she refused to leave Featherland. Her trip to Ottawa and Montreal in 1967 had reinforced her conviction that she would rather spend all her time with her feathered family. So instead they packed a lunch and climbed the slope to picnic in the upper bowl.

The day was perfect, with fluffy white clouds slowly moving across the intensely blue sky. From their scenic vantage point they overlooked distant Victoria and the Pacific. After the climb, they lay back and relaxed in the deep moss, soft as a blanket and multi-colored with tiny wildflowers.

"I still remember that first time we hiked up here," Adele said. "Today feels even better — it's almost as if we're sharing our Eden through the book."

The sunny summer day was the happiest they had experienced for years. After their long struggle to get the book published, the Hyndmans thoroughly enjoyed basking in the warm afterglow of all the praise it received.

Adele unpacked the lunch basket as Cecil uncorked a bottle of wine and poured two glasses.

"I propose a toast." Cecil raised his glass. "To all those publishers, editors, and agents who said the book couldn't be done."

"But we did it." Adele raised her glass.

For the first time in decades, the future looked bright and promising — thanks to one magnificent and remarkable creature.

"To our golden gal, Susan, the Queen of Featherland," Adele toasted.

seventeen

THE GRASP

Late June found Cecil busy making last-minute schedule changes for his upcoming trip east to promote the book. Originally he had booked a rail ticket to Toronto, intending to return to the West Coast by air. His New York agent, Ruth Aley, had interested an American publisher in the possibility of reprinting *The Grasp* and wanted Cecil to fly to New York.

The positive book reviews had indeed created a demand for *The Grasp*, and the Hyndmans were swamped with book orders.

One nonprofessional review pleased Cecil more than all the others. His father, now aged ninety-five, wrote from Ottawa:

I never was so proud of anything in my long life as I was when I read your book The Grasp. *I want to congratulate you on this wonderful achievement. I am very proud of you as I know what the book meant to you under these difficult circumstances. You certainly are entitled to great credit for your courage and pluck in the face of many obstacles.*

The letter moved Cecil. For most of his adult life, Cecil had considered himself the black sheep of the family for not undertaking a professional career path as his parents had wished. As a youngster he had displayed an aptitude for law, yet Cecil never entered law school as his parents had hoped. Nor did he complete his medical studies. For many years Judge Hyndman had supported Featherland. Now his investment was finally paying off.

After stops in Toronto and New York, Cecil traveled to Ottawa at the end of June to see his father. While there he staged a Canada Day promotion, "flying in" a bird from Featherland. He picked up Natoma the goose at the airport and took it to Parliament Hill, where a press photographer took dozens of shots. The wire service photo appeared across Canada.

Although the promotional stunt exhibited the showman side of Cecil, his letter home to Adele showed his philosophical side:

In Ottawa, people by and large are as cold and hard as their steel and concrete jungle disguised as culture. People create an environment in keeping with their nature. Here materialism and status reign supreme. Here smiles are mere grimaces and clothes and grooming are surface graces. Here people live ersatz emotional lives. They zoom about modishly in posh juggernauts and never have time to think anything out. . . . Let's have our birds and their love if we can. I'll have your love and the birds if I can.

After flying back from his exhausting trip, Cecil filled Adele in on the highlights and on his business discussions with the experts in the publishing field. Ruth Aley had introduced him to a number of editors and publishers in New York. Disney had expressed "keen interest" in the book and possible film rights. An eastern TV producer had approached Cecil about obtaining the TV rights to Susan's story.

Adele shared her own good news. The *Winnipeg Free Press* had called, proposing to serialize the book in their weekend magazine. And the local school board had contacted them about making the book part of their recommended reading program, which could result in a huge order of up to 600 copies.

The good times continued through the summer and well into the fall. Sales of the book remained steady and Cecil ferried across to Vancouver to get a quote from a printer for resetting the type and reshooting the photos to improve the quality of *The Grasp*.

In late fall of 1969 Cecil flew east again. He met the son of Alfred Knopf, who expressed interest in putting out a revised edition of *The Grasp*. Although the discussions went well with "the friendly giant" (Knopf stood almost six foot seven), Cecil returned to the West Coast without a contract. But he remained buoyed up by the potential breakthrough; he knew American publishing firms' minimum press runs were at least ten times the number of copies he had self-published.

When Cecil arrived home he was saddened to learn that Darwin, one of the great horned owls, had died. But life went on at Featherland. He wrote to Ruth Aley,

Since my arrival home four more birds, including a crow and towhee, were brought to Featherland for us to try to save them. One is on the road to recovery already.

Today we have been working on the overgrown hoofs of Antonio Sibelius Cavazos, our Mexican donkey. It is tricky, Tony being an artist in the use of teeth and feet, and one can lose some knuckle skin in the course of the job.

You would be amused had you been present with us tonight. There was a vocal hubbub among three little hawks in our bird room. The

cause: A very cute little screech owl sitting on the branch of a tree just outside the window, his big eyes observing with keen interest the little United Nations assembly visible through the pane.

His agent replied in late October, mentioning where she had recently sent the book and the reaction it had received. Once again, publishers were gripped by the story, but found the writing not up to professional standards.

The agent ended her letter by saying that another publisher in California was interested, and a large New York publishing house wanted to read a copy. She also promised to send the book to her London agent.

The hectic year, with all its travel and the stress of getting the book out, caught up to Cecil late that fall. Once again he had thrown himself at a project with an enthusiasm and concentration that exceeded his body's capacity, exhausting his energy reserves — both physical and psychological. He collapsed into bed.

In early November Cecil was still recovering from several bouts of illness when a windstorm struck. The violent gusts lifted parts off the roofs of some of the outbuildings. On the morning of November 5, something large banged against the window. At first Cecil thought a dead tree limb might have fallen. Suddenly the gulls outside let out a collective scream. Alarmed by the nearly hysteric cries, the Hyndmans watched as "a large dark form burst across" their view, "skimming the netting not more than a few feet from the window." The form disappeared as quickly as it had appeared.

"Bald eagle!" they both shouted excitedly as they raced toward the window.

"The words were hardly out of our mouths when the storm-driven form appeared again, swooping at high speed to hit the net with such force to partially break through. The huge wings were flailing away," Cecil wrote in his journal.

Adele rushed out through the door in her blouse and slippers, while Cecil, undressed, struggled "like a Keystone Cop to pull my pants on." He was still weak from his long illness and barely awake.

By the time he reached the door he had his pants on, but he had forgotten his shoes. He was startled to see that Adele, who wore no protective clothing or gloves, had caught the invader's taloned feet with her bare hands.

"Cec, it's a young golden eagle," she called excitedly. "It can't be, but it is."

Upon Cecil's arrival the bird of prey began to struggle. For a brief moment Cecil stood frozen to the spot. While his eyes took in all the obvious identifying marks of a juvenile golden eagle, his mind refused to accept the possibility. A cross outburst from Adele finally made him react.

He rushed back inside and, "panicking around . . . found gloves and in bare feet, got them out to her as she pinned the wings and got the beauty in her arms." Now fully awake, Cecil yelled at Adele to "get inside with him before you catch cold." He threw a coat over her shoulders and held the door open for her.

Adele walked inside and managed to hold the eagle firmly while Cecil scrambled to find his camera, then load it. Cecil later wrote,

How Adele does these things is almost beyond belief. But that fiery invader fell under the potent spell Adele casts and simply relaxed in her arms like a contented baby.

As Adele sang and gently talked to the youngster, Cecil took photos. Within minutes, the newcomer calmed enough for Adele to feed it beef from her fingers.

The golden eagle stayed quietly in her lap until Cecil arranged quarters in an outbuilding. All this time, "Susan sung away in her room, quite unaware of the whole happening."

After setting up temporary quarters for the golden eagle in Talon Hall, the Hyndmans excitedly discussed the extraordinary event. Cecil had not yet handled the eagle; Adele commented that "it must have been starving, it weighed no more than a bag of feathers. Only a starving eagle would have persisted in attacking the gulls through netting."

Adele voiced her concern that the poor condition of the eagle could be the result of some illness. From its juvenile plumage, Cecil was sure the eagle had been hatched earlier that year. An immature eagle, not knowing any better, could have tried soaring in the gale and been swept across the strait by the winds coming from the direction of the mainland.

"What a Christmas present," Adele sighed. She went on to express what Cecil was afraid to even hope — that this newcomer might accept him. Although he had never lost any of his affection for Susan, it still pained him every night when Adele slipped into Susan's room for her nightly visit while he had to stay outside.

Over the next few weeks the Hyndmans continued to monitor the immature eagle's health. Cecil was delighted to discover it was a female. He named it Kluane II, after the male golden eagle in whose company he had spent so many hours writing many years earlier.

Two events saddened the holiday season that December at Featherland. Early in the month, Sheba the Queen, a red-tailed hawk who had been with them since 1957, passed away. Then, just two days before Christmas, Doctor Archibald — Archie the South American caiman — died.

The Hyndmans quietly celebrated the arrival of 1970. They had reason to be cautiously optimistic about the year. The success of their self-published book had confounded their detractors; the revenue from sales had already repaid almost all of their costs. Now the publication of Susan's story promised to open other doors.

A reprinting of *The Grasp* looked almost certain, as well as a serialization in a national magazine. The provincial education department was still interested in making the book part of the recommended reading program. Cecil had already started on a complete rewrite of *The Grasp*, based on the suggestions offered by his New York agent. And while he continued to explore the various publishing avenues open to him, he started carefully preparing for the next step in building Featherland's reputation: obtaining recognition for their work in the scientific community.

Early in January, Adele became very worried about Susan after a photography session with her. Carefully, Adele had coaxed her into position with her bill pointed at *The Grasp* and her taloned foot beside the book. The photo pleased Adele, but Susan's behavior caused her concern; the Queen seemed listless.

Susan had not produced an egg in over a year, for the first time since 1964. The Hyndmans were not overly concerned; if anything, they were relieved, as on more than one occasion she had seemed in distress before and after laying.

There certainly was no sign from Susan that her affection for Adele had slackened. Her hostility toward Cecil remained, as she made perfectly obvious with her aggressive stance every time she spied him.

On Wednesday, January 7, Susan rejected food and seemed very quiet. Adele tended to her off and on most of the day. By Thursday morning her condition had worsened. By 5:00 p.m. her wings drooped, and when Adele fed her, she promptly threw up her food.

On the following Saturday, January 10, Susan laid her fifteenth egg at 8:30 p.m. Cecil recorded it as "immaculate bluish white except for one very tiny blood streak near large end. . . . The egg weighed just under four ounces."

Adele massaged Susan's abdomen with lotion, and this action seemed to ease her discomfort somewhat. She began to move without pain. Clearly, Susan's egg laying was both a blessing and a curse. While the feat was remarkable, there was no doubt Susan suffered during egg laying. And her difficulty was becoming progressively worse as the size and weight of the eggs increased.

Cecil informed the press of Susan's latest accomplishment. She slowly recovered from her ordeal, helped by Adele's massage therapy.

The rest of January sped by, with Cecil struggling to rewrite and update the book about Susan. He also worked on his scientific paper and recorded words from Shadow the raven. And in the evenings, Cecil always found time to visit Kluane II. The visits did more than energize Cecil. He could sense a bond slowly developing between them. He wrote in his journal, "I wonder if Kluane II will accept me and fill the void left by Susan's stinging rejection so many years ago. Only time will tell how far our relationship will progress."

Sunday, February 1, 1970, was a day the Hyndmans never forgot. At 8:00 p.m. Adele followed her usual routine of feeding the various birds in their separate rooms in Talon Hall. She fed the female great horned owl Talon at about 8:10 p.m.

Cecil joined Adele twenty minutes later, and as they walked down the centre of Talon Hall, Adele caught sight of a steaming, warm egg in full view on the floor of Talon's enclosure.

"It can't be," she said.

For a moment, both Hyndmans were so stunned neither moved. Finally Cecil stepped forward for a better look. Talon's wings spread aggressively at his approach. But the owl made no objection to Adele entering her room and taking the egg.

When they later sat and talked about the astonishing event, they berated themselves. The signs had been there for some time but they simply had not recognized them. Over the past few years, Talon had indicated she favored Adele. About two weeks before laying her egg, Talon had shown definite signs of hostility toward Cecil.

"On the day of the lay," he wrote, "she developed an almost frantic interest in Adele. Her outbursts of vocalizing were remarkable, especially as her voice changed. She made three quick sounds before the usual sequence."

Cecil vowed that they would not be caught off guard again. He kept a close eye on Talon over the next few days, since an owl's normal clutch can contain up to three eggs. Cecil described the preparations:

Adele built Talon a nest of straw and twigs on the floor. Talon pulled fluff from her chest and dropped the soft down in the nest. She continued to welcome Adele excitedly. She flew into a rage at my appearance so I stayed out of her room. Vocally she nearly boomed herself breathless.

On Thursday, February 5, their long vigil was rewarded. Talon laid a second egg at 4:00 p.m., then sat on it in the nest for several hours. Adele photographed her there. But Talon rejected and destroyed a chicken egg the Hyndmans put in her nest as an experiment.

Later, Adele brought Cecil the second egg to weigh. It was "a shade over two ounces, equivalent to a large poultry egg. The off-white shell had a high sheen splattered with haemorrhaged blood."

Cecil wrote a news release, and used it in a number of letters:

Talon's egg laying is a virtual sequel to Susan's. Talon was hand-reared here from the baby fluff stage, [and] has lived happily ever since in her own room in Talon Hall, named after her years ago.

Like Susan, Talon has never seen another of her own species — or any owl for that matter — and has known only human association.

Talon's relationship with Adele is roughly similar to Adele's relationship with Susan. Susan laid in her tenth year and Talon in her ninth. I am quite safe in saying that no one else in North America has a collection of golden eagle eggs and great horned owl eggs laid by their own birds on their own premises.

The significance of the event as a sequel to Susan, and one of extreme rarity, lies not in the mere fact of a great horned owl laying eggs. Needless to say, owls do so in a wild state and with a mate of their own kind. It is the fact Talon, being hand-reared like Susan, attached herself to Adele. Such a bird must be healthy and very happy to lay at all. Laying requires a very forceful stimulus — in this case a human one — to bring about an active ovary. I know of no other great horned owl who laid under such conditions.

Although he never admitted it in his journal, Cecil was falling in love. His passion rose as spring gave way to heat of summer, his favorite season. He felt young again, full of vitality and energy only the young possess. He began to secretly stay out late with his lover. Despite being a night owl, he often snuck out of the cottage before sunrise to be with her.

Adele knew all about Cecil's midnight and early morning rendezvous with the young female. She did not mind, and even encouraged, the relationship. After all, she too was in love with a golden eagle and knew exactly how Cecil felt about Kluane II.

Although it had been ten years since Susan had rejected him, Cecil had never lost any of his affection for her. He joked that

Sue's a heart-breaker; she used to love me, then turned around and tried to kill me. Next she kicked me out of my own bedroom, stole

my wife from me, and took up with her. But I've never blamed her and she's still the great love of my life — besides Adele.

Although Kluane II often displayed a belligerent attitude toward him, Cecil accepted this as part of the eagle's youthful zest for life. He always encouraged ego in birds, as he felt it was vital for their well-being.

"Life was full, life was good," Cecil wrote about this happy period at Featherland.

Cecil often described the late 1960s to mid-1970s as "Featherland's golden period." While remaining focused on Susan and the other birds, in the summer of 1970 Cecil finally started preparations for the scientific paper he proposed to write. To document his findings, he bought a new camera and enlarger, and invested in a new microscope.

Cecil also bought his first cassette tape recorder. Up to 1970 he had used a variety of reel-to-reel machines. While all produced professional-quality sound, they were extremely clumsy and meant as studio recorders. Cecil could carry the smaller portable recorder anywhere, including Talon Hall. This motivated him to continue work on his series of cassettes of talking birds and bird sounds.

He also continued working on inventions, coming up with an idea for a relief printing process he called Signaface, which he later patented. Part of each day was also taken up with teaching various birds to speak. The Hyndmans also continued their mallard sexing study, raising eight mallards that year.

That summer the Hyndmans celebrated their twenty-fifth wedding anniversary on June 25. On the same day, Cecil spoke to the American publishers about his revised version of *The Grasp*. In July Cecil and Adele visited the Gull Islands three times to collect cormorant, gull, and black oystercatcher eggs. Their final collecting trip took place on August 10, when they returned for more gull eggs; only three had survived from their earlier trips.

But no matter how busy their schedule, they prided themselves on never turning away an injured bird. Most of the year, some five to ten injured birds could be found recovering in their cottage — often triple that number during the summer nesting season.

November brought "black sky and gusts," Cecil noted in his journal as he awaited a response from the U.S. publisher. The approach of the bleak and blustery winter conditions affected Cecil, who shared with his birds a dislike for winter. He had seen too many of his feathered family die during winter. And his misgivings proved well founded; below-freezing temperatures came early that November.

The loss of sunlight also seemed to affect Susan, who was now sixteen. Although some captive golden eagles had lived over twenty years, there was little scientific knowledge about their average life-span. But there was no denying Susan, like the Hyndmans, was entering the last phase of her life.

Over her years at Featherland, she had often displayed a loss of appetite in winter. "Sue's been off her food for the better part of a month now," Cecil recorded in his journal when this behavior persisted. "Adele's worried, although she managed to induce her to eat oolicans and some strips of beef."

Cecil's mood slowly darkened to match the shortening days as Susan's lethargy continued. When she began to lose weight, the Hyndmans started treating her with antibiotics administered twice daily. Adele carefully monitored Susan's condition, visiting her room every few hours.

The bleak weather also brought a series of further setbacks. The Winnipeg *Free Press Weekly* magazine decided against serializing

The Grasp

The Grasp. Jerry Fairbanks' Hollywood company sent an associate to visit Featherland, but the obstacles involved in restaging Susan's life story as a film — either fictional or documentary — proved overwhelming. The University of British Columbia science journal rejected Cecil's scientific paper on the shell pigmentation of golden eagle eggs.

Ruth Aley forwarded another rejection letter from a publisher. Where only a year ago the prospects of an American publishing house reprinting *The Grasp* had looked promising, Aley admitted she had exhausted her contacts. The revised draft of *The Grasp* was now in the hands of the last publisher on her list.

The worst blow came from an unexpected source close to home. The provincial department of education, which had recommended *The Grasp* be placed on the recommended reading list for B.C. schools, had negotiated with Cecil a special price for the book. At stake was a huge order, as many as 600 copies — more than the initial print run. That winter, without warning or explanation, the recommendation was canceled. The reversal stunned the Hyndmans, especially as they had already discussed the reprint with local printers.

Cecil and Adele visited the superintendent of education. It turned out that he "had not bothered to read the book," and when he did, he "promptly blew a fuse . . . and ordered cancellation of the recommendation." Cecil wrote:

> When pressed, he admitted that the new appraisal was based solely on disagreements with our views and not, as pretended, on the quality of the book. He said I represented a point of view repugnant to traditional religious dogma.

Cecil suspected the superintendent might also have become anxious after hearing Cecil's pro-evolutionary views on a radio program. It was only a few days after he had appeared as a guest on a local radio show that the letter reversing the rating of the book arrived. On the three-hour radio program, Cecil had held out his view that "forms of life have a common root or origin — each is genetically related to every other — however removed." He maintained, "There is no impediment to the possession in common of specific faculties of brain. The very fact of evolution makes my premise perfectly consistent."

The Hyndmans moved up the bureaucratic ladder, contacting the deputy minister. The administrators involved in the earlier decision found themselves in an uncomfortable position. One admitted to Cecil he feared being fired. Cecil knew he had the education department officials in a bind. Even if they rationalized their decision to cover what Cecil termed the "unspoken religious influence within the education system," they could not excuse "their practice of passing judgment on books to be recommended for school without reading more than a fraction of the book." Clearly, this constituted "dereliction of duty."

Finally they contacted the minister of education. He eventually sent the Hyndmans a reevaluated book review, which read in part:

[The Grasp] *is the story, with photographic illustrations, of the experiences and observations of the author and his wife with a captive golden eagle. Reviews have noted the novelty of the topic and the sincerity and careful observations of the author. A few minor printing errors and some aspects of the treatment of the theme have been the subject of some criticism. The account may have considerable interest for pupils of junior and senior secondary school levels.*

Cecil checked with his local school district superintendent, who confirmed the review was "sent to all superintendents, principals, and teachers in the province," and assured him, "this is probably the best circulation that can be given to support any publication. I really expect you will be hearing directly from various districts."

The Grasp was thus reinstated, but on the lower "general book list" instead of the higher "recommended listing." Cecil wrote bitterly in his journal:

> *[one] narrow-minded man, rather than go against his religious views, sacrificed my financial interests, my prestige, my competence as a writer in an attempt to make it appear the removal of* The Grasp *from the recommended listing was on the basis of writing and the caliber of the book — when in fact it was based solely on opposition to views I expressed.*

As Christmas approached, Susan slowly regained her strength, but the slow pace of her recovery worried Adele. Finally Susan began to vocalize, a promising sign that not only her health, but her spirit, was back to normal.

Susan's "voice" also figured prominently in three promising commercial ventures the Hyndmans embarked on that December. For years Cecil had been producing tapes of his birds, but although he had sold some of them privately, no company or audio producer had ever tried to market them commercially — until a radio producer at a Vancouver station expressed interest.

The Vancouver producer was so intrigued by the tapes of unusual bird sounds, including Susan's love song, that he asked Cecil what he would want for eighty of them, one minute long each. Instead of accepting the offer, Cecil proposed to do "two or three scripted productions gratis for him to test on the air and then finances could be taken up."

After preparing the pilot tapes, Cecil returned. The producer now asked Cecil for a quote on producing 250 of them to sell to other stations. The money involved was considerable — plus the potential sales to the public.

When the Vancouver radio station suddenly withdrew its offer in the fall, Cecil approached a production manager at a Victoria radio station. After a lengthy meeting, the producer decided to take the next step. In mid-December they recorded two pilot productions in an audio studio. After these audio productions were packaged, the producer planned to offer the series to various radio networks.

Jerry Fairbanks, the Hollywood producer, had also expressed an interest in Cecil's audio tapes. Cecil obliged by mailing him some samples. His accompanying letter explained:

> Over the years, I've recorded: speech from three gulls, the rather extraordinary attempt at a full sentence by Fuey the goose, and the vocalizing of a hand-reared black oystercatcher called Beeper; reflecting every conceivable mood from elation, alarm, desire for attention, hunger, contentment, and even the misery of illness.

Cecil described his previous audio productions: *Quiz Kids of Featherland*, "featuring mynas and other talking birds"; *They Speak for Themselves*, which incorporated a number of productions; *The Night of the Owls*, featuring five different owls, a snoring cormorant, and Goliath the raven, "who made a language out of one word 'hello,'" and, when Cecil had hay fever one year and "sneezed like hell, he picked up the *'achoo'*"; *Owl Serenade*, featuring "three little screech owls . . . found in a nest at Featherland"; *Music from the Treetops*, which sounded "as though you were out on a field on a summer day, lying on the grass listening to pheasant and quail, ravens overhead and robins — as well as little song sparrows"; and *The Shadow Knows*, featuring the raven Shadow, who had an amazing ability to speak but "wouldn't permit recording in his presence," forcing Cecil "to secretly record him from a window outside, . . . usually between 2:00 and 4:00 a.m."

Cecil told Fairbanks how he had produced some forty or fifty cassettes, mostly from reel-to-reel recordings. He had "310 reels of this stuff, mostly 1000-foot reels, stored outside in outbuildings."

Unfortunately, while both the Victoria-based radio producer and Fairbanks wrestled with the problem of how to use these unique recordings commercially, neither could find a solution to justify the time and money needed to mass-produce and market the tapes.

Although disappointed by this setback, Cecil continued to record bird sounds as part of his research, concentrating that winter on Talon.

Of all his recordings, Cecil was proudest of the "Song of Susan," the highlight of his cassette *They Speak for Themselves*. He wrote of it:

> *There's never been another recording of that song in the world. And you'll never hear it again as it's a love song for a mate. In the wild you couldn't get close enough to hear the song — even if they did sing it. It took me two years to put the "Song of Susan" together. At the end of it, her voice rises and rises, like an eagle itself soaring high up into the sky.*

Christmas came early that December as Talon showed signs that she was about to lay again. Adele prepared a nest for the owl while Cecil recorded her "peculiar vocalizing, with her succession of notes markedly different." On December 15, 1970, at 4:00 p.m., Talon laid. Three days later she laid the second egg of the clutch, and proceeded to sit on both.

As he had done with most of Susan's eggs, Cecil drained Talon's two eggs. The Hyndmans ate them, scrambled. Cecil reported that "they tasted mild and palatable — much like poultry eggs. The yolks were normal but smaller than in hens and pale, appearing close to faded lemon color instead of orange."

The year 1971 brought heavy snow in early January, coating Featherland in white. Cecil captured the scene with photographs, commenting how "Featherland had been transformed into a fairy wonderland setting, the trees coated with what resembles thick white icing."

The fairylike appearance was not without cost, however. A series of deaths saddened Featherland during the cold period. On January 12, the parakeet, Blossom, died in his sleep of old age. The "superb little song and dance man" had been at Featherland twenty-four years.

Cecil developed a sinus inflammation, which was becoming an almost yearly event. He went to see a specialist, who put him on antibiotics. To aid his recovery, he rested, spending his time answering a request from an eastern magazine planning to publish an article on Susan. The editor wanted Cecil to clarify the sleeping arrangements — where did all the seagulls that occupied their bedroom sleep at night? The editor also asked for a description of their cottage and Featherland. He answered the specific question thus:

Our hand-reared [gulls] have been accustomed all their lives to coming into our bedroom on name late at night and being lifted into their own individual carton beds. None make any sound until they go out again late the following morning.

After the article appeared, Cecil wrote his New York agent, hoping news of the latest publicity about Featherland could help get a U.S. publisher for his book.

In her reply, Ruth reminded Cecil she had now contacted all of the New York publishing houses, and all but one publisher had rejected the revised manuscript of *The Grasp*.

"What will we do if they say 'no'?" Adele asked Cecil when shown the agent's letter.

"Unless this publisher expresses interest, I don't think we should reprint the book ourselves," Cecil told his wife.

"So this publisher is our last chance?"

The Grasp

"Looks that way."

After months of waiting, a letter arrived from the managing editor of the last American publishing house that had expressed interest in *The Grasp*. The letter opened encouragingly, but the final paragraphs delivered the bad news: "I regret, however, that we are not in a position to publish the revised edition of *The Grasp*."

The rejection shook Cecil's confidence. He confessed his frustrations in his journal:

I feel I've been the object of the old lift-him-up, knock-him-down routine. One reviewer makes reference to The Grasp's *"smooth prose." Then a publisher rejects it due to my non-professional writing. Next my literary agent states "the whole story is so unusual and impressive." How my book can be this sort of thing and pitifully poor writing at the same time is mystifying — but so goes literary lingo.*

What am I to think? I know that The Grasp *is a published book in Canada, not doing too badly. Dammit, if my book draws interest, appeals in some ways and sells, I don't care if it is "a distinguished literary work" — whatever that is — or not. Could it be that I'm still a very infantile innocent abroad in the world of bookish letters?*

eighteen

TWILIGHT YEARS

Adele encouraged Cecil to move on to his next challenge: proving that he was a legitimate researcher and not just an eccentric with a golden eagle living in his bedroom. This was a first step in an ambitious, long-term plan to build on Darwin's work to establish that birds and man shared certain faculties. Even a scientist with higher degrees in ornithology would have trouble proving such a bold and provocative theory. Cecil, who had not even finished university, rated his chances at "slim to none."

His years of studying mallards and developing a sexing method had not brought him any recognition. Nor had his decades of research into hand-rearing seabirds. Never had he received any research grants. But Cecil was determined to change all that. To accomplish this, he desperately needed Susan's co-operation.

In late February, Susan began to exhibit behavior that often preceded her laying an egg. Although she had laid one in late February in 1967, the majority of her eggs had been laid earlier in the winter. Adele began to check on Susan more often, especially as Cecil needed outside confirmation of details he had written in his scientific paper. Although no one had ever lived in more intimate closeness to golden eagles than the Hyndmans, Cecil realized this meant nothing to professional science journals, which demanded independent and qualified scientific verification.

On April 5, 1971, Susan provided the necessary proof by laying her sixteenth egg while Adele looked on. Susan became very excited afterward, racing around her room. Adele retrieved the egg only seconds after it was laid, while Cecil anxiously waited just out of Susan's sight so not to cause her stress.

Adele's fingers and hand were stained red from handling the egg. When she passed it to Cecil, blood from the egg ended up on Cecil's thumb and forefinger. While Adele saw to Susan, who appeared quite healthy after the delivery, Cecil checked the egg. If he could separate the red blood on it from the wet mucous coating, he might have the proof he so desperately needed to validate his theory: that haemorrhaged whole blood was the substance on golden eagles' eggs.

Cecil immediately called his contact, pathologist Dr. George Anderson at the Royal Jubilee Hospital. After taking the sample to the hospital, Dr. Anderson confirmed under a microscope the presence of blood. Cecil had his proof.

The egg itself was weighed and measured — it was as large as the previous record-breaking one.

A delighted Cecil excitedly phoned CKDA news, the provincial game branch, and a number of scientists at the University of Victoria, who congratulated him.

A second egg had seemed likely, but ultimately did not appear. Susan regained her appetite, and her right foot, which sometimes stiffened as the result of laying, cleared up. She was soon "flying and her old vigorous self again."

This was the second time in two years that Susan had laid a single egg and not her normal clutch of two. Cecil and Adele were concerned about the effect egg laying had on Susan's aging body. She was now over sixteen years old. As there was no definite knowledge about how long female golden eagles continued to lay eggs, the Hyndmans were entering uncharted territory.

That summer an unusually high number of abandoned and injured birds were brought to Featherland, and several writers and producers visited the avian sanctuary, following up on Susan's story after the publication of *The Grasp*. Many of the buildings at Featherland badly needed painting, as well as maintenance work that could only be done during the summer.

Cecil grew frustrated as the hectic summer left him little time to complete his scientific paper on Susan's eggs. Finally he secluded himself in an outbuilding and informed Adele to tell anyone phoning that he was unavailable. It took until July, but at last he completed the research paper and mailed it off.

Only a week later, a brush fire erupted on the neighboring property that had once belonged to the Hyndmans. Fearing the blaze might spread to their outbuildings, they helped put out the fire. Inhaling the smoke did not help Cecil's breathing problems.

Perhaps it was the smoke, but Cecil was not the only one to experience breathing difficulties. Adele became worried about Susan, whose voice became quite "husky, with the loss of highs." Like Cecil, Susan had always been susceptible to sinus problems.

Given her past medical problems, the Hyndmans took Susan's difficulty seriously. The golden eagle was immediately put on antibiotics, and in addition to her nightly visits, Adele often stopped by during the day to monitor Susan's condition. Very quickly Susan's voice showed signs of improvement, but other indicators of her health were not as encouraging.

In late September, the Hyndmans were awakened by a violent crashing noise around 2:00 a.m. The loud thumping seemed to be coming from inside the cottage.

"It's Susan," Adele cried.

She jumped out of bed without any clothes on. Fearing the worst, Adele quickly ran into Susan's room to find the eagle crashing into the walls. Despite Adele's attempts to calm her, Susan continued her panicked flight, crashing around her room and flying with force against the door — as if trying to escape.

Although Susan made no attempt to attack, Adele was forced to duck time and again to avoid Susan's wings whipping the air in "a frenzy of fear," as Cecil later wrote. Something had clearly terrified Susan. Adele had never seen her so agitated, and she worried that Susan would injure herself by flying against the wall.

Finally Susan's outburst subsided as unexpectedly as it had begun. When the golden eagle landed and tucked in her wings, Adele cautiously approached Susan, noting she still had her hackle feathers raised. In her soft, singsong voice, Adele managed to calm her. The feathers relaxed and Adele could feel the tension leave Susan's body as she gently stroked her. She remained in the room for some time, until she was sure Susan had totally recovered from whatever had caused the panic attack.

Cecil anxiously waited outside in the Plume Room. When Adele finally left Susan's room, she could offer no explanation for Susan's bizarre behavior. Cecil checked outside and found no sign of any obvious cause. Later, the Hyndmans learned that tremors from an earthquake had occurred at that moment. They assumed Susan was sensitive to the vibrations.

Although Susan fully recovered from the earthquake experience within a day, she showed no signs of a full recovery from her sinus problems. The Hyndmans could do nothing but wait until the course of antibiotics was over.

Susan was not the only bird of prey the Hyndmans had trouble with that month. They faced the combined wrath of the golden eagle Kluane II and the great horned owl Talon. The areas of roof over both of their rooms in Talon Hall needed repairs. Earlier in the summer Cecil and Adele had started the job, then postponed it as both Kluane II and Talon had become very disturbed at the hammering above them. With the autumn rains and winds approaching, they could not put off the necessary repairs any longer.

During the roofing repairs, Talon became so distressed that she somehow managed to squeeze out between the bars. The great horned owl flew free in Talon Hall "until evening feeding time when Dell caught her in the bald eagle Lightning's pen and returned her in her coat to her own room. Then she put up wire mesh over the bars," Cecil tersely noted in his journal, understating the drama of a slight woman intervening between these two great birds, mortal enemies in the wild.

Kluane II rebounded from the roofing ordeal quite quickly. Cecil noted in his journal:

she gently took my ear in her bill and, after my kissing her in the face, she bent down and gently held the end of my nose in her bill. Her eyelashes were less than two inches from mine. Her amber eyes staring directly into mine. Two weeks ago she held my ear in her bill. A phenomenal demonstration of two-way affection.

While Cecil was experiencing these encouraging signs from Kluane II, Adele's concern for Susan's health deepened. Susan showed no definite improvement in her thickening voice from the antibiotics. The Hyndmans discussed Susan's condition and decided to try another antibiotic.

October arrived and Adele was alarmed to find lumps on Sue's jaws.

"After all my sinus trouble, I know how she feels," said Cecil sympathetically.

Adele worried the eagle might have tumors, but Cecil assured her, "It's likely just a swollen sinus." Nonetheless, Adele's question worried him; tumors had accounted for the most deaths at Featherland over the years.

On Monday, October 11, the Hyndmans were scheduled to begin Susan's new treatment. That day Cecil received news that his father had died. The death was not entirely unexpected, as Judge Hyndman was ninety-seven and had been in poor health and confined to his house in Ottawa for some years. But no amount of mental preparation could ease the blow.

Distressed as he was over his father's death, Cecil had little time to mourn as Kluane II became ill. On the 23rd of that month, Cecil wrote in his journal: "Now Kluane II has developed a swelling on her jaw. Started antibiotics to reduce swelling under right jaw."

By late October neither Cecil nor Adele was sleeping well. They both had good reason to be concerned. On the 24th Cecil noted, "Despite two courses of antibiotics over a month, Susan still has voice trouble. Now will start new type of antibiotic twice daily."

The Hyndmans grew so anxious and tense that neither spoke more than a few words to the other. They were both afraid to express their deepest fear — that the two golden eagles had the same infection. Susan's infection seemed untreatable, and while she was not critically ill, she had lost her appetite and her energy. If her physical deterioration continued at this rate, she would not survive the winter.

The prospect of losing both these beloved eagles, within weeks of his father's death, disturbed Cecil to the point where he found sleeping next to impossible. Each night he would stroll out back and up the slope, hoping the physical exertion of the climb would tire him. Contributing to his worry was his lack of knowledge. When Susan had nearly died many years ago, he had been able to examine her. That option no longer existed.

As the days, then weeks, slipped by, neither eagle improved. On November 13, Cecil wrote, "Kluane II's swelling is now such that there is no feathering over the area."

Nor was Susan much better. Her eyes had now become swollen, and were obviously very painful. Adele's usually pleasant disposition hardened into an edginess that became close to explosive. She worried that the spreading infection might blind the Queen of Featherland. After consulting an eye, nose, and throat specialist for medical advice, the Hyndmans decided to try a sulfa preparation.

Adele began applying the medicine to Susan's eyes. But over the course of a week, Susan showed no improvement. By now her eyes were almost swollen shut.

"Sue'll soon be better," Adele surprised Cecil by announcing on November 29.

"When I last looked through the grille, her eyes were still swollen," Cecil sounded skeptical.

Adele explained that her prediction was not based on any physical sign. Instead, she described to Cecil an eerie experience she had while walking out back. The familiar sound of an eagle's wing froze her in midstep. She not only recognized the sound immediately, but realized the eagle could not be far above her head.

"I looked up after hearing this swishing sound above and saw a mature bald eagle swooping low, as if paying Featherland a visit." After gliding silently, its white head inspecting her, the bald eagle had resumed its flight across Featherland.

Within days of Adele's prediction, Susan's eyes responded to the new combination of medications. The swelling eased and her voice improved slightly. In a startling coincidence, Kluane II's swollen glands also began to recede.

Within a week, both Susan and Kluane II improved so dramatically they were "taken off the 'danger list,'" although Kluane II still had some puffiness around her bill and eye.

Cecil celebrated the recovery by making his annual pilgrimage up Burble Creek, which was burbling for the first time that season. This habit had begun back in the late 1940s after the Hyndmans had hauled rock to construct waterfalls and pools, then moved ferns and trees alongside the creek to provide a scenic backdrop. Over the years, nature had taken over. Tiny saplings they had planted had grown into trees, their limbs crisscrossing the creek. The sword ferns grew to such a size many visitors considered them the largest in all of Victoria. The tips of the fronds dipped gracefully into the water like "curved, green lace."

Silt carried by the creek and moss carpeting the sides of the pools covered all signs of human hands. Most visitors commented on the natural beauty of Burble Creek, with its rocky waterfalls and swirling ponds; Cecil did not have the heart to tell them that most of the more scenic parts were carefully constructed.

Long after the need to repair the ponds or rebuild the waterfalls had passed, Cecil continued his winter trips. Usually he undertook the hikes by himself, pausing to listen to a winter wren song over the sound of rushing water. It took some years before he realized what drew him back each winter: the flow of the winter creek invigorated him, as if he renewed himself by breathing in the mist rising from the water. He called it his "winter baptism."

That evening, Cecil returned to the cottage exhausted but looking forward to his first good night's sleep in what seemed like months. Before heading to bed, he offered the starling Lingo a piece of grape and was pleased to hear him answer the offer by saying, loudly and excitedly, "here."

Adele's flushed appearance as she entered the bedroom told Cecil right away that something had happened. She excitedly informed him Talon had celebrated December's arrival "by beginning to sing the same three-single-note sequence she sang earlier in the year at the time of her lay."

They went out to see the great horned owl in Talon Hall. Cecil was not welcome in Talon's room, so he stayed outside while Adele induced her to sing.

After spending some time listening to her singing, he decided to drop in to see how Kluane II was doing. He was overjoyed when she took his ear in her bill "with the gentleness of silk." He noted she had shed one of her flight feathers, which measured 20.5 inches long.

Sleep should have come quickly to Cecil that night. Both golden eagles were now out of danger. Talon's behavior suggested she was about to lay. Yet instead of falling sleep, Cecil found himself tossing and turning. The cause of his insomnia was Susan. After Kluane II arrived, he had thought he might get over "the second great love of his life." But her recent illness had revealed to Cecil just how much she meant to him. Even the thought of her passing had devastated him. He wrote:

> *Susan had been in our home for over sixteen years. Like all our birds, we treated her as a feathered personality. Our approach was — we belong to them as much as they belong to us. To lose her would be like losing everything.*

Although Susan's voice returned to normal as the swelling receded, it took her body much longer to fully recover. The two-month illness had put an enormous strain on her aging body, so much so that she laid no eggs the following year. Since laying her first clutch in November of 1964, she had averaged two eggs a year.

The Hyndmans were generally pleased that Susan wasn't laying, since she had shown signs of distress over her last few eggs. Adele often told Cecil she hoped Susan would never lay again. Certainly she did not need to add to her remarkable accomplishment of laying seventeen eggs in captivity. Adele worried whether Susan's aging body could take the continued stress of laying eggs each year. Talon, as if making up for Susan's inactivity, laid one egg in March and a clutch of two eggs in November of 1972.

The summer of 1972 a copy of the American ornithological science journal *The Condor,* arrived at Featherland. Inside appeared Adele and Cecil Hyndman's scientific paper "The Shell Pigment of Golden Eagle Eggs." Seeing the article in print in many ways made Cecil even prouder than the publication of *The Grasp.*

When he had first broached the subject with Adele over four years ago, Cecil warned that they faced an almost insurmountable obstacle: a long-standing scientific belief that had remained unchallenged for so long it seemed set in stone. "The ornithological fraternity was extraordinarily insistent that the shell pigmentation in the golden eagle was from glandular sources," complained Cecil. Respected authorities like the *New Dictionary of Birds* said that "the colors of egg shells are due to two main pigments — red-brown and blue-green, which are responsible for the entire range of hues." Even Audubon had referred to the coloration of eggs as coming from pigment glands.

The Hyndmans had positive proof to the contrary. Close study of Susan's newly laid eggs had revealed that in fact "the coloration of the eggs of the golden eagle is dried blood proper from haemorrhaged blood vessels in the oviduct and vent." But challenging the widely held theory was doubly difficult for Cecil and Adele. Their claims were refuted by some of the most respected bird experts. Without any advanced degrees, government research grants, or scientific recognition, they simply had no credibility. Yet they knew that few ornithologists were in the position to observe the process of egg laying as closely as they had. Certainly few — if any — others had experienced receiving a golden eagle's egg in their hands.

When Cecil had first submitted a report on his and Adele's research to several Canadian scientific journals, it was rejected by them all. So he rewrote the paper and submitted it in 1970 to *The Condor*, which was edited by the Smithsonian Institution in Washington, D.C.

Cecil's reputation again defeated him. The prestigious American publication advised him on April 5, 1971:

Two external advisers have reviewed your enclosed manuscript on the pigments of golden eagle eggs. Neither one is convinced that you have made a sufficiently strong case that the normal pigmentation is simply blood. I do not believe we should publish your paper unless you can satisfy the questions raised.

Cecil wasted no time in replying:

On the day your letter was mailed to me, rejecting our paper, Susan laid her sixteenth egg at 6:30 p.m. in our home. We observed blood and a swab of the colored matter was collected. The egg and the swab were taken to the Royal Jubilee Hospital pathology lab where microscopic examinations were carried out. The director of the pathology lab agreed the coloration was blood — with red corpuscles. This can only come from ruptured blood vessels, not from the secretion of pigment glands.

This time the paper was accepted, edited for length, and finally published in the summer of 1972. At last Cecil had the scientific

recognition he had so long wanted! Letters of congratulation poured in from university biology departments around the world. Other research facilities in Alaska, New Mexico, West Germany, Portugal, and England wrote to request reprints and information.

Over the next year, Cecil could barely keep up with answering the ever-growing piles of correspondence resulting from the publication of his article. He had had no idea the amount of interest that his paper would generate. He personally answered every one of the dozens and dozens of letters he received, often typing out four-page responses.

Cecil's one great regret was that his father did not live to see this triumph. Judge Hyndman's illustrious law career had rocketed after a high-profile murder defence case built around his own studies into the make-up of blood. Cecil recalled how his father had been asked to defend an immigrant farm worker charged with the horrific axe murders of the whole family he worked for near Red Deer:

The defendant was found covered in blood and so was the axe. The case against him was so convincing no lawyer would take the case. As Dad had very little business in his law office in Alberta, he had nothing to lose and took the case.

Dad researched blood and found, at that time, you couldn't tell the difference between the blood of a pig and that of a human. He argued the blood found on his client could be from a pig, as the farm had a lot of pigs. As the prosecution couldn't prove the blood found on the axe and his client was human blood, the defendant went free. Dad got tremendous publicity over his brilliant defence and that helped start his successful career.

But Judge Hyndman had contributed, in a sense, to Cecil's research. Upon his death he had left some of his estate to Cecil, thus alleviating Featherland's financial burden and allowing the Hyndmans to concentrate on avian research.

With the proceeds from the estate, Cecil bought a new microscope to document his research into avian blood. He intended to build on the recognition his article brought him. He began by extending his research into shell coloration. He strongly believed the shell pigmentation of other species of birds was also caused by hemorrhaged blood.

Cecil also wanted to study avian red blood cells and their nuclei. Over the next few years, he studied numerous eggs and blood taken from birds. One notebook alone, filled with hand-drawn sketches, covered over 120 birds ranging from bald eagles to saw-whet owls. Cecil examined the blood using his new microscope, sketching the variation in size and shape of red blood corpuscles and often photographing the prepared slides with his new equipment.

Cecil's aim was the comparative study of blood from different birds. He knew human blood analysis could be a useful tool; blood cells, for example, could provide early warnings of cancer. Cecil hoped eventually to establish an avian blood analysis system that could also be used as a diagnostic tool.

Cecil's Christmas letter of 1972 was long and positive. He wrote proudly how Featherland had entered a new phase, reflected in its new name: Featherland Bird Research Farm. "We again received a federal research permit to continue our seabird research, journeying to the Chain Islets," he wrote, adding how "a rotten egg exploded in the car on the way home, leaving a terrible odor. Only now, months later, do we find the incident amusing."

He told of Talon's egg laying, and of how he had had some success selling his tape productions, including a number of copies of *They Speak for Themselves*. He was working on another production involving Shadow the northern raven.

Above all, he was upbeat about the research into avian blood, which looked so promising, and about another project that involved studying "the size of chick in relation to the size of egg in various species."

Finally, his Signaface invention, which produced a relief image, was in the midst of patent processing.

The Hyndmans quietly celebrated that Christmas with their feathered family. As so often happened at that time of the year, their small cottage "swelled with extra 'Christmas guests'" in what had become "a tradition of sorts" necessitated by a cold spell. "If only they could sing Christmas carols," Cecil wrote.

One high, soaring bird song stood out among the cacophony of avian sounds that filled the cottage during Christmas: once again Susan began to sing her love song to Adele. The beautiful and expressive notes were a cause for both delight and alarm. Susan's love song often preceded the laying of eggs, and since her last few lays had been difficult, Adele and Cecil feared another lay might permanently damage Susan — if not threaten her life.

Adele closely monitored Susan over the next few days, noting her loss of appetite. "Yesterday she was very thirsty, and the same today," Adele informed Cecil just before the new year.

Other than giving her more water, the Hyndmans could only wait and watch over the next few days. The weather had turned unseasonably warm, giving them a little more peace as they could return Pertino and the other Christmas guests to their regular quarters.

After helping Cecil clean the pens in Talon Hall all day on Friday, January 5, Adele went back to the cottage to check on Susan in the early evening. Within minutes, she ran back to Talon Hall.

"She's not well," Adele told Cecil. "She's ill and her wings are drooping. Even her walk is clumsy."

The next day, Saturday, Susan's condition continued to deteriorate, but she took some food. Other than giving her more water, Cecil and Adele could only wait and watch. By now both Hyndmans were convinced Susan was about to lay another egg.

When Adele got up the following day, Sunday, January 7, 1973, she found Susan ill on the floor of her room. Adele stayed with her, wiping her feathers with a wet cloth and comforting her. Her great wings sagged as if heavy weights tugged on them. She tried to walk, but had difficulty even standing, as her legs buckled under her. Adele observed that Susan's vent area was silky soft and relaxed. Her pelvic bones were loosely apart as she strained painfully to expel her egg.

Cecil paced in the cottage outside the Queen's room, as nervous as an expectant father, making pot after pot of coffee.

Finally, at 5:00 p.m., the exhausting and painful ordeal ended as Susan laid an egg. After being with Susan all day and watching her difficult delivery, Adele remained with the eagle, observing how Susan's vent area tightened up within twenty-five minutes of the expulsion of egg.

When Susan seemed out of danger, Adele left Susan's room. She could barely walk, as she had knelt on the hard wooden floor for so long comforting Susan during the stressful laying. Physically drained and emotionally overcome, she collapsed into bed after handing the precious egg to Cecil.

He measured and weighed it. Susan's seventeenth egg turned out to be the largest of all, measuring three and a quarter inches in length and weighing four ounces. Susan was eighteen and a half years old.

While Susan had made it through the delivery, Cecil and Adele worried that Susan might lay another egg soon. They feared her body might not be resilient enough to withstand the process.

The next few days were tense inside the cottage as Adele stayed with Susan. The golden eagle's recovery was painfully slow. She continued to refuse food, her long wings almost touching the floor as she shuffled in discomfort in her room.

Adele's long vigil was interrupted when another member of the Featherland family suddenly became ill. Cecil found the Mexican donkey, Tony, collapsed in his stall. He immediately called the vet,

who confirmed Tony's heart was causing the trouble and administered adrenalin by needle. Cecil remained with Tony while Adele
returned to nurse Susan.

By nightfall, Tony had recovered enough to stand. But Susan's
recovery took much longer. But by Saturday, January 13, Cecil noted
with relief in his journal, "Sue seems to be on the mend. Today she
stood on her perch and started eating a little." As it had now been
almost a week since she laid, the critical period had passed. Cecil
was now convinced Susan would not lay a second egg after all.

As if to celebrate, that evening Cecil drained Susan's seventeenth
egg, carefully weighing the contents. Its fate was the same as
many previous ones: "The yolk tasted delicious, fried separately and
sprinkled with salt. The white becomes like colorless, translucent
jelly in the fry pan."

While relieved that Susan seemed to slowly be regaining her
strength, both Hyndmans were worried over what might happen
in the future should Susan ever lay another egg. As it turned out,
however, the Queen of Featherland would never again lay an egg.
Her seventeenth turned out to be her last.

Over the next few weeks, Adele nursed Susan, massaging her
and bathing her daily. Each night Adele and Cecil talked before
going to bed. The question Cecil asked was always the same: "How
is Susan?" He did not need a verbal reply. Adele's expression told
him everything.

Adele harbored a secret fear that the recent lay had permanently
weakened Susan's aging body. While she took food, and was able to
shuffle across the floor, her once-buoyant spirit sagged as much as
her wings. Never before, even after her most difficult lay, had she
taken this long to recover. Adele could see the difference in not
only her body language but her eyes. Ordinarily Susan's amber eyes
radiated such an intensity that visitors often said her stare literally
froze them in one spot. Now her eyes were dull and lifeless.

As the weeks dragged by, Cecil stopped asking Adele about Susan, especially as he was also going through a difficult period with Kluane II. His problems were the exact opposite of Adele's. Where Susan showed no spark of her former spirited nature, Kluane II had become very aggressive, "not unlike a younger version of Susan, who had also gone through periods in her development where she was exceedingly belligerent," he wrote.

Cecil blamed himself, because he had made the mistake of trying to record Kluane II's voice inside her room. She had lunged at the microphone, and Cecil barely made it out of her room safely. Cecil wrote that her "fiery mood persisted for some days, a not unusual event with a young and powerful female golden eagle, and one we went through with Susan."

He had no choice but to feed her from the outside of her room. Unfortunately, he soon discovered her bill had overgrown to the point where she had trouble eating. After discussing catching techniques for clipping it, the Hyndmans decided against their usual approach, which involved Adele switching off the light while Cecil swooped in and caught her in a thick blanket. That method depended on split-second timing and agility and Cecil admitted to Adele he was no longer as agile as he had once been.

Now sixty-two, Cecil had trouble with his right leg. Often the pain prevented him from walking, and at times he experienced a loss of feeling in his leg and foot.

"Given Kluane II's violently ferocious mood, we came up with another plan — a full frontal approach," Cecil wrote. "I entered her room armoured to the hilt — even shielded." The capture was bloodless and Cecil managed to keep Kluane II confined within the thick blanket while Adele trimmed her bill.

That evening the Hyndmans reminisced about their troubles capturing Susan in the years gone by. Cecil remarked how "Susan had drawn more blood from my flesh than she ever shed in her layings."

"Remember your Man From Mars outfit?" Adele laughed.

"And now you go into Sue's room in the nude," Cecil said.

The nostalgic conversation made Adele very quiet. Cecil realized that she felt Susan might never fully recover.

A week later, on a cold night in early February, Adele entered Susan's room. Instead of standing listlessly, waiting for Adele to hand-clean her, the eagle was splashing in her tub. Before her last egg laying, she had often liked to stand in the water, cleaning herself and then spraying the water as she fluffed her feathers.

Adele could barely contain her excitement over this dramatic improvement. When she started her nightly chore of cleaning the floor, Susan followed her around, her long talons scraping on the wooden floor. It was a game they had often played in the past, where Susan attempted to help Adele clean her room.

Within a few days, Susan recovered to the point where her old playfulness returned. "She has a new lease on life," Adele delightedly told Cecil late one night. That evening Susan had surprised Adele by closing her bill on a roll of newspaper. Her expression and gestures indicated she wanted to play. So Adele threw the roll of newspaper, tied like a bat.

Adele noticed the bright flash back in Susan's eyes. What she described as "that haughty and regal sparkle" had returned — a stare so powerful it seemed capable of lasering through the wad of newspaper. In a lightning move, Susan caught the rolled-up paper Adele tossed. She grasped it so hard her talons left an imprint on the paper.

Cecil related his own good news to Adele. Kluane II's dangerous mood had mellowed. When he brought her supper, he was able to put his lips close to a slice of beef beside her bill. As she had done a number of times before, Kluane II deferred to Cecil when he took the slice she intended for herself.

After their shared supper, Kluane II had lifted Cecil's hat off and dropped it on the floor. She seemed to be inviting him to stay. Next, Kluane II played with Cecil's eyelashes and eyebrows, preening them with her open bill. He wrote that she was like his lover becoming more and more intimate; "she gently plucked hairs from my head, caressing the skin down the back of my neck under my shirt with her bill." That a razor-sharp bill, intended to kill prey, could also be used with such tenderness constantly amazed Cecil.

"On her own, she rubbed her face and bill against my cheek. All the while she supported most of her weight on my bare left hand — around which she wrapped her talons," he wrote. "The extreme gentleness of her talons, used to crush prey, showed her other side. She could be extremely sensitive."

Cecil's experience with the eagle that night was unprecedented. Kluane II had become excited, making a breathless "het-het-het" sound. She flapped to the floor and spread her wings, her backside to Cecil. When she raised her tail, Cecil realized what she wanted. For a moment he hesitated.

"Kluane II was now in a wildly sexual state," Cecil later told Adele. After shaking her wings, she again took off in an almost uncontrolled flight around her room, coming close to bouncing off the walls. She landed and repeated her mating stance, continuing her breathless "het-het-het" while raising her tail.

Cecil complied, manually bringing her to orgasm. "She had a real orgasm, you could feel by the contractions. I doubt if anybody else knows — but there's orgasm in an eagle."

Kluane II screamed at climax, got up and flew around her room. This exuberant display was just the start of an emotional outburst, perhaps the most intense Cecil had ever witnessed. Next, the eagle "picked up her toys, tins, and plates and threw them all over the place, creating a noisy racket. It was a wild reaction to the manipulation — just like a human being."

Later back at the cottage, Cecil could feel his body trembling when he explained this bizarre sequence of events to Adele. She was surprised but not shocked by Cecil's admission.

"My experience with Kluane II could well be unique in the history of birds — certainly I know of no one else," Cecil said. While some falconers work to get semen and to inseminate their birds, the process is a surgical affair.

As they discussed the remarkable events of the evening, Adele reminded Cecil that Susan never needed such stimulation, yet had produced seventeen eggs. They compared the two female golden eagles' behavior. Susan, when she was ovulating, about a month before the lay, would start singing to Adele. Other behavior reflected her rather exuberant mood prior to egg laying.

Adele remarked that Susan's labor was as difficult as any human birth. Over the years these "deliveries" had become more and more difficult. Seeing Susan in pain, watching her blood flow as the egg came out, was a traumatic event for both women — human and feathered. Cecil also had shared the joy and agony, watching Susan laying eggs right into Adele's hands.

"Do you think Kluane II will produce eggs?" Adele asked.

"Only time will tell," Cecil answered.

As the evening lengthened, their conversation began to fade. Again it was Adele who voiced what was on both their minds. How would the public react to the information that Cecil had physically sexually stimulated Kluane II?

"Remember how the provincial school system rejected *The Grasp* because of that reference to Susan being in love with me?" Adele said.

He had been considering that very question all evening. Although he did not have any moral reservations about what he had done, he knew only too well how many years it had taken to build up their credibility and overcome their reputation as eccentrics. To release information about such highly sensational behavior to the general public, or even to the scientific community, would severely damage — if not destroy — their lifetime of research at Featherland.

"It will have to remain our secret," Cecil said.

nineteen

FAREWELL

The mid-1970s became a "Renaissance period" at Featherland as Cecil and Adele settled into a comfortable, if somewhat bizarre, lifestyle. Freed from the pressing financial worries of their first three decades at Featherland, they were at last able to indulge their passion for birds to the full. Without visitors touring Featherland, they each spent a good portion of the day with the respective female golden "mates."

Adele especially needed this closeness with Susan after her mother, May Gordon, died in Ottawa. Her mother's death opened old and painful wounds, and was the occasion for family strife. In the early 1970s, Adele had become worried when her letters home to her mother were not answered. She discovered her aunt had her mother admitted to a psychiatric hospital, then a home. Adele's aunt also had assumed the power of attorney — without consulting

Adele. Adele had been told all her life that she was adopted, but she suspected there was more to the story. After her mother's death, Adele requested the papers relating to her birth and adoption but her aunt would not reveal all the details. To add to her suspicions, Adele was left only a small amount of her mother's estate while her aunt received the bulk of the estate.

The Hyndmans hired a lawyer and located a baptism certificate. With this evidence, and some clues from conversations Adele had overheard, they came to a startling conclusion. Adele was May's child after all, born to her while May was still in her teens. The family had hidden the shame of a child born out of wedlock with a life-long subterfuge. An uncanny resemblance between "adoptive" mother and daughter was thus explained, and a mystery that had long worried Adele solved. But the years it had taken to learn the truth affected Adele. In the mid-1970s, she became distant and spent even more time with Susan. Although Cecil tried to be supportive, he worried about Adele's behavior. She seemed to retreat into her own "feathered world, where Susan was her confidante" and even Cecil was excluded. He could not criticize Adele, however, as he was spending more and more time with his eagle mate, Kluane II.

The daily routine during this era varied little. Mornings were spent feeding birds and cleaning up pens. Repairing fences, Talon Hall, and the other outbuildings meant a fair amount of physical work, especially as much of the fencing and some buildings now were over thirty years old. The manual labor had one great benefit: both the Hyndmans were in good physical shape.

Occasionally old friends dropped by, or sometimes a reporter, but ordinarily the afternoons were free. After supper, Cecil and Adele both trained birds to talk. Cecil had rigged overhead microphones throughout the cottage. After their evening speech training, Adele would retire to spend time with Susan, while Cecil left to visit Kluane II.

"Night owl" Cecil often continued his research into avian blood late into the night after Adele had retired for the night. He had placed a microphone outside Kluane II's room. Wires ran to a speaker next to his bed. He called this set-up his "eagle-activated alarm system." Kluane II would rise and begin playing with the sturdy metal tins and plates in her room. Often Cecil was awakened early, around 7:00 a.m., to the noisy clanging of metal on metal.

Although Cecil rarely got to sleep before 2:00 a.m., often much later as he suffered from insomnia, he would rise and go out to feed and play with Kluane II. This daily routine had evolved because Kluane II was at her best in the morning.

"When I started for her house she somehow sensed it and when I was fifty feet away she would become vocal, welcoming me," he wrote.

Cecil found Kluane II very alert in the mornings, "tweetering responsively . . . with expressions of excitement." Often Kluane II engaged in one of her favorite games, playing with Cecil's hat, then greeting him with an affectionate bill rub. As usual, Cecil hand-fed the eagle, taking strips of beef from a plate. He could gauge her mood by attempting to take back the raw beef from her mouth.

After his early-morning session with Kluane II ended, Cecil would often go back to bed, sleeping for a few hours until it was time to take the gulls outside for the day.

He recorded one morning in his journal, "In the faint light of early morning, I couldn't sleep with a little screech owl's big round orbs staring into mine from a position above my bed." So he got up again, walking quietly inside the cottage so not to wake Adele and the forty-odd birds that shared their small quarters. He made a pot of coffee, then went to Susan's room. Carefully he moved the bamboo curtain and peeked inside.

Shafts of sunlight streamed into Susan's room. While Kluane II was an early riser, Susan had adapted to the Hyndmans' routine and slept late. Susan's eyes were shut as she slept, her body moving slightly, as if she was dreaming. Cecil savored the magic moment as the sunlight caused Susan's feathering to glow gold.

He wrote, "She wasn't aware of my close presence as I stood there watching her sleeping on her stomach. Unlike any other eagle anyone has ever seen, she often used to sleep in that undignified position." Like Cecil, Susan loved the warmth of the sun. He often caught her sunbathing during the day. "Sometimes, as she stood regally on her box warming herself in the sunlight streaming in, she would nod and close her eyes."

The perfect symmetry of the image of Susan in front of him cried out to be captured on film. Cecil tiptoed to the desk, picked up his camera and then quietly set up his tripod. As he put his eye to the viewfinder, a deep "caw" from one of the ravens almost made him jump. Susan also reacted, moving her head slightly and ruining the composition of the shot.

Cecil left the tripod in place and went to wake Adele. He found that one of the gulls had joined Adele on the bed. The gull lay on its stomach next to Adele, and both were sleeping peacefully. Although he wanted to photograph the scene, Cecil did not want to disturb the sleeping pair. Besides, years earlier he had photographed Adele and a gull sleeping together in bed.

He returned to his camera, set up outside Susan's room. In the early morning quiet, he reflected on the two scenes of Susan asleep on her floor and Adele sleeping next to the gull:

Here at Featherland, Susan and our other birds didn't experience any fear at all and so were able to absorb another way of living, another relationship. By hand-rearing birds from an early age we were able to make them part of our feathered family. Watching Susan sleep so contentedly, in such a relaxed state, moved me.

Finally Susan stirred again. Cecil stepped back, afraid she might see him and become aggressive. Instead, she settled back, stretching on the floor, her head now visible through the viewfinder. Cecil snapped the shutter. It was the last photograph he took of the Queen of Featherland.

Cecil and Adele were with Susan when she died in 1978. The previous year she had begun to fade, slowing down her movements. Cecil described her final months thus:

> *She weakened, losing body weight and we could do nothing. There was no illness, it was really a case of old age catching up. Over the months, she gradually got weaker and weaker and passed away peacefully after a long life with us here in the cottage. She had hatched in 1954, so she was twenty-four at the time of her death.*

The next morning, Cecil lifted Susan's once-powerful body, now lifeless, for the first time in many years. As he picked her up, he recalled her strength and the way she had struggled the last time he had held her while Adele trimmed her bill. Her lightness surprised him as he tucked her nearly eight-foot wings close to her body. The Hyndmans buried Susan outside in the "soft earth of Featherland below the window of her room."

Susan's death deeply affected them both, but Adele even more than Cecil. Her grief seemed inconsolable, and for days afterward she could barely function, shuffling in a daze inside Ookpik Cottage. Often Cecil saw her wander toward Susan's room as if she expected Susan to still be there. Then Adele would stop and stand motionless before reaching the bamboo curtain.

After almost a week passed and there was no change in Adele, Cecil began to worry about his wife's physical and mental health. He knew only too well what Susan had meant to Adele. She had been more than a member of their feathered family; she had been the love of Adele's life. He also knew how this death, coming so closely after her mother's, "was a deep psychological double-blow."

Listless and lacking any sense of direction, Adele withdrew deep inside herself. Cecil tried to be supportive, taking care of her and encouraging her to grieve in the hope that she would release the repressed emotions eating away at her.

But he, too, found it hard to deal with Susan's death, though he deliberately held back his own grieving while trying to help Adele recover. Although his legs were not as strong as they used to be, he found himself again climbing up the rocky path by Burble Creek. The tension that filled the once lively cottage drove him outside. Where Adele had retreated inside herself, Cecil retreated into nature.

Often he climbed late at night, using the moonlight to illuminate his path. As he picked his way up along the edge of Burble Creek, he could feel the tension leave his body. By the time he made it up top, his legs ached, "but it was a good pain — physical and not emotional." At the top, Cecil sat on the soft mossy slope, "listening to the silence" as his eyes took in the "faint flickering of the city below and the stars above."

Alone in the velvet darkness, his thoughts seemed clearer. "It was as if the night draped all the petty details, allowing me to distinguish what was important from what was merely clutter." His main worry was how to pull Adele out of her emotional nose-dive.

In the weeks since Susan had died, Adele had regained some semblance of her earlier self and had resumed part of her regular bird-feeding routine, but she moved through the motions without emotion. Cecil found himself watching impotently, unable to draw her out of her state. He thought of taking her on a cruise — to get away, lose herself somewhere, anywhere, hoping the fresh perspective would snap her out of her moody withdrawal.

But Adele wouldn't hear of it. Featherland was her home and her birds were her family. Here she belonged and here she would stay.

Her feistiness pleased him — if nothing else, she was regaining some of her usual vigor.

A few days later Cecil again started up the slope before twilight. He was forced to stop at "scenic rest points" along the way as his aging legs slowed his ascent. Many of the points had whimsical, yet apt, names: steep Huff and Puff Hill bordering on the lowlands; Poplar Plaza, a grove of trees; Quack Lake, a pool he and Adele had made for ducks; the Grotto, a rocky waterfall along Burble Creek; and Sway Bridge, which crossed the creek.

At his first rest stop, Cecil sat on the rustic seat he had built under the gnarly limbs of an oak tree. His legs felt the way the twisted limbs looked: contorted and in pain. Yet somehow this made his "advancing old age more . . . acceptable, knowing this giant of a tree, with its twisted limbs, was already old and scarred" before he was born.

As he sat catching his breath, Cecil's thoughts turned to Adele. When they first arrived at Featherland, she called it her Eden — an idyllic retreat cut off from the real world. Cecil worried that she had been drawn too deeply into the world of birds. She often talked to him in the same high-pitched voice she used to talk to the birds. At night she would sing to the birds in Talon Hall.

"There seems to be a very thin line between obsession and madness — it's called passion," Cecil often said. The same passion that led them to give up their lives to birds now threatened to engulf Adele. Cecil realized that they had so isolated themselves from the rest of the world that they now "were in too deep to turn back" even if they wanted. There was nothing for Adele on the "outside" — Featherland was her only world. Adele's strength was her weakness; she cared too much, loved too much. And losing Susan, the greatest love of her life, had left an enormous hole in her life — one she could never fill. For Adele, life would never be the same again.

Cecil got up from the bench to continue his climb. He passed one of his favorite vantage spots, one he often sketched at. Below him he could see the "lush green rolling fields across the road, which sloped toward a gorge, changing color at every season." But for the first time the scenery failed to move him.

A bald eagle swooped low far below, then gained height as it flapped toward the sea. Cecil could feel a great sadness begin to overwhelm him as the eagle grew smaller and smaller. His thoughts turned to Susan. He recalled her life, from the day in 1955 when he had peeked into the large wooden box from the Yukon, and four inches of talon shot through the air hole, through her near-fatal bout with pneumonia and her days as his "second wife," to her rejection of him in favor of Adele and the egg laying that had astounded bird experts. He thought of Susan's fame, and of her love song, which he had recorded. Melancholy engulfed him as he heard the notes of Susan's song — or was it the breeze through the trees? Finally he relived writing Susan's story in *The Grasp* and publishing a scientific account based on her eggs in *The Condor*, finally receiving the public and scientific recognition he had so long worked for. Yet Cecil would have gladly traded all that acclaim to have Susan back again. Although it had been many years since he rubbed her neck feathers and felt her bill against his cheek, he could still recall how she smelled, the softness of her feathers. Although she had injured him a number of times, he had never lost his love for her.

Now she was gone. The emotions he had suppressed for so long flowed out in a torrent of tears. Standing on the rocky, exposed slope, Cecil wept. The loss of Susan meant far more than the end of Featherland's most famous bird — it was the end of an era. Life, for both Cecil and Adele Hyndman, who had formed a strange but passionate attachment to the fierce, glorious golden eagle known as Susan, would never be the same again.

Epilogue

In many ways, the end of the story of this unique three-way, two-species love affair is a sad one. Susan's death truly broke Adele Hyndman's heart; she was never quite the same again, though she lived twelve more years. In the early 1980s she suffered her first stroke during a December snowstorm. She had several more, over the years, until a serious one in February of 1986 left her hospitalized for months. The strain of looking after Featherland without Adele's physical or moral support took its toll on Cecil's health. In the fall of 1986 both were in hospital. Separated from Adele and his feathered family, Cecil nearly despaired. This time, Adele was no longer coherent or strong enough to "will him to live."

In perhaps the cruellest blow of all, the Hyndmans lost all their feathered companions during this period. As Cecil was not expected to live, his brother Lou arrived from Edmonton. The SPCA became involved and put down the birds remaining at Featherland.

"They were family to us — we never traded or sold a bird," wrote Cecil, devastated. "You don't do that to family."

Adele was moved to an extended care facility called the Priory; her condition had deteriorated to the point where she needed a wheelchair and was only lucid for brief moments. After seven and a half months, Cecil was discharged, to return to an empty Ookpik Cottage, which had been looted while he was in the hospital.

He could hardly avoid thinking of Susan as he sat in the silent living room, looking into Susan's now-empty room. Her eggs rested in a place of honor in the living room, Cecil's oil painting of her hung on the wall, and his favorite photo album rested on the coffee table. Her long flight feathers, collected over the years, hung carefully arranged in rows in the cottage. Even when he walked outside, he encountered memories of Susan; her body was buried by the cottage.

Cecil slowly built up his wasted muscles and regained part of his strength. He needed this to lift Adele in and out of her wheelchair when he picked her up at the Priory for visits to Featherland. Sometimes she only spoke a few words.

Christmas of 1989 was the last Adele and Cecil spent together. They quietly exchanged gifts and Cecil played tapes of Adele singing to Susan. He placed his hand in hers. When Adele heard Susan's love song on tape, she cried.

On April 17, 1990, Adele passed away. Cecil had her remains cremated, and carried her ashes up the rocky slope to the secluded bowl that was her favorite spot at Featherland. "Terribly upsetting and I wept and wept," he wrote in his journal.

I took the rest of the ashes of my dearest Adele and scattered them among the wildflowers in bloom around the rock outcropping and the fields. Some I poured into the base of the beautiful oak trees and in the tall grasses of parts of Featherland Adele and I used to walk around together — and in the places Adele used to go on her own to think her own private thoughts. I called on her to look down from above. How I hope she could hear me. She is now part of the land she loved.

The final stop on his walk was the most painful. Cecil paused before Susan's grave. The two women he loved so much were now dead. He dug up the earth below him with trembling hands, then scattered the last of Adele's ashes on the golden eagle she had loved so much, reuniting them in death.

Cecil remained at Featherland, taking his solitary nature walks, and dividing his time between assembling material for his long-imagined "post-Darwin" manuscript he still hoped to write and renewing his sagging spirits by quietly observing nature and painting nature scenes.

Realizing he needed companionship to fill the void in his life, Cecil bought a two-and-a-half-month-old African gray parrot. Once again the wooden walls of Ookpik Cottage echoed with bird sounds. Cecil named the silky silver-and-crimson-tailed parrot Quite So, and he quickly became a night owl like Cecil, staying up until 2:00 a.m. to watch TV. He often sat on the chair behind Cecil, providing a running commentary. Cecil observed: "A dramatic and fiery explosion on the screen might bring a 'Holy Smoke!' 'Wow!' or 'Whoopie!' from Quite So — all part of his vocabulary. He seems to associate these words appropriately with the action on the screen."

He accompanied Cecil everywhere, riding on his shoulder in the kitchenette when he prepared food. He ate with Cecil and liked to share a spot of tea served in a bowl. His table manners made Cecil laugh. "His legs are on the short side and he often trips over a spoon and, like an irate human, vents his anger by knocking the spoon to the floor."

Cecil's ambitious book project became mostly a question of cataloguing his forty-five years of accumulated material. His photo collection alone eventually amounted to over ten boxes — an estimated 10,000 negatives. The tapes amounted to 300,000 feet of bird sounds, spanning four decades. A meticulous note- and record-keeper, Cecil filed away everything of value — and much that had little or no value. The accumulated lifetime of writing, notes, journals, blood studies, and manuscripts filled boxes stored in rooms in the cottage as well as spilling over to Talon Hall. The staggering mass of written material far exceeded even the size of his tape and photo collection.

He worked on this book project in the evenings, spending the warmer days walking, noting his observations in his journal. Of one spring walk out back, he wrote:

acorns splitting open and taking root behind cottage along path up rock wall. First lily of valley and the horse chestnut tree has dozens of clusters of blossoms. In the bowl beside the huge oak, the dogwood is in flower. Deer seem to be eating wildflowers in bowl.

He often watered those oak seedlings struggling to establish a foothold on the dry slopes.

Cecil also wrote poetry, something he had done with some success in earlier days, even impressing his father the judge. "At odd times in the middle of the night, he would get out of bed and sketch out a few words." He put together his own chapbooks, which he circulated among his family and friends. Some of his poems appeared in magazines, his last poetry appearing in 1996 in a poetry journal called *Quarter Moon Quarterly*.

Epilogue

But for all that his final years were quiet and a little melancholy, Cecil had the satisfaction of seeing many of his theories, scorned earlier in his life, become widely accepted. Jane Goodall's work with chimps, and Dian Fossey's with gorillas, were evidence of a huge shift in public opinion. The general public accepted the intelligence and personalities of primates. In Cecil's opinion, Goodall's work substantiated his long-held view that "we're not the only form of life that has the ability to work things out in a reasoned way."

Like Cecil, Goodall lived with the objects of her study, with no degrees or training — just passion.

Other scientific projects studied animals' ability to acquire language to communicate with man. Primate researcher Francine Patterson taught sign language to a female gorilla called Koko at Stanford University. At the University of Hawaii, researchers trained dolphins; some dolphins progressed to where they understood 3,000 different sentences.

Cecil read about these projects with bemused delight. What he had predicted decades ago was being proven in these well-financed projects. He took more than a little pleasure in realizing he had been ahead of his time and years in advance of the scientific community.

In the mid-1940s, the little budgie Macdougal's incredible ability to speak had convinced Cecil that birds shared some human faculties, including intelligence. Now in the 1990s, he read of Dr. Irene Pepperberg's work with an African gray parrot named Alex, who demonstrated an ability to use speech correctly, and with meaning. When a researcher held up two keys and asked, "Alex, how many?" the parrot answered "two." Alex was able to correctly identify which key was bigger and distinguish whether or not it was made of wood.

Pepperberg reinforced what the Hyndmans had known decades earlier. Dr. Pepperberg has said, "A parrot is not just a bundle of bright feathers. A parrot is a creature with mental capabilities beyond what we would have guessed — a creature that deserves respect." Pepperberg found she had to gain Alex's trust and affection before he would speak.

Cecil tried to keep up with Alex's progress, enjoying the unofficial competition. Up to the mid-1990s, Cecil's parrot Quite So surpassed Alex in the number of words spoken. The irony of an old and frail man, working alone and unfunded, besting the well-financed efforts of a large university team always brought a twinkle to Cecil's blue eyes.

When the strict behaviorists had argued that animals have no thought processes, no awareness, Cecil knew otherwise. He and Adele strongly believed birds had emotions and personalities, much like humans. He put it thus:

To the scientists decades ago, this was heresy. But it's true that they have faculties that we have, some absolutely the same but others completely different and what intrigued me was finding the ones we shared. I need another hundred years to explore them all. I'm firm in my belief, we're not entirely separate. According to Darwinian theory, we all started from amoeba in the ocean and from that point of view there's no reason we shouldn't share some characteristics and connections.

In the final years of Cecil's life, the scientific community was implicitly endorsing some of his theories and methodology. But there was still something they could never duplicate, he insisted.

Scientists always draw a line. But you simply can't do the things we did here in white suits in a lab. The lab experiments only get data, not things we accomplished here. Our relationships with birds went far beyond just friendliness. That takes your whole life, night and day.

I admire people who go out in the woods, take tape recorders or cameras into the wilderness and endure harsh conditions to record natural behavior. But I've seen things that they'll never see and known things that they'll never know.

Cecil gained satisfaction from reflecting on the fact that he and Adele had lived a life no one else had ever attempted — in intimate contact with creatures they loved. Although they had broken new ground, enduring poverty to support their life work, they had not achieved riches, fame, nor any scientific acclaim. But the affection he had been given by Susan was more than enough return. He had loved and been loved in return. There is nothing more important in life — love is life itself.

After a bad fall and a fight with emphysema, Cecil Hyndman died peacefully in 1997, at 11:00 a.m. on April 17, the same date his wife Adele passed away on seven years earlier. He was eighty-five.

The simple burial took place on April 21, 1997, in Victoria. The words "HE LOVED" were engraved on his gravestone. An eagle soared overhead during the burial — a more fitting tribute than any eulogy.

Acknowledgments

A *number of people* helped make this book possible. Debbie and Bryan McGill deserve special mention. Debbie became very close to Cecil Hyndman, often visiting him and even climbing up on his roof to repair a leak after a storm. After he had died, she erected a bench in his memory. Nelson Doucet of Stoddart Publishing saw the potential in my original proposal and took the time to help reshape it. His subsequent encouragement kept the project on track. Jan Atkinson-Grosjean, a writer and editor and fellow Federation of B.C. Writers board executive, helped organize my proposal. Cathy Gibson assisted with the typing. My family also pitched in: my father Emmett Burns helped hang the mildewy papers of Cecil Hyndman, and my daughters Danielle and Cehra were "underpaid assistants."

Dr. Andrew Glen kindly offered me free lodging when I interviewed Cecil in Victoria. Other family members, friends, and fellow writers helped and encouraged me: Ed Griffin, Trish Webb, Hugh Wilson, and the talented Wilson clan of writers: Lucy, Len, and Isabel. Special thanks to editor Jim Gifford at Stoddart, who helped shape and polish the book throughout its various drafts. Editor Elizabeth d'Anjou's restructuring suggestions were invaluable, and she performed miracles by polishing my clunky prose. Finally, Cecil's brother Jim Hyndman, and Cecil's friends George Bligh, Marie and Jerry Thomas, Brian Roberts, and Lon Wood gave of their time generously.